Labour and Justice

Labour and Justice

The worker in Catholic social teaching

Gavan Duffy

GRACEWING

First published in 2008

in the United Kingdom by
Gracewing
2 Southern Avenue,
Leominster
Herefordshire HR6 0QF

in Australia by:
Freedom Publishing Pty Ltd
582 Queensberry Street
North Melbourne
Victoria 3051

All rights reserved. No part of this publication may be reproduced, stored in a retrieval system, or transmitted in any form, or by any means, electronic, mechanical, photocopying, recording or otherwise, without the written permission of the publisher.

© Gavan Duffy 2008

The right of Gavan Duffy to be identified as the author of this work has been asserted in accordance with the Copyright, Designs and Patents Act 1988.

ISBN 978 0 85244 686 7

Cover image taken from The Power House Mechanic by Lewis W. Hine

Typeset by Action Publishing Technology Ltd,
Gloucester GL1 5SR

CONTENTS

Acknowledgements xi
Preface
by George Cardinal Pell, Archbishop of Sydney xiii
Introduction 1

Chapter 1 **In the beginning** 5

Chapter 2 **The biblical worker** 9
    The worker in the Old Testament 9
        The Psalms 9
        Deuteronomy to Ecclesiasticus 10
        Trades and crafts 12
        The prophetic writings 14
        The Hebrew concept of social justice 15
        The social security of Deuteronomy
          and Qumran 17
        Change in attitude to work 18
    Slavery in the Old Testament 18
    The worker in the Gospels 24
    Jesus and work 26
        Summary 30
    The worker in the epistles 31
    Slavery in the New Testament 34
        Summary 38

Chapter 3 **The worker in the patristic era** 42
    The social teaching of the early Fathers 42
        The necessity of the crafts 44
    All entitled to a livelihood 44
        Solidarity and subsidiarity 45
        Stewardship 47
        A variation on the golden rule 49

	The common good	51
	Summary	52
	Slavery in the patristic era	53
	Summary	56
Chapter 4	**The medieval worker**	59
	The decline of slavery	59
	The influence of the monks	59
	Slavery to serfdom	64
	A philosophy of work and the evolution of the guilds	67
	The guilds	69
	The guilds in everyday practice	71
	The doctrine of the 'just price' (*justum pretium*)	75
	Just wage	77
	Summary	78
Chapter 5	**The rise of the proletariat**	81
	The Reformation	81
	Dissolution of the monasteries	85
	The Catholic social movement and the proletariat	89
	The Catholic social movement in Germany and France	89
	The Fribourg Union	94
	The Catholic social movement in England and the United States	95
	Conclusion	97
Chapter 6	***Rerum Novarum* – The Magna Carta of the social order**	99
	The decade before 1891	99
	Leo XIII	101
	On the condition of the working classes	101
	Labour and capital	102
	Solidarity	104
	Trade unions	104
	A living wage	106
	Working conditions	107
	Private property and the worker	108
	The worker and the state	109
	Biblical references	110
	The legacy	110

Contents   vii

Chapter 7	**The Chesterbelloc era**	116
	Background	116
	Capitalism	117
	The proletariat and the servile state	120
	Distributism, property and the worker	123
	The worker-priest experiment	127
Chapter 8	**Pius XI – *Quadragesimo Anno***	132
	Background	132
	Pius XI	133
	The encyclical	135
	Labour and capital	135
	Trade unions	136
	The individual and social character of labour – worker participation	138
	Wage determination	140
	Evolution of labour law	143
	Worker and property	144
	Vocational groups	144
	Conclusion	146
Chapter 9	**Pius XII and the national episcopal conferences**	150
	Background	150
	The community and the natural law	151
	The dignity of labour	152
	A community of work	153
	Worker participation	153
	The class struggle	154
	Capitalism	155
	Wages	155
	The worker and property	157
	National episcopal conferences	157
	United States Catholic bishops	157
	Australian Catholic bishops social justice statement 1943	158
	Australian Catholic bishops social justice statement 1947	160
	Australian Catholic bishops social justice statement 1948	161
	Hierarchy of Quebec	163
	Statement of bishops of Ohio	164

Chapter 10	**Mater et Magistra**	166
	Background	166
	Mater et Magistra	166
	Wage justice	167
	Worker participation	170
	The International Labour Organization	173
	Trade unions	173
	Worker cooperatives	173
	State intervention	175
	Summary	176
Chapter 11	**Gaudium et Spes**	178
	Background	178
	Unjust economic structures	180
	The worker	180
	The primacy of labour	181
	Wages	182
	Trade unions and strike action	183
	Working conditions and structures	183
	Worker participation and codetermination	184
	Summary	185
Chapter 12	**The Social Encyclicals of Paul VI**	188
	Background	188
	Populorum Progressio	188
	Work	188
	Worker participation	189
	Trade unions	189
	Octogesima Adveniens	189
	Urban proletariat	189
	Wages	190
	Trade unions – political strikes	190
	Worker participation	190
	Synod of bishops 1971	191
	Summary	191
Chapter 13	**John Paul II**	193
	Background	193
	Laborem Exercens	195
	Theology of work	195
	Solidarity and the worker question	197
	Labour and capital in conflict – the priority of labour	198
	Worker participation	200

	Materialistic economism	204
	Indirect employer	206
	Wages	207
	Trade unions	209
	Centesimus Annus	211
	Alienation	211
	Worker participation	213
	Capitalism – yes or no?	213
	Summary	214
Chapter 14	**Recent Statements of national episcopal conferences, *Deus Caritas Est* and other church documents**	217
	United States Catholic bishops	217
	Worker participation	218
	Trade unions	219
	Wages	220
	Employment	221
	Sacred Congregation for the Doctrine of the Faith – *The Instruction on Christian Freedom and Liberation*	221
	The Canadian Catholic bishops	222
	Australian Catholic bishops' conferences	224
	Vatican Intervention at the World Summit on Social Development, Copenhagen 1995	227
	Pastoral Letter of United States bishops 1991	227
	Catholic bishops' conference of England and Wales 1996	228
	Deus Caritas Est	229
	Summary	230
Chapter 15	**Catholic social teaching and the worker in the neoliberal capitalist era**	232
	Globalization and globalism	232
	Injurious policies of the indirect employer	233
	Laissez-faire and neoliberal capitalism compared	233
	Employment and wages	236
	Trade unions	242
	Worker participation – a move towards more just work structures	247
	Reform of the institution of the corporation	250
	Worker cooperatives	252
	Conclusion	253

Chapter 16	**Epilogue – The binding threads**	257
	Justice	257
	Service	257
	The equality of all before God	258
	Stewardship	258
	The common good	259
	The dignity of the human person	260
	The magisterium	260
Bibliography		261
Index		273

Note: Scripture references are taken from The Jerusalem Bible.

ACKNOWLEDGEMENTS

In the course of writing this book some three draft manuscripts were produced. My gratitude is due to Les Savage for his assistance in editing the final draft. His advice was invaluable. Thanks are also due to Bruce Nickel and Sean Duffy for the proofreading of the early manuscripts and to my typist, Kathryn Wood, for her patience in transcribing my tapes accurately, a task which would not have always been easy. Finally, I express my appreciation to my wife Anne, for her support and encouragement over the nearly three-year period of writing this book.

PREFACE

The tradition of Catholic social teaching provides invaluable guidance on a diverse range of issues. Some of the more important heads these issues fall under include the nature and configuration of the political community; responsible stewardship of the environment; liberation from injustice and poverty; and the fruitful promotion of peace. Since the nineteenth century the social teaching has developed into an integral guide to the Church's mission in the world, with a considerable degree of variation as it is applied to particular circumstances and conditions. Underlying these particular applications, however, is a constant concern with meeting the requirements of justice in societies which are increasingly dynamic and rapidly changing.

Living in the world but not of the world, the Church acts as a leaven throughout the course of human history. In social terms, this leaven translates into a vision of the common good and it is this vision which is pursued and upheld by the social teaching of the Church. But as this teaching has developed over time, and as it has addressed political and social concerns particular to certain crises in human history, a tension has appeared between two sometimes competing tendencies at work in the pursuit of the common good.

Catholic social teaching is not an ideology. It is based on a realism about the human condition which seeks a balance between the competing demands of subsidiarity and socialization. Either of these principles, when sundered from Christ and left unbalanced by the other can lead to problems. Subsidiarity can be pursued in a way that comes to make it resemble a radical form of individualism, with the individual as 'the smallest unit' trumping considerations based on the common good. In a similar way, when socialization is taken as the supreme principle of social life, the freedom of individuals and groups can be eroded, and the door left open to different forms of the totalitarian impulse, with its disdain both for life and the dignity of the human person.

Subsidiarity and socialization need to go together, and the principle of solidarity is indispensible in helping to ensure that they are harmonized in the service of the common good. But the commitment to solidarity needs to be anchored in faith in Christ, and a personal and prayerful relationship with him. The social teaching of the Church depends on the anthropology which arises from Christian revelation, just as the Church's justice work depends on faithful discipleship. It is always a temptation for us to forget that it is God who gives the increase and blesses our efforts with whatever success they might enjoy. This can be a particular danger in justice work, and meditating on the social teaching the Church in all its fullness can help us to avoid this.

Solidarity is based on the intrinsic social nature of all people and serves as both a social principle and a moral virtue. When we stand in solidarity with others we should also bear witness to the life in Christ which is at the centre of the Church's social teaching, and its understanding of the relationship between individual flourishing and the common good. At the same time, however, the social teaching is a gift all people of good will, particularly in its vision of the person and society and in its identification of fundamental principles which should inform our thinking about the shape and quality of life in common. The social teaching takes the dignity of the human person and projects into the social world that we all inhabit. In doing this the Church puts its expertise in humanity at the service of all those, believers and non-believers alike, who are concerned with how to build and sustain a decent, just and prosperous society.

One area where this is particularly apparent is the field of human work. In this book Gavan Duffy seeks to analyse the development of the rights and duties of the worker in Catholic social teaching. Central to a clear understanding of the nature of work in the social teaching is the emphasis on the human person and the way that the needs of the individual must also be included in any social discourse relating to work. 'The Church is convinced that work is a fundamental dimension of man's existence on earth' (*Laborem Exercens*, II. 4), and the relationship between God, society and the work we do, is a central theme of the book.

Duffy embarks on a systematic historical approach seeking to establish the biblical foundations of the centrality of work in a person's life. He traces the development of the Hebrew attitude to workers and examines the later influence of the New Testament and Pauline literature on these same attitudes. Work in the Greco-Roman world, and especially menial work, was something left to slaves, and Duffy introduces us to the specific contributions made by the Church Fathers in their efforts to apply Christ's teachings to offset at least the worst abuses that were concomitant with slavery in the Roman world.

Duffy then examines the decline of the Roman world and the disruption caused by the Barbarian invasions, and the way the Church responded to the need to regulate and renew economic life. The Middle Ages saw the emergence of the guilds, the precursors of modern trade unions and professional associations, and also the first attempts to deal with the way the guild system could inhibit competition and initiative. This system was itself sent into decline by a new wave of social unrest and religious protest. The Reformation brought significant change to the course of European history and one of these transformations became identified with the rise of capitalism as an economic and social force. In this process, as some have argued, the world began to move from the dualism of freeman and serf to what would later be identified as the dichotomy of capital and labour, or the dualism of to the capitalist and the proletarian. Today, our understanding of what actually took place is considerably more complex than either Marx or even Weber described, and against this standard the social teaching of the Church has fared very well.

It was in the context of emergence of the threat of wage slavery and the dangers of unbridled capitalism and atheistic socialism that Pope Leo XIII wrote *Rerum Novarum* in 1891. Duffy begins with this great encyclical, which has stood the test of time remarkably well, and proceeds to work through the various encyclicals on social questions which succeeded it, right up to the time of Pope John Paul II. In doing this, Duffy is not so much concerned with historical anecdotes or vignettes but is focused on the antecedents of Catholic social thought and on its influence in mediating between the articulated differences between capital and labour.

Duffy shows that work is consistently presented within the social thought of the Church as something more than an economic endeavour, more than an activity which places an individual in the service of an impersonal marketplace. It in this framework that the Church's definition of work as any activity 'beginning in the human subject and directed toward an external object' (*Laborem Exercens*, II. 4) begins to strengthen the principle that it is not the human person who exists for work, but work which exists for the human person. This means that the laws and conventions governing work should not be determined by economic factors alone. Pope Benedict XVI reinforced this basic principle of the social teaching on the feast day of St Joseph the Worker in 2005 when he expressed his hope 'that work will not be lacking, especially for young people, and that working conditions will respect always the dignity of the human person'.

The coming of the twenty-first century has brought with it new social problems that can also be analysed and clarified by the social teaching of the Church. Globalization, for example, brings many benefits to those people capable of accessing these advantages, but quite rightly Duffy focuses on the plight of the disadvantaged in a global economy. What makes this book stand out is its central claim 'that the social teaching of the Church directly challenges and confronts' that which stands in the way of 'the attaining of a just distribution of the world's goods, the dignity of work and the mutual dependence of capital and labour.'

Labour and Justice: The worker in Catholic social teaching is a valuable addition to the literature on the social teaching of the Church. Gavan Duffy places the reader in the centre of a dialogue about the presence of Christ and the mission of the Church in questions of social and political responsibility. It is a dialogue that needs to be taken seriously and better known, among Catholics and other Christians, and also among all those concerned with building a good society.

✠ George Cardinal Pell
ARCHBISHOP OF SYDNEY
July 2008

INTRODUCTION

This work examines directly the development of Catholic social teaching in respect of the rights and duties of the worker.

Beginning with the Old Testament, a comparison is made between the attitude of the Hebrew people as expressed in Scripture to those who performed the tasks associated with the crafts or with labour. This examination demonstrates how the attitude of the Hebrews to workers, in comparison with the attitude of surrounding peoples, was ameliorated by their belief in a just God who spoke to them in Scripture and through the prophets. In its examination of the New Testament, the work extracts gospel and epistle references to the worker, particularly from the Pauline texts on the subject. This examination reveals a change in attitude to the worker from the Old Testament to the New.

Next examined are the writings of the Church Fathers and their application to the worker. It can be seen from this that the early Church Fathers, whilst not directly developing a body of teaching in respect of the worker, developed a philosophical platform for its later development. It is shown that the teachings of the Church Fathers, in their application of the teaching of Jesus in the Gospels to the prevailing attitudes of Roman society, contributed to the further amelioration of the condition of slaves in the later empire. When speaking of the worker in Greco-Roman society, one is in effect speaking about the institution of slavery.

Further changes in attitude to the worker which followed the decline of imperial authority in the West are then dealt with. It is seen here that the role of the Church and its teaching regarding the dignity of the human person and the place of work in the scheme of redemption had an ameliorating effect on the treatment of slaves in the various barbarian kingdoms which arose in the West following the extinguishment of Roman authority. It is suggested that it was the influence of Christianity which ultimately led to the evolution of the condition of slavery as it was known in the Roman Empire and during the Carolingian period, to that of the serfdom of the Middle Ages.

There follows a discussion of the guild system of regulating and controlling the crafts. The guilds were a society, in part cooperative but mainly composed of private owners of capital, whose corporation was self-governing, and was designed to check competition between its members in order to prevent the growth of one at the expense of the other. The functioning of the guilds is examined, and it is explained why some Catholic writers, such as Hilaire Belloc and Gilbert Keith Chesterton, regarded the guilds as an excellent example of the practical application of Christian principles to work and economics.

This work continues with an examination of the effects of the Reformation and the rise of liberal capitalism on the guild system, and discusses how they both contributed to its decline. Consequent upon the decline of the guild system and the onset of liberal capitalism, society came to be divided into two classes: the capitalist class and the proletariat. The factors which contributed to it are discussed. It is shown how the division of society into capitalist and proletariat, haves and have-nots, resulted in the development of a class war and the antagonism between labour and capital. It is suggested that under the liberal capitalist system, the conditions of the working class came to resemble, in the words of Leo XIII, 'a yoke, almost of slavery'.[1]

What follows is an analysis of the manner in which the antinomy between capital and labour gave birth to the philosophy of Marxism in 1848, an event which followed the publication of the *Communist Manifesto* by Karl Marx and Freidrich Engels in that year. It discusses how the development of the two antagonistic classes of capital and labour was viewed by the Church as an aberration or distortion of the social order and how, in response to the rise of the philosophy of Marxism, Leo XIII responded with his great social encyclical *Rerum Novarum*, promulgated on 15 May 1891, an encyclical which was to earn him the title of 'The Workers' Pope'.

The social teachings and encyclicals of Popes Pius XI, Pius XII, John XXIII, Paul VI and John Paul II are treated sequentially in ensuing chapters. Mention is also made of Benedict XVI's first encyclical *Deus Caritas Est*. All of these popes, in some way, expanded upon and developed the social teaching of the Church in its application to workers. In many ways it could be said that these later encyclicals have 'fleshed out' *Rerum Novarum*. During this period, numerous advances have been made in the fields of technology, and there has been a considerable improvement in the conditions and wages of workers. In its consideration of the social encyclicals since *Rerum Novarum*, this work discusses the way in which the popes have developed and expanded Catholic social teaching in respect of the workers as changes in technology and various structural changes to the financial system have thrown up new and complex challenges to the creation of a just social order in which the dignity and the rights of workers are fully respected.

The manner in which the popes since Leo XIII have confronted the injustices associated with these developments, and their detailed recommendations for action, would be viewed by many in this age of neoliberal capitalism as quite radical.

In the later chapters of this book the writer identifies the deleterious effects upon the rights of workers of global neoliberal capitalism. It is asserted that in the early years of the twenty-first century there are already signs that some of the less desirable traits of nineteenth-century laissez-faire capitalism are once again rearing their heads. Its effects are seen in such developments as the 'hollowing out' of the middle class and the concentration of wealth in fewer hands. It is also seen in the slow but sure erosion in the working conditions of employees and in their level of remuneration. It is seen in developed countries in the trend towards longer working hours and the increasing casualization of the workforce.

In the context of the world economy, a gap continues to widen between the developed and undeveloped nations, whilst inequitable trade agreements tend to confine the developing nations to the status of providers of raw materials to the industrialized world – an inequity which, more often than not, finds itself imposed upon the working men and women of the developing nations in the form of long hours, low wages and poor conditions. Besides placing the development of Catholic social thought and the worker in an historical context, it is this writer's intention to show how, of necessity, the social teaching of the Church directly challenges and confronts the philosophy of neoliberal capitalism in its national and global forms, and moves toward the attainment of a just distribution of the world's goods, the dignity of work and the worker, the priority of labour, and the mutual dependence of labour and capital.

Note
1 *Rerum Novarum*, para. 6, p. 7.

Chapter 1

IN THE BEGINNING

With sweat on your brow shall you eat your bread.
                                                    Gen. 3:19

The early chapters of Genesis indicate that Yahweh is a worker. He is an active and powerful God who is perfect in all that he does and has no weaknesses. Yahweh performs all of the works of creation described in Genesis. He is incessantly at work, defending, helping, championing, exciting Israel. The early chapters of Genesis open with the striking description of Yahweh fashioning the world with his own hands like a potter. He takes the dust of the earth and forms a figure out of it, and then breathes the breath of life into it and it becomes a living being (Gen. 2:7). His work, just like any human work, is arduous (Jer. 2:21). The God of the Hebrews is surely a God who does not shrink from work.[1]

This Old Testament concept of Yahweh as a worker is in sharp contrast with the pagans' notion of their gods. As Gideon Goosen says:

> We can get some idea of the immense difference between pagan and Hebrew concepts of work by contrasting the Greek god Hephaestus with Yahweh. Hephaestus, in spite of enormous strength and in spite of all the admiration the ancient Greeks had for work, is depicted as physically lame. He is constantly referred to as 'the illustrious lame god' and 'the lord of the crooked foot' and elsewhere Homer remarks, 'He limped but was nimble enough on his slender legs'. His weaknesses are not limited to the physical. When he traps Ares and his adulterous butterfly wife, Aphrodite, he visits all the other gods and Zeus to complain to them that Aphrodite has always despised him for his lameness. Ares was handsome and sound of body, but Hephaestus was born a cripple and cursed the day of his birth. However the other gods seeing how cleverly he trapped Ares and Aphrodite, remarked 'Hephaestus may

be lame, but his craft has won the day.' From these episodes we get an image of Hephaestus as a god of great physical power and skilful craftsmanship, but with a certain touchiness about his deformity and inability to cope with his whimsical wife.[2]

What a contrast this is with the Hebrew God, Yahweh. The God of the Hebrews is not afraid to work with his hands, whereas neither Zeus nor Jupiter deigned to do so, relegating this kind of activity to lesser gods. Thus, Yahweh, by working, has given work a value far above that which it enjoyed in Greco-Roman civilization.

The worker and work are the subjects of frequent mention in Scripture. In Genesis, the references to Yahweh's work as a creator are accompanied by exhortations to humanity: 'Be fruitful and multiply and fill the earth and subdue it' (Gen. 1:28). Later, after the fall, the original blessing of work contained in the very mystery of creation and connection with humanity's elevation as the image of God, is contrasted with the curse that sin brought with it: 'Accursed be the soil because of you. With suffering shall you get your food from it, every day of your life.'[3] John Paul II in *Laborem Exercens* comments that this toil connected with work marks the way of human life on earth and constitutes an announcement of death: 'In the sweat of your face ye shall eat bread till you return to the ground for out of it you were taken.'[4] John Paul II makes the interesting observation in *Laborem Exercens* that the Bible contains reference to some twenty-eight different callings and occupations.[5]

Paul Gauthier, writing on the redemptive role of labour, says that humanity redeems itself by labour[6] and by the command of the Creator that 'in the sweat of his face shall he eat bread until he returns to the ground' and the exhortation to subdue the earth: 'Be fruitful, multiply, fill the earth and conquer it. Be masters of the fish of the sea, the birds of heaven and all living animals on the earth.'[7] This is not a negative punishment. It is the ready participation in the redemption because the seed of the woman shall break the head of the serpent. In the New Testament the Redeemer himself decided to labour as a carpenter in order to save humanity. For man, to labour is to take part in his own redemption, in time and in eternity, on earth and in heaven, materially and spiritually.[8] Gauthier says that on the spiritual, eternal and celestial plane labour allows man to cooperate with God, who has charged him to go forth and dominate the earth, take possession of it, and complete the creation. Labour allows a man to save himself from sin by offering up the fatigue and pain of labour. Labour allows humanity to commune with the carpenter of Nazareth and through Him with all his brothers and sisters and with the Father himself, who 'labours unceasingly'.[9] The material and spiritual dimensions of labour referred to, whilst distinct, are not separate. As Gauthier says, there is a Marxist interpretation of labour which is a mere caricature of the true redemption. But there is also a Christian interpretation of labour which redeems in the name of Christ. On the terrestrial, temporal and material plane, humanity can free itself from want. Even in work, mankind can reach a certain fulfilment. Not only does labour permit a person to earn his or her bread, but it also allows them to become more human, to share human solidarity and take their part in the construction of the terrestrial city.[10]

After Yahweh created the world, he put mankind in the centre to cultivate it. In other words, he intended humanity to work right from the beginning. Mankind was to devote itself to agricultural pursuits in the Garden of Eden, whereas in the golden age of Hesiad and Lucretius mankind was free of labour and the earth brought forth her fruits without any effort on the part of mankind. As Goosen says, herein lies one of the big differences between Greco-Roman civilization and Judaism. The Hebrews accepted work as being natural and willed by God. The Greeks and the Romans considered it unnatural.[11]

For the non-Hebrew of biblical times, the complete man, the moral man, liberated his hands and his soul from the servitude of manual toil, and a beneficent nature has foreseen and provided a slave for his master just as he had provided the body to be the servant of the soul. The ideas held in antiquity concerning the condition of those who work with their hands attest that the opprobrium which was attached to work was not merely the haughtiness of an intellectual. This opprobrium had the thought and the universality of a social fact and of a collected presentation of a reality.[12]

Reliable witnesses of the average opinion on manual labour in Greece in antiquity are Xenophon and Herodotus. Herodotus said that it was established amongst the Thracians, the Scythians, the Persians and the Libyans and the majority of the barbarians that those who learnt mechanical arts and their children were looked upon as the lowest class of citizens. On the other hand, he said, the noblest exercised no mechanical art and were principally those who were destined for the profession of arms. He said that all of the Greeks had been educated in those principles, particularly the Spartans. He did, however, make an exception of the Corinthians who made much of their artisans.[13]

These ideas were normally translated into institutions. In Thebes, for example, shopkeepers were prohibited from holding the office of magistrate and had no access to such a position until the expiration of ten years after their retirement from business. At Epidauros, the ignominy attaching to manual labour compelled the state to constitute it an administrative service, entrusted to the slaves of the state. In Sparta the law forbade a citizen to take upon himself the servitude of any manual occupation.

Given the dignity and the nature of work imparted to it by Genesis, one may well ask, as does Gauthier, how it has come about that labour has become one of the most frequent and most serious occasions for the exploitation of one person by another and of human degeneration? The exploitation of a person made in the image of God by another in the same image, which now degenerates into a satanic caricature, is no new phenomenon but one which has persisted through the ages to our own time. Once it was called slavery, then serfdom. Now it is called the wage system. However, it is an exploitation of which the Church has not been unmindful and to which it has turned its mind in every age.

Notes
1 Goosen, p. 5.
2 Ibid. pp. 24–5.
3 Genesis 3:7.
4 *Laborem Exercens*, p. 104.
5 Ibid. pp. 100–01.
6 Gauthier, p. 8.
7 Genesis 1:28.
8 Ibid. p. 9.
9 Ibid. pp. 38–9.
10 Gauthier, pp. 38–9.
11 Goosen, p. 27.
12 Borne and Henry, p. 30.
13 *Herodotus, The Histories,* tr. Aubrey de Sélincourt, p. 196.

Chapter 2

THE BIBLICAL WORKER

The worker in the Old Testament

Throughout the Old Testament the concept of justice, particularly in its relationship to Yahweh's poor (the 'anawim') looms large. This is the case in respect of both the prophetic books and other biblical texts. I shall deal firstly with the non-prophetic texts as the prophetic texts, will require further elaboration.

The Psalms
Some twelve of the Psalms contain references to what may be termed 'justice' or issues pertaining to justice. Frequently the reference to justice is to the poor and the weak as in Pss. 41 and 82. Other times it is to the orphan, the needy, and the oppressed as in Pss. 82, 94 and 72 and others, to the innocent as in Pss. 15 and 94. Ps. 99:4 says, 'God, righteous and holy king, You are a king who loves justice, insisting on honesty, justice, virtue'. In Psalm 72, the Royal Psalm of Solomon, certain attributes are expressed as being desirable in the king. In verses 1–2 it is stated, 'God, give your own justice to the king, your own righteousness to the royal son, so that he may rule your people rightly and your poor with justice'. In verse 4 it is stated, 'May he defend the cause of the poor of the people, give deliverance to the needy and crush the oppressor'. In verses 12–14, 'He will free the poor man who calls to him and those who need help; he will have pity on the poor and feeble, and save the lives of those in need; he will redeem their lives from exploitation and outrage, their lives will be precious in his sight.'

Ps. 37:21 describes a virtuous man as being one who is 'generous and open handed'. Ps. 15 states who it is that has the right to enter the Temple of Yahweh as His guest (Ps. 15:5).

> Lord, who may enter your Temple?
> Who may worship on Zion, your sacred hill?
> A person who obeys God in everything
>   and always does what is right,
> whose words are true and sincere,
>   and who does not slander others.
> He does no wrong to his friends
>   and does not spread rumours about his neighbours.
> He despises those whom God rejects,
>   but honours those who obey the Lord.
> He always does what he promises,
>   no matter how much it may cost.
> He makes loans without charging interest
>   and cannot be bribed to testify against the innocent.[1]

Psalm 112 says that a virtuous man is one who does not charge interest on loans and is honest in all his dealings.[2] Psalms 58, 82 and 94 deal with corruption in public life and state how it is the duty of those in authority, particularly judges, to see that the weak, the orphan, the needy, the virtuous and the innocent receive justice. In Psalm 41 it is said that 'happy is the man who cares for the poor and the weak; if disaster strikes, Yahweh will come to his help. Yahweh will guard him and give him life and happiness in the land' (Ps. 41:1-2). Psalm 106 makes the broad statement 'Blessed are they who observe justice' (Ps. 106:2).

In the Book of Leviticus, first reference is made to the Great Commandment: 'You must love your neighbour as yourself'.[3] It is not difficult to draw from this that loving one's neighbour as oneself would include being just in all one's dealings with servants and employees.

Deuteronomy to Ecclesiasticus
Deuteronomy[4] is more explicit:

> You are not to exploit the hired servant who is poor and destitute, whether he is one of your brothers or a stranger who lives in your towns. You must pay him his wage each day, not allowing the sun to set before you do, for he is poor and is anxious for it; otherwise he may appeal to Yahweh against you, and it would be a sin for you.

The biblical worker

In Ecclesiasticus, a direct reference is made to the various trades and crafts, their function and the dignity of the work of tradesmen and craftsmen:

> Leisure is what gives the scribe the opportunity to acquire wisdom;
> The man with few business affairs grows wise.
> How can the ploughman become wise,
> Whose sole ambition is to wield the goad;
> driving his oxen, engrossed in their work,
> his conversation is of nothing but cattle?
> his mind is fixed on the furrows he traces,
> And his evenings pass in fattening his heifers.
> So it is with every workman and craftsman,
> toiling day and night;
> those who engrave seals,
> always trying to think of new designs:
> they set their heart on producing a good likeness,
> and stay up perfecting the work.
> So it is with the blacksmith sitting by his anvil;
> he considers what to do with the pig-iron,
> the breath of the fire scorches his skin,
> as he contends with the heat of the furnace;
> he batters his ear with the din of the hammer,
> his eyes are fixed on the pattern;
> he sets his heart on completing his work,
> and stays up putting the finishing touches.
> So it is with the potter, sitting at his work,
> turning the wheel with his feet;
> constantly on the alert over his work,
> each flick of the finger premeditated;
> he pummels the clay with his arm,
> and puddles it with his feet;
> he sets his heart on perfecting the glaze,
> and stays up cleaning the kiln.
> All these put their trust in their hands,
> and each is skilled at his own craft.
> A town could not be built without them,
> there would be no settling, no travelling.
> But they are not required at the council,
> they do not hold high rank in the assembly.
> They do not sit on the judicial bench,
> and have no grasp of the law.
> They are not remarkable for culture or sound judgement,
> and are not found among the inventors of maxims.
> But they give solidity to the created world,
> while their prayer is concerned with what pertains to their trade.[5]

Again in Ecclesiasticus it is stated:

> A meagre diet is the very life of the poor,
> he who withholds it is a man of blood.
> A man murders his neighbour if he robs him of his livelihood,
> Sheds blood if he withholds an employee's wages.[6]

It is difficult to imagine the rights of the worker to a just wage being expressed in stronger language.

With an example of Genesis (chapters 2 and 3) it could probably be said that for the Hebrews agriculture became the prototype of work both in time and status. Furthermore, historically speaking they had been promised land by Yahweh. This was Yahweh's land and he would point it out and hand it over to them. After their long period of slavery in Egypt, we can imagine the pride and joy of the Israelites in having their own land to cultivate. In giving them the land, Yahweh in Lev. 25:3–6 laid down rules for its cultivation from the beginning. Thus it can be appreciated that the Israelites, called by Yahweh to be the people of God, and their consciousness of themselves as being a farming people, were two concepts inextricably tied up together from the beginning.[7]

That the Israelites were an agricultural society is reflected in their history. The patriarchs Noah, Abraham and Isaac were all farmers. Amos was one of the shepherds of Tekoa (Amos 1:1). David was a shepherd (1 Sam. 16:11). This meant that in the eyes of ordinary folk the status of work was enhanced. If their leaders were artisans, there was nothing to be ashamed of in working with one's hands. Furthermore, the point has been made that in the Old Testament, when Yahweh has something important to communicate to someone, he frequently does so while that person is at work. Gideon was threshing and cleansing wheat when the angels of the Lord appeared to him (Judg. 6:11); Saul was looking for asses when he met Samuel and continued to plough the fields after he was made king (1 Sam. 9:4,18 and 1 Sam. 11:5). From these examples it can be seen why the Hebrews concluded that Yahweh's blessing was on their work.

Trades and crafts
With agriculture being the dominant occupation of the Hebrews, trades and crafts received somewhat less attention. This may have been due to the fact that for a long period of time the Hebrews were mainly nomadic farmers and only later

did they settle in the towns. The trades and crafts that they subsequently learnt were learnt from the pagan peoples who lived around and amongst them. However, Gen. 4:22 indicates that amongst the Hebrews certain trades at least had an early origin. This passage refers to Zillah, who gave birth to Tubal-Cain, who was referred to as the ancestor of metalworkers, in bronze or iron. It stands to reason that the Hebrews, who in the course of their history came to grips with many of the warlike peoples who surrounded them, would have had to have knowledge of metalwork for the manufacturing of weapons. However, it may well be that, apart from the manufacture of weapons, the trades may not have been widely practised amongst them.

In Exodus reference is made to the construction of the sanctuary for the Ark of the Covenant and to several skilled trades such as work in gold, silver or bronze, stonemasonry, wood carving, engraving, weaving and embroidery. So it would seem that, even if to a limited extent, the various trades and crafts were known to the Hebrews.[8]

It seems clear from the Old Testament that Yahweh is personally interested in the work of the Hebrews. Yahweh himself gave the design for the tabernacle. He puts wisdom into the hearts of every craftsman. It was not the need of dignity for Yahweh to assist the workmen among the people, for he had ordained the work in the first place. Yahweh was infinitely closer to the Hebrews than any pagan gods had ever been to their followers. As stated in Deuteronomy: 'And indeed, what great nation is there that has its gods so near as Yahweh our God is to us whenever we call to him?'[9]

Whilst it appears the trades and crafts may not have been as esteemed amongst the Hebrews as was agriculture, pride in craftsmanship is clearly evident in the erection of the temple. This occurred during the reign of Solomon, and everyone was intensely proud of it. The preparation for the construction of the temple were made by David, whose dream and idea the temple was. These preparations made by David are described in 1 Chron. 22:1–8, and the details of the construction and materials used are detailed in 1 Kings 6. The great detail given by the author of 1 Kings reflects his natural pride in the undertaking. The workers worked with joy and love considering what they did to be the work of Yahweh. Significantly, Solomon addressed the people at the opening ceremony and thanked Yahweh who had carried out by His hand what was promised to David; in other words, it was God's work from beginning to end.[10]

Goosen draws an interesting analysis between the construction of the temple and the construction of the Tower of Babel. He uses the analysis to differentiate how work can be for either good or evil. He states that the word 'ba-bel' can in fact mean 'gate of God' and that the construction of the tower was the attempt to establish contact with divinity. The evil in this story might be taken to be an attempt to try to force Yahweh to come down to men. Goosen sees this dichotomy as being the ambiguity of work in that it can be either God-oriented or self-oriented, for good or for evil.[11]

Oliver O'Donovan expresses the view that originally and fundamentally the existence of Israel as a people was mediated through the land. Possessing the land was a matter of observing that order of life which was established by Yahweh's judgement; on the other hand, possessing the law was a matter of enjoying that purchase on the conditions of life that was Yahweh's gift. As stated in Ps. 37:29: 'The virtuous will have the land for their own, and make it their home forever.'

In Josh. 24:13 Yahweh says 'I gave you a land where you never toiled, you live in towns you never built; you eat now from vineyards and olive groves you never planted.' Although as stated in Lev. 25:23 ownership was still vested in Yahweh, the Hebrews were in effect leaseholders from Yahweh. 'Land must not be sold in perpetuity, for the land belongs to me, and to me you are only strangers and guests' (Lev. 25:23). On the one hand, Israel as a whole possesses the land as a whole. On the other hand, each tribe and family has its share, its own way of participating in the gift of God to his people. O'Donovan says that this gift is both collective and distributive.[12]

The notion of the collective and distributive nature of Israel's ownership of the land in some ways foreshadows the patristic writings on stewardship of the second to the fourth centuries AD, to the effect that property was held by its owner in trust for all.

The prophetic writings

It has been said that the prophets sat in judgement on the institutions of Israel and became the conscience of the nation. This judgement on the nation constituted a new role in the religions of the Near East, and it has become part of the tradition of western culture since that time.[13] The pre-exilic classical prophets addressed social morality. This sometimes earned for them the designation 'social prophets'. Whilst the prophets make no direct reference to the worker, their social message

The biblical worker

has direct application to the situation of the worker and to all those in a situation of weakness, need, or dependence. The social message of the prophets was admittedly a major emphasis, but an explanation is to be found in the function of an Israelite prophet: serving as a conscience for his people in precisely those matters where conscience was needed. As stated in the *Jerome Biblical Commentary*, against the backdrop of Israelite history, prophetic social doctrine fits into its proper place and is not out of proportion. The prophets themselves could only have been puzzled by the designation 'social'. They were only insisting on the social virtues inherent in the doctrines of election and covenant, virtues which had been flagrantly violated in an Israel that had largely abandoned its ancient ideals, assimilating itself to Gentile ways. In presuming a social character to the religion of Yahweh, the prophets were proposing nothing new but recalling a known, although much ignored, morality.[14]

The Hebrew concept of social justice

Townsend's view was that from this prophetic emphasis emerges an Old Testament theme that becomes a major assertion and extends into the New Testament doctrine of the kingdom of God: 'How happy are the poor in spirit; theirs is the Kingdom of heaven' (Matt. 5:3). This theme is that of Yahweh's poor, the anawim – that is, of the socially oppressed whose redress could only come from Yahweh. The prophets did not sentimentalize poverty, although it was regarded as an undesirable thing. What they promulgated was the fact that the poor man was not a just man simply because he was poor, but rather that poverty and unjust oppression were frequent companions. It was the evil of others that had created this situation, and the whole of prophetic effort was directed against the evil. It was the evil of oppression and injustice that they railled against.

It could be said that if the Jews had a more acute sense of justice than other nations, it was due to their religious faith and the prophets. The prophets were particularly active during periods of both great material prosperity, which turned the Jews away from their religion, and periods of national catastrophe in which they fell into despair. The prophets spoke out like the voice of conscience denouncing the sins of society, especially religious hypocrisy and economic exploitation. The remedy they advocated was a return to the love of God and the keeping of His law. For the prophets, righteousness (including justice in the modern sense) was not only a duty imposed by religion, but was identical with true religion. In both the Old and the New Testaments 'righteousness' goes deeper than 'justice'; it is not satisfied by conformity of social behaviour to legally prescribed norms and accepted principles of equity, but requires also an inner quality of loyalty, service and compassion of person to person, modelled on the faithfulness of God to His people, which was manifested in history especially by His saving acts in their times of adversity.

Townsend argues that what the prophets denounced was not that the northern kingdom had grown rich on agriculture, nor that the southern kingdom had prospered on trade, but that neither recognized that God was concerned with these activities. The prophets declared that God is the lord of economics and politics no less than of religion. Their denunciations were prompted not by mere conservatism, but by a refusal to condone a social order which made a mockery of godliness and religion by neglecting the claims of humanity.[15]

The Jews had a conviction that there was a divine plan in history and that it required their active cooperation as a people. It never entered the heads of the Jews to suppose, as Christians have sometimes been inclined to do, that morality is concerned with the private lives of the individual rather than with the public concerns of society, economic and political. They shared the ancient conception of morality as essentially concerned with the community. Their religious experience of God's dealings with them confirmed it. As long as the Jewish nation lived, righteousness and sin were social conceptions, and the preaching of the prophets made a point of condemning social injustice as a crime which made nonsense of the worship of the Lord. But following the destruction of Israel and the Babylonian exile, the stress of prophetic preaching changed. It was then placed on personal responsibility before God.[16] This is not to say that the post-exilic prophets lost sight of the concepts of social justice. In the eyes of Ezekiel who made provision in his planning for a fair distribution of land amongst the people when they should return to their country (Ezek. 47:13, 21–3; 48:1–7, 23–9), and of all the post-exilic prophets, religious renewal and social reconstruction were identical claims. The Jews did not distinguish between the 'spiritual' and the 'secular'. For them, human beings and their societies were unities of both, and both had to be brought into the service of God.

S. C. Carpenter makes the comment that the prophetic vision

of the prophets was always concerned chiefly with the plain man. There was room on the canvas for the upright, noble ruler, who was a glory to the state, but the main interest is with the masses. It was also his view that the counsel the prophets gave to their contemporaries on social duty was very uncompromising.[17]

The social security of Deuteronomy and Qumran

Deuteronomy lists certain practices aimed at aiding and assisting the poor. In 24:17 it says, 'You must not pervert justice in dealing with a stranger or an orphan, nor take a widow's garment in pledge'. In 24:19, 'When reaping the harvest in your field, if you have overlooked a sheaf in that field, do not go back for it. Leave it for the stranger, the orphan and the widow.' In 24:20, 'When you beat your olive trees you must not go over the branches twice. Let anything left be for the stranger, the orphan and the widow.' In 24:21, 'When you harvest your vineyard you must not pick it over a second time. Let anything left be for the stranger, the orphan and the widow.' In 23:25–6 it says 'If you go through your neighbour's vineyard, you may eat your fill of grapes, as many as you wish, but you must not put any in your basket. If you go through your neighbour's standing corn, you may pick the ears with your hand, but you must not put a sickle into your neighbour's corn.'

These practices known as 'gleaning' were a significant element in the Deuteronomic code. The *New Jerome Biblical Commentary* refers to gleaning rights as a significant element in Deuteronomy's 'social security system'.[18]

The Damascus document of the Dead Sea Scrolls makes reference to what may be described as one of the earliest references to something resembling a social security system apart from those measures listed in Deuteronomy. There is a section headed up 'This is the rule for the congregation by which it shall provide for all its needs.' It goes on to say that the members of the community 'shall place the earnings of at least two days out of every month into the hands of the guardian and the judges, and from it they shall give to the fatherless, and from it they shall succour the poor and the needy, the aged, sick and the man who is stricken [with disease], the captive taken by a foreign people, the virgin with no near kin, and the maid for whom no man cares ...' and this is the exact statement of the Assembly ...'[19]

The statement of the rule is fragmented, but there is

sufficient to indicate that the members of the Essene community engaged in work of some kind for which they received earnings, and from these earnings a sum was deducted on a regular basis for the maintenance and welfare of the disadvantaged in the community.

Document 4Q159 of the *Ordinances or Commentaries on Biblical Law* from Qumran modifies Deut. 23:25-6 to a minor extent. Whereas in Deuteronomy it is stated that a poor man may eat ears of corn in the field of another person, but is not allowed to take any home, the Qumran statute indicates that on a threshing floor he may both eat and gather provisions for his family.

Change in attitude to work

Goosen asserts that in the Old Testament there is a noticeable shift in emphasis on the question of work after the Babylonian exile. He says that the authors become less enthusiastic about work and stress the need for wisdom. In the wisdom literature work is portrayed as sometimes pleasant, sometimes painful, but always a necessity of life. The prosaic fact is that one must work in order to live and, moreover, as work is a natural law, one must fulfil the law. On the other hand, idleness is condemned as it leads to poverty and hunger. The idler is a burden to himself and runs the risk of dying of starvation (Prov. 21:25; 10:4;), he has nothing to eat (13:4) and he is stupid (24:30). Elsewhere in Proverbs it is asserted that there is nothing like hunger to stimulate one to work (Prov. 16:26); the idler is comparable to a lump of dung and is avoided by everybody (Eccles. 22:2). For the man of private means and a man who works hard, life is pleasant (Eccles. 40:18). 'Do not shirk wearisome labour, or farm work, which the Most High created' (Eccles. 7:15-16).[20]

The Book of Proverbs, which is full of worldly wisdom, reminds us that the good businessman will rise to the top; he will come to serve kings (Prov. 22:29); an honest worker should take no notice of the prosperity of a sinner since one never knows what turn his career might take (Eccles. 9:16). One should be meticulous in one's work in order to advance (Prov. 19:1).

Slavery in the Old Testament

There is a dichotomy between the concept of slavery as it existed for the Hebrews and for the pagans. According to Aristotle's theory of slavery, the association which existed between the master and the slave was an association as natural as that between a man and his wife. Just as the wife is made for the husband, the slave is made for the master. For Aristotle there are men, who, by their nature, are destined to govern and to command, because their reasoning faculty is capable of foresight, and there are men destined by nature to submission and to servitude because, as they are incapable of foreseeing by themselves, they are only capable of realizing by their bodily strength the provisions of their masters. In nature, indeed, there is no resemblance to the faulty artisans of the human world. Nature understands that a perfect instrument is that which serves only a single purpose; it is for this reason that the slave serves only to obey; a being capable at one and the same time of ordering and obeying would be imperfect; nature's definition would be equivocal. His very being would be branded with an uncertainty.[21]

The notion that slavery could possibly be based upon injustice and violence is (according to Aristotle) scarcely to be examined. If nature had not wished for slaves, she would have endowed shuttles with the property of spinning and weaving cloth automatically, without human attention. The slave is the living property of the master; he or she is nothing but an instrument, though the first of instruments. The relationship between the master and the slave is one-sided; it binds the slave to the master, but not the master to the slave.

Borne and Henry hold that the wisdom of the ancient Greeks entertained no suspicion that man could possibly be in himself a centre and a whole; if every man is a part of the world, the slave can quite well be a part of his master. In the worker, the artisan, the wisdom of antiquity was unable to recognize the man. Everything goes to prove the deliberate and universal scorn of work; the theories of the philosophers just as much as the philosophy which appears spontaneously from language: the Greek *ponos* and the Latin *labor* mean at the same time both work and pain. Slaves and masters were different beings in their bodies and in their minds. Work was a servile thing, because it focused upon the soul a resemblance to the matter which it worked upon and modified; it was human in proportion as it was the service by means of which a few persons were allowed the privilege of enjoying leisure. The slave who was a cook could both live and die happily, if his toil makes possible the existence of a Lucullus.[22]

Work in the pagan world enjoyed neither the beautiful nor the good, for enjoyment is an end in itself, and labour is but a means to an end. The only activity which is human in the fullest sense of the word is leisure which renders possible a political life, or a life spent in the activities of contemplation. The intoxication of disinterested knowledge, which was the marvellous discovery of Hellas, caused it to disregard the eminent dignity of service. Borne and Henry argue that it was reserved as the function of Christianity which imparted dignity to the idea of *labor,* to set free the children of the worker, Martha, without omitting to glorify the children of the contemplative Mary.[23]

Under the Mosaic law, slavery was accepted. If the slave concerned was a Hebrew, his service lasted for six years, and if he declared his love for his master he could remain in his service for all time.[24] Slavery was sometimes a punishment for thieving, for if a thief could not make full restitution he ought to be sold into slavery.[25] Furthermore, it sometimes happened as seen in Nehemiah[26] that the Hebrews had to barter their sons and daughters to obtain sufficient corn to survive.

John Byron speaks of the Hebrew nation that, having been freed from slavery in Egypt, they were now slaves of God. He said that the nuance of the debt-slavery laws made it impossible for an Israelite to lose status as an Israelite while serving a fellow Israelite. He said that Israelites were not to be the permanent slaves of anyone except God, who had released them from slavery in Egypt.[27] Referring to Exodus 21:2 Byron says that the 'serve' and 'going out' were representative of the theme in Exodus of Israel's 'service to' and 'going out' from Egypt. He said that just as Israel 'served' Egypt and then 'went out', the Hebrew slave who 'served' another Hebrew must also 'go out'. The theme of Exodus clearly emphasizes that Israel has been released from slavery and is disqualified from permanently serving another.[28] This Hebrew concept of 'slavery to God' has a later parallel in the New Testament where Paul depicts himself as a slave for the gospel.[29]

Dale Martin says that the slavery to Christ to which Paul alluded was an example of his playing upon the soteriological meanings of metaphorical slavery by showing that his own self-lowering will bring not only the salvation of his converts, but his own eschatological salvation as well.[30]

Other than the manumission which occurred in the sabbatical year, slaves could be liberated in jubilee years, which occurred every fifty years. The Jews were constantly reminded by their sacred writings that they had once been slaves and had been liberated from the Egyptians by the intervention of God. The sacred memory of God's compassion inculcated an attitude of

The biblical worker

humanity which benefited foreign slaves as well. Exodus says:

> This is the ruling you are to lay before them: when you buy a Hebrew slave, his service shall be for six years. In the seventh year he may leave; he shall be free, with no compensation to pay. If he came single, he shall leave single; if he came married, his wife shall leave with him. If his master gives him a wife and she bears him sons and daughters, wife and children shall belong to her master, and the man must leave alone. But if the slave declares, 'I love my master and my wife and children; I renounce my freedom,' then his master shall take him to God, leading him to the door or the doorpost. His master shall pierce his ear with an awl, and he shall be in his service for all time. If a man sells his daughter as a slave, she shall not regain her liberty like male slaves. If she does not please her master who intended her for himself, he must let her be bought back: he has not the right to sell her to foreigners, thus treating her unfairly. If he intends her for his son, he shall deal with her according to the ruling for daughters. If he takes another wife, he must not reduce the food of the first or her clothing or her conjugal rights. Should he cheat her of these three things she may leave, freely, without having to pay any money.[31]

In Leviticus it is stated:

> The servants you have, men and women, shall come from the nations around you; from these you may purchase servants, men and women. You may also purchase them from the children of the strangers who live among you, and from their families living with you who have been born on your soil. They shall be your property and you may leave them as an inheritance to your sons after you, to hold in perpetual possession. These you may have for slaves; but to your brothers, the sons of Israel, you must not be hard masters.[32]

Deuteronomy says:

> If your fellow Hebrew, man or woman, is sold to you, he can serve you for six years. In the seventh year you must set him free, and in setting him free you must not let him go empty handed. You must make him a generous provision from your flock, your threshing floor, your wine press; as Yahweh your God has blessed you, so you must give to him. Remember that you were a slave in the land of Egypt and that Yahweh your God redeemed you; that is why I lay this charge on you today.[33]

In Jewish law if a slave suffered grievous bodily harm at the hands of his master, he was granted freedom, whereas under the code of Hammurabi the slave was compensated by a sum of money. 'When a man strikes at the eye of his slave, male or female, and destroys the use of it, he must give him his freedom to compensate for the eye. If he knocks out the tooth of his slave, male or female, he must give him his freedom to compensate for the tooth.' [34]

It would seem that the purpose of these laws was to relieve the situation of those whom misfortune had reduced to a position of dependence. Such laws, however, would not always have solved the problems of those who had been forced into a position of servitude. The situation of the slave after his or her release must have been very precarious, since he or she would seldom have had access to the resources necessary in order to establish themselves as a free citizen in the community. The mere emancipation of the slave did not solve the problem of his or her rehabilitation, and the fact that the law found it necessary to exhort the master to furnish his or her slave with generous provisions upon release as shown above in Deut. 15:12-15 is surely a recognition of this difficulty. The slave, although subject to an obligation to observe certain constraints imposed upon him or her by his master, may often have preferred to remain in servitude than to be set free to face the possibility of destitution. It was therefore not without reason that the law permitted the slave to remain in bondage if he or she so wished (Exod. 21:5-11; Deut. 15:16-17), and it may well have been in his own interests to do so. It would therefore seem that the institution of the seventh year with its demand for the emancipation of Hebrew slaves after six years of servitude would not always have provided relief for the poor debtor who may have felt that his master could offer him the protection and support which he may have lacked had he been set free.[35]

It is interesting that under Hebrew law a slave was able to obtain his or her freedom by the simple expedient of running away. Deut. 23:15-16 provides, 'You must not allow a master to imprison a slave who has escaped from him and come to you. He shall live with you, among you, wherever he pleases in any one of your towns he chooses; you are not to molest him.' This provision highlights the huge difference between the situation of slaves in Hebrew law as against their situation in the pagan lands which surrounded them. It seems that it was possible for slaves to become free by an act of their will: by simply deciding to escape. In essays entitled *Ethics as Deconstruction* and *The Ethics of Deconstruction*, David J. A. Clines states that the Hebrew Bible does not report the abolition of slavery as a real social phenomenon, but it does announce a conceptuality according to which traditional slavery is, strictly speaking, inconceivable. He says that if slavery is no more than a matter of a choice that slaves make, the ethical problem of slavery has well-nigh disappeared.[36]

Other near-eastern societies of the time had no such law. The laws of Eshnunna, for example, explicitly imposed a fine for harbouring a runaway slave, while the code of Hammurabi made it a capital offence. In the Alalakh Tablets from Syria there is evidence of a reward being paid to a person for apprehending a runaway slave.[37]

David Clines asserts that Deut. 23 and Exod. 21 give rise to a concept of voluntary slavery which is deconstructive of the whole concept of slavery as it is traditionally understood. He says that slavery is in a sense abolished under Hebrew law when it ceases to be a state that a person is forced into against their will. It still survives as a social institution indeed, but, in that the line of distinction between slave and free has been blurred, it has lost its conceptual force.[38]

It can be said then that, in general, slaves were better off in Hebrew culture than in any other cultures of those times. They were not permitted to work on the Sabbath, were not regarded as a commodity, and were admitted to the communion of the cult. Slaves were accepted into the household to various degrees, and frequently the master would seek the opinion or the advice of a slave as did Saul in 1 Sam. 9:6. They were often entrusted with the responsibility of managing their lord's household affairs and business interests. In Hebrew culture, it was customary to greet a slave with a blessing. Boaz, for example, greeted the slaves picking ears of corn with the greeting: 'Yahweh be with you'. (Ruth 2:4). So then, among the Hebrews we find a greater appreciation of work than among the pagans, we also find a more humane treatment of slaves; in fact, the word used for servant, *ebed,* means 'worker', and the biblical phrase 'servant of the Lord' was a title of great honour. Significantly absent from the Hebrew mentality is not only the pagan disdain for manual work, but also the association of certain types of work with slaves, which is common in other cultures of all times:[39]

> You have only one slave? Treat him like yourself,
> since you have acquired him with blood.
> You have only one slave? Treat him as a brother.
> since you need him as you need yourself.
> If you ill-treat him and he runs away,
> which way will you go to look for him?[40]

The delivery of the Hebrews from slavery in Egypt was an event which they were to celebrate annually. This event defined who they were as a nation. They were a people that had been set free. The Hebrews were established in their own land, not as slaves, but as a free people. Their land was equitably divided amongst the people according to tribe and family. This was important. Yahweh was acknowledged as the owner of the earth, and he distributed amongst his people justly and fairly because they were all equally his children.

Engerman, Drescher and Paquette list twenty-five excerpts from Exodus, Deuteronomy and Leviticus concerning the manner, duration, and conditions for entry into the state of slavery by Hebrews.[41] It is clear then that the Hebrews regarded the enslavement of fellow Hebrews unfavourably and established conditions for their early emancipation.

The worker in the Gospels

We do not find a detailed theology of work in the New Testament. However, we do find a general and useful orientation to the subject. There is a perspective which a certain section of humanity has been able to apply to the situation in which it has found itself throughout the course of history. This perspective examines the Gospels or their application to the subject of work and the worker. This involves a consideration of the cultural ambience of the New Testament – that is, how it was similar to other cultures of the era, though somewhat more civilized and refined. The same social patterns as elsewhere are found: the slaves and servants, manual workers and scholars, idlers and the unemployed.[42] There are those who were dishonest and clever in administration.[43]

In the Synoptic Gospels one's attitude towards work is necessarily tied up with the problem of riches, which received special attention, particularly at the hands of Luke. The hoarding of possessions is roundly condemned (Luke 12:16–21), for the fool said to himself after he had amassed plenty, 'Take things easy. Eat, drink, and have a good time'. In the Old Testament the problem was sometimes expressed in either pursuing riches, wisdom, work or pleasure, *theoria* or *praxis*, whereas in the New the problem is cast in the terms of either God or money (Matt. 6:24). The plain truth is that those who have many possessions will find it difficult to enter the kingdom.[44] The message appears to be simple. If the object of work is to supply the needs of the body and personal fulfilment, then work solely for the purpose of acquiring wealth, or with an undue emphasis on acquiring wealth, is evil. As is said in Matthew: 'No one can be the slave of two masters: you'll either hate the first and love the second, or treat the first with respect and the second with scorn. You cannot be the slave both of God and of money.'[45] If it is sometimes said that the kingdom of Heaven is the reign of God in the souls of men, this is made clear from this extract from Matthew and from Luke: 'So in the same way, none of you can be my disciple unless he gives up all his possessions'.[46] Jesus demanded of His followers a total surrender involving a change of heart, as in Matthew it is said, 'If anyone wants to be a follower of mine, let him renounce himself and take up his cross and follow me. For anyone who wants to save his life will lose it; but anyone who loses his life for my sake will find it. What, then, will a man gain if he wins the whole world and ruins his life?'[47]

Although riches are seen as an obstacle to entering the kingdom, idleness is not to be encouraged. We are exhorted to use our talents. Sloth is condemned in the Gospels and work is therefore implicitly advocated. As the parable of the talents indicates, some kind of work is necessary in order to develop one's talents.[48] The emphasis is on doing, not passivity. The Last Judgement scene is an illustration of this point. Some will be condemned for being idle, others for sins of omission.[49] The letter of James underlines the importance of being a doer of the word 'but you must do what the word tells you, and not just listen to it and deceive yourselves'.[50] Later in the same letter he says in even stronger language when speaking of faith: 'Faith is like that: if good works do not go with it, it is quite dead'.[51] What we see here is a close parallel with the Old Testament Hebrew emphasis on *praxis* and personal conduct. What a person knows and learns should be translated into practice.

In working, in developing our talents, there is always a social dimension that comes into the picture. Being a good steward always involves others. A father works, for example, so that he can give his son bread, not a stone;[52] likewise, the fruit of one's work, bread, will be an obvious thing to offer the unexpected visitor.[53] This social dimension of work is a fundamental aspect of the Christian approach to work. The fruits of our labour provide for our needs and the needs of others. However this social dimension is one which capitalism is constantly threatening to submerge. The Gospel sees work in the context of service to others. Liberal capitalism sees work as a function of the productive process.

Jesus and work

Although the kingdom of God is a kingdom of the spirit, it is in some ways a visible kingdom. This physical sense is gathered from the practise of Jesus and his followers. In the Gospels the Kingdom begins to take shape as a community of disciples, especially the twelve, gathered around Jesus. It is not a community withdrawn from the everyday world and indifferent to its affairs; it is a community whose members work and live in the world around them giving witness by their examples in living, and preaching the Gospel of Jesus. The community acts on the world like yeast on flour (Luke 13:20–1). This was what Jesus said and did. It is the view of this writer that this is what all Christians are called upon to do whether in their factories, farms, offices, workshops, social institutions, homes or at their places of recreation and leisure.

The Gospels contain numerous references to workers. Jesus himself was a worker and, like Amos, Saul and David, came from the artisan class. Like His earthly father, Joseph, Jesus was a carpenter, or the more frequently used term, artisan. As an artisan He was not expected to be either learned or wise, as we see from the reaction of the Nazarenes when He visited His home town: 'This is the carpenter's son, surely? Is not His mother the woman called Mary, and his brothers James and Joseph and Simon and Jude? His sisters, too, are they not all here with us? So where did the man get it all?'.[54] This reaction of the Nazarenes to Jesus exhibits the attitude to artisans indicated in Ecclesiasticus in which it is indicated that the manual worker is supposed to be occupied only with his own trade and not to have the wisdom or intelligence of the scholar.[55]

In the years before His public ministry, Jesus worked as a carpenter with Joseph and Mary. Nothing is said in the Gospels of this time, but it is probable that He experienced all of the frustrations and satisfaction of any tradesman. As a tradesman He would have served the people of Nazareth and the surrounding district in the same way as other tradesmen in the village. So even before His public ministry, His working life was an orientation of service to others, an orientation which was to be a feature of His whole life: '. . . just as the Son of Man came not to be served but to serve, and to give His life as the ransom for many' (Matt. 20:28).

It may be argued that the Gospels and the example of Jesus indicate that work is of little value and Jesus' work as a tradesman counted for very little. It may also be argued that His ministry was His 'work'. The Apostles abandoned their nets to follow Jesus; therefore, worldly occupations must be of little importance. Here we are beginning to touch on the eschatological value of work. However, the Gospels show that life possesses values and work is part of that value system. Making a decision according to one's values is a part of life. The Apostles had to make such a decision in leaving their nets to follow Jesus, but most of us are not presented with the necessity for making a choice of such a radical dimension.

There is, as Garriguiet points out, at one extreme, a school of thought which asserts that Jesus' intention was exclusively of a religious nature and that He was only concerned with questions of the spirit and largely indifferent towards everyday affairs. Some proponents of liberation theology may place an undue emphasis on Jesus as a radical social reformer. Neither view, it is submitted, is a valid interpretation of the gospel message. His primary mission was the establishment of a spiritual kingdom, His Church. The incarnation occurred for humanity's redemption. But even if Jesus came on earth to free humanity from sin, if His first care was the spiritual good of the individual, it does not follow that He was indifferent to his temporal welfare. 'Having come to perfect man, He took the whole man, and placed him in the setting assigned to him by providence. He took him with his body, his social destiny, his numerous wants, his duties of every kind and in his necessary relations.'[56]

It is sometimes suggested by those unfamiliar with the dichotomy between doctrinal teaching and social teaching that Catholic economics are useless because they are part and parcel of an antiquated social fabric. At this stage a distinction must be drawn between the doctrinal and economic teachings of the Church. This objection would indeed be destructive if Jesus had given us a dissertation on the social problems of His time. Christian dogma can never admit a distinction between speculative and practical truth; it can never be accommodated to current usage or thought. On the other hand, Christian economic teaching, while based on immutable principles of justice, is not identical with those principles. It deals with their application to practical life, and its findings will vary as often as the concrete data. What Jesus actually gave us in the Gospels was a more or less disconnected series of precepts and counsel, from which human reason could deduce a number of principles of necessary truth on which the social teaching of the Church has its foundation. These are the principles of justice in one's dealing with others, charity, service, truthfulness and the centrality of God. The impersonality and detachment from contingencies of Catholic social teaching facilitates its ease of adaptation. It is suitable for every society because it was not given to any one particular society. As Garriguet said:

> In the gospel we have something better than a system. Systems fit into a definite setting; outside it, they do more harm than good. Christianity gives us something worldwide and permanent, a frame of mind, an orientation of energy from which may be obtained, at each stage of social development, the greatest possible amount of justice.[57]

Christian social and economic teaching, while based on immutable principles of justice, is not identical to them. It deals with their application to practical life, and its findings will vary as often as the nature of the situation to which the social principles are applied. The major premise, derived from revelation, is necessary and constant. The minor premise will change as conditions vary, and the conclusion will change with it.

Some Catholic sociologists contend that the very essence of Christianity is to be found in the Sermon on the Mount. It is here also that we discover the most telling exposition of Jesus' social and economic teaching. We are told that we cannot serve both God and money (Matt. 6:24), and it is also in the Sermon on the Mount that Jesus says, 'Set your hearts on His Kingdom first, and on His righteousness, and all His other things will be given you as well' (Matt. 6:33-4). In the same sermon, Jesus enunciates what has been termed 'the golden rule': 'So always treat others as you would like them to treat you; that is the meaning of the law and the prophets' (Matt. 7:12). It is a reasonable assumption that treating others as you would like them to treat oneself would include the payment of a just wage to workers and the provision of healthy and proper working conditions. As Patrick McDowall says, we have here the epitome of Christian economics. We have the source of all human rights in the absolute dominion and the universal fatherhood of God.[58]

Whilst the exhortation to seek first the kingdom of God is a great practical rule of life, these words were never intended to mitigate the punishment of fallen man: 'With sweat on your brow shall you eat your bread, until you return to the soil' (Gen. 3:19). The difference is that labouring man now has a new sense of values. The primary object of his working is the glory of God. If one's work is attended by success, then one should guard against the danger of avarice. One has to remember at all times that riches were created for humanity, not humanity for riches. As we have seen, it is in Genesis where all of creation is placed at the service of humanity (Gen. 1:28). If man's hope of heaven is endangered by riches, then it is dearly bought. If man fails in his work, he is not to be discouraged as if he had lost all that was worth having. He needs to find comfort in the fact that the real prize may still be his, and that his very poverty and suffering can be used to bring it nearer.

One of the cornerstones of Jesus' teaching is the concept of being a 'servant' or a 'worker' for all. Time and again Jesus makes the point that we are to be servants of others just as he made himself a servant for us. In Luke 22:25-7 he says,

> Among pagans it is the kings who lord it over them, and those who have authority over them are given the title 'benefactor'. This must not happen with you. No; the greatest among you must behave as if he were the youngest, the leader as if he were the one who serves. For who is the greater: the one at table or the one who serves? The one at table, surely? Yet here am I among you as one who serves!

Later, at the Last Supper, Jesus re-emphasizes again strongly the necessity of service to each other:

> Do you understand, he said, what I have done to you? You call me master and Lord, and rightly; so I am. If I, then, the Lord and Master, have washed your feet, you should wash each other's feet. I have given you an example that you may copy what I have done to you. (John 13:13-15)

In Mark, when the Apostles were arguing over which of them was the greatest, Jesus said to them, 'If anyone wants to be first, he must make himself last of all and servant of all' and again he says, 'Anyone who wants to become great among you must be your servant, and anyone who wants to be first among you must be slave to all. For the Son of Man Himself did not come to be served but to serve, and to give His life as a ransom for many' (Mark 10:43-5). John F. Dowd describes Mark 9:35 to 10:43-5 as containing a litany on service that reaches its crescendo of ultimate liberation in the death of the servant. The reference is to Jesus himself. He says it is in sharp contrast in style to the attitude to power embodied in the emperors and kings of old and in authoritarian regimes of the present day.[59]

Summary

It is evident from the Gospels that Jesus recognized that both individual and social reform was needed. Jesus was not a reformer of the political kind in advocating the improvement of laws and institutions governing and administering society. He enters into no detailed discussion of the social order at all. However, a transformation of the social order would inevitably, though indirectly, take place by the change of mind and heart to which He called all humanity. It would seem to follow from the nature of the gospel teachings that the Christian reformer is a person who abstains from violence and rash behaviour, and a person of patience and hope who works for the interpenetration of humanity and society by a new spirit.

Henry Townsend emphasizes the question well when he says that every person, being both an individual and a member of society, leads his own private life and at the same time serves in the corporate life of the community. He can no more forgo the one than the other; but he can neglect one for the other, becoming either a self-centred individualist or an impersonal collectivist. A sound social doctrine must accommodate these tendencies of human nature, not by cutting them back but by unifying them. Jesus' teaching makes this possible by providing a common aim for both, so that by reaching out in the same direction they can be made to work harmoniously together. It seems to bring about a change in men, a conversion of heart and mind (the basic meaning of 'repentance') which will draw them into the right relationship with God and with one another, thereby introducing them into a new kind of life, beginning on earth and reaching full maturity in heaven. That life is to be a life of love, initiated and sustained by God: love for God issuing in, and measured by, love of man for man. Thus the kingdom which Jesus announced is an interior kingdom, but an interior kingdom which is to overflow into men's relationship with one another.[60]

Jesus' ethical doctrine concerns itself primarily with the personal behaviour and conduct of one person to another. However, that does not make it individualistic and of no relevance to the affairs and challenges of economic life, politics and the state. Jesus wanted men and women to live righteously in common; but he dealt directly with social affairs only insofar as they involved questions of moral principle and then only as they confronted him.[61]

C. A. Anderson-Scott, delivering the Hulsean Lectures in 1929, makes interesting deductions in respect of Matt. 5:42:

The biblical worker 31

'Give to anyone who asks, and if anyone wants to borrow, do not turn away.' He said that these words, literally applied, would be open to all the obvious and well-grounded objections with which we are familiar. He says that they are to be understood literally, but not literally applied. Once more, Jesus is dealing with what is understood to be one of man's natural rights, the right to have property, the right to do what he likes with his own. It is to be observed that Jesus nowhere denies this right, and Scott says that it may be correct to speak of Jesus as a revolutionary. But if so, He is a revolutionary in morals, not in economics, however possible it may be that a wide extension of His revolution in morals would lead to an economic revolution as well. Scott then quotes Dr Bethune-Baker, who asks the question: 'Are you to give to everyone that asketh you?' His answer is, 'Certainly not' and thus, he says, 'Pay your poor rates willingly; and don't try to cut down wages to a minimum; and give all the help you can to individuals you know are out of work because there is no work for them to do.' He concludes by saying that our attitude to money, power, and property should be one of detachment. It should be such that these things in themselves would never be a hindrance to our giving help to our neighbour even at cost to ourselves.[62]

There is a small passage which appears in each of the Synoptic Gospels during the narrative of the feeding of the five thousand. The Apostles turn to Jesus suggesting that He send the people away so they could go to neighbouring villages to buy food. Jesus' reply in all three Gospels is 'Give them something to eat yourselves.' (Matt. 14:16; Mark 6:37; Luke 9:13). Are not these words in their calling to charity and service an exhortation to humanity to take responsibility for one's neighbour? It is an exhortation to act rather than be a passive onlooker of events and situations affecting the needs and rights of our brothers and sisters in the secular environment. Is it a call to put into practice the principles of distributive justice? It is this writer's view that the answer is 'Yes' to these questions, although the answer is not necessarily the sole answer.

The worker in the epistles

The letter of James contains three passages with elements pertaining to workers. In 2:1 the author says, 'My brothers, do not try to combine faith in Jesus Christ, our glorified Lord, with the making of distinctions between classes of people.' In calling the faithful to avoid making distinctions between classes of people, the Apostles treat each other equally, and: 'to keep the supreme law of scripture: you must love your neighbour as yourself', (Jas 2:8). Later in the same letter the Apostle says, 'Labourers mowed your fields and you cheated them – listen to the wages that you kept back calling out.' Realize that the cries of the reapers have reached the ears of the Lord of hosts' (Jas 5:4).

The denunciation of the withholding of wages or otherwise defrauding workers is a recurring theme in both the Old and the New Testaments. Lev. 19:13 says, 'You must not exploit or rob your neighbour. You must not keep back the labourer's wage until next morning' and again in Deut. 24:14, 'You are not to exploit the hired servant who is poor and destitute.' Also Eccles. 34:22 says, 'A man murders his neighbour if he robs him of his livelihood, sheds blood if he withholds an employees wages.' The first letter of John contains a strong admonition to those who say that they love God:

> Anyone who says, 'I love God'
> and hates his brother,
> Is a liar,
> Since a man who does not love the brother that he can see
> Cannot love God, whom he has never seen.
> So this is the commandment that he has given us,
> That anyone who loves God must also love his brother.[63]

In Philippians, Paul speaking of how Jesus came to be the servant to all, said:

> His state was divine
> Yet he did not cling
> To his equality with God
> But emptied himself
> To assume the condition of a slave,
> And became as men are;
> And being as all men are,
> He was humbler yet,
> Even to accepting death,
> Death on the cross.[64]

He also says, 'Always consider the other person to be better than yourself, so that nobody thinks of his own interests first but everybody thinks of other people's interests instead' (Phil. 2:3–4).

On one occasion Paul had reason and the necessity to exhort the community of believers to work. Earlier he had spoken to

The biblical worker

them about the Parousia, and it appears that some of them thought that it was so imminent that they would cease all activity and await its coming. Paul's advice to them was:

> We gave you a rule when we were with you: not to let anyone have any food if he refused to do any work. Now we hear that there are some of you that are living in idleness, doing no work themselves but interfering with everyone else's. In the Lord Jesus Christ, we order and call on people of this kind to go on quietly working and earning the food that they eat. (2 Thess. 3:10)

Paul thought the problem so serious that he went on to say,

> My brothers, never grow tired of doing what is right. If anyone refuses to obey what I have written in this letter, take note of him and have nothing to do with him, so that he will feel that he is in the wrong; though you are not to regard him as an enemy but as a brother in need of correction.[65]

Paul also gave the Thessalonians his own example in telling them that when he was with them he was not idle but worked day and night so as not to be a burden on any of them. This was done as an example to them.[66]

Goosen is of the opinion that Paul's views on work were in line with Old Testament ideas, in that he insisted on work as a means to economic independence and freedom. This, he said, is understandable and logical, given Paul's religious training. But he also urges people to work so that they can give charity and support to those unable to work. Goosen interprets Thess. 3:12 as Paul saying that work guarantees a 'quietness' of spirit (2 Thess: 3.12). The person who is busy with his work possesses a tranquil spirit and has neither the time nor the inclination to pry into matters which do not concern him.[67]

In Ephesians, Paul, writing as a prisoner in Rome, says:

> I therefore, a prisoner of the Lord, beg you to lead a life worthy of the calling to which you have been called, with all lowliness and meekness, with patience, forbearing one another in love, eager to maintain the unity of the spirit in the bond of peace. There is one body and one spirit, just as you were called into one and the same hope when you were called. There is one Lord, one faith, one baptism, one God and Father of us all, who is above all and through all and in all.[68]

In this passage Paul is exhorting the Ephesians, whether they be freeman or slave, to work diligently for God's sake, not for man's.

In carrying out the work of his trade as a tentmaker, Paul gave an example to all. He plied his trade so as not to be a burden on the community. Goosen says that Paul's practice of his trade whilst also evangelizing was the common practice of rabbis at that time. Like Jesus, Paul's apostolic teaching becomes his all-absorbing 'work'. He plants and waters, but God gives the increase. Goosen says that Paul saw his total mission as the 'work' of labour (in the sense of giving birth). The shaping of the Christians after the form or model (*morphe*) of Christ is the goal of his endeavours.[69]

Slavery in the New Testament

In the Gospels and epistles of the New Testament we see the beginnings of the change of attitude towards slavery which began to permeate the empire in parallel with the expansion of Christianity. This change of attitude did not express itself in opposition to the institution of slavery as such but rather involved, as we shall see, a change in attitude towards the person of the slave and of the dignity of human labour. Both of these developments were to be at the core in the future unfolding of Catholic social thought.

In the kingdom of God the prevailing atmosphere is one of freedom and not constraint, because fraternity, and not fear, is its cohesive force. However, nowhere in the Gospels is it recorded that Jesus spoke out against the institution of slavery which, more than any other practice in ancient times, denied the essential brotherhood and sisterhood of humanity. This silence has puzzled many people and was used by some through the ages to justify their position in respect of slavery.

Townsend says that slavery continued among the Jews in New Testament times, though on a smaller scale and with more humanity than elsewhere. He says that in the Gospels Jesus seemed to be aware of the practice around him and to advert to it openly, not in condemnation of it but in illustration of his teaching – for the royal and baronial households in which slavery continued offered in some ways an analogy with the kingdom of God. For example, in the parables of the householder who planted a vineyard and of the great wedding feast, the 'servants' and 'steward' of our translations were domestic slaves (Matt. 21:33–43; 22:1–14). In the first parable they stand for the Jews, as the priests and Pharisees were quick to recognize; in the second they represent the prophets in the Old Testament and the Apostles in the New who were sent by God

The biblical worker

as His messengers to invite first the Jews, then the Gentiles into the kingdom.[70]

In the Gospels the relationship between Jesus and His disciples is frequently referred to as that of servants (slaves) to their Lord and Master. However, in John's version of the Last Supper, Jesus reverses this role and takes upon Himself the role of the slave in washing the feet of the Apostles (John 13:2–17). After He had done this, He said to them, 'Do you understand what I have done to you? You call me Master and Lord, and rightly; so I am. If I, being the Lord and Master, have washed your feet, you should wash each other's feet. I have given you an example so that you may copy what I have done to you' (John 13:13–15). A little later he declares the Apostles emancipated when He says to them, 'I shall not call you servants any more, because a servant does not know his master's business,' (John 15:15). Certainly, in His portrayal of His relationship with His disciples – as slave to Lord and Master – Jesus challenges the prevailing attitudes of His time and of the Roman world on the use of authority and power. Dowd says that, just as the teaching of Jesus on sharing wealth breaks the spiral of greed that makes for rich and poor, so His teaching on power as a service loosens the grip of false political power. Jesus' style of being a servant and calling His disciples into servanthood is a new way of establishing relationships in contrast with the prevailing style and practice.[71]

Paul, in 1 Corinthians says,

> Let everyone stay as he was at the time of his call. If, when you were called, you were a slave, do not let this bother you; but if you should have the chance of being free, accept it. A slave, when he is called in the Lord, becomes the Lord's freedman, and a freedman called in the Lord becomes Christ's slave. You have all been bought and paid for; do not be slaves of other men. Each one of you, my brothers, should stay as he was before God at the time of his call.[72]

He is saying that believers who are slaves should be content with their condition, but if the chance to become free presents itself, they should accept it. In 1 Cor. 7:21–4 Paul reinforces the basic principle which punctuates his advice throughout the chapter, that of contentment in one's life situation. Circumcision and slavery, two great social dividers touching the questions of race and social class, appear as examples of Paul's point. One should not be anxious to change one's situation of life when the call of God to salvation is received, no matter whether such external circumstance relates to circumcision, slavery, or, by implication, marriage.[73]

Paul's words to the Christians who were in slavery – 'Do not let this bother you' – were not unique in the first century, as 'inner-freedom' was probably regarded as more important and could be endured irrespective of one's legal or social status. However, the context in which Paul gives this advice determines its special meaning: 'Since you have been called by God, your legal status no longer determines your existence. Stop being concerned about it for you are already a "freedman in Christ".'[74]

In Colossians Paul says:

> Slaves, be obedient to the men who are called your masters in this world; not only when you are under their eye, as if you had only to please men, but wholeheartedly, out of respect for the master. Whatever your work is, put your heart into it as if it was there for the Lord and not for men, knowing that the Lord will repay you by making you his heirs. It is Christ the Lord that you are serving; anyone who does wrong will be repaid in kind and he does not favour one person more than another. Masters, make sure that your slaves are given what is just and fair, knowing that you too have a master in heaven.[75]

It would seem from this passage that Paul uncritically accepts slavery as a social institution. However, it is also clear that for Paul, for those who are in Christ all human distinctions of race, social status and sex are transcended. Houlden says that Paul's belief in Christ as the new Adam leads him to this conclusion.[76]

In Galatians 3 Paul preaches of the equality of all believers in Christ, whether they be Jews or Gentiles, slaves or freedmen. He says,

> You are, all of you, sons of God through faith in Christ Jesus. All baptized in Christ, you have all clothed yourselves in Christ, and there are no more distinctions between Jew and Greek, slave and free, male and female, but all of you are one in Christ Jesus. Merely by belonging to Christ you are the posterity of Abraham, the heirs he was promised.[77]

However, as far as the institution of slavery is concerned, there is here no call to action. Paul's main concern is that the faithful should immerse themselves in Christ and exhibit the attributes of Christ. Houlden raises the possibility that the fact that Paul made no call to action on the question of slavery may have been because of his possible view that the second coming was imminent and, in any case, Christians were hardly a significant political force.[78] Houlden also asks the questions as to whether a Christian slave would have been content, as Paul was, to leave the matter on this exalted plane? It is this writer's view that, given the prevailing mores of the time, the morality of the institution of slavery per se would not have been given any consideration at all.

For Paul, work was seen in the context of service, and slavery was just one of the institutions of those times. Christian slaves could be distinguished by their spirit of service. Paul urges them to respect their masters, and even more so if their master is a Christian himself, because the person who has the benefit of their services is close to God. Goosen says that Paul's optic turns the whole master–slave relationship around and sees the master as the privileged recipient of the services of the slave.[79] Paul in fact sees himself as a slave to the Gospel.

In the letter to Philemon, Paul appeals to Philemon to take back and treat with kindness the slave Onesimus. It is not clear from the passage whether Onesimus is a runaway slave or how he came to be with Paul. However, it does appear that Philemon was the master of Onesimus, and Paul, who was at this time a prisoner in Rome, had decided that Onesimus should be returned to Philemon. In the course of the letter he says that Onesimus should return to Philemon, not as a slave, but as something much better than a slave, as a dear brother and a brother in the Lord (Philem 16).

The concept of all men being children of God and brothers of Jesus is again evident here. It is as if he is saying to Philemon that if he is really a child of God, he should treat Onesimus as a brother, for he is one too.[80]

The only other epistle to make reference to slaves is 1 Peter. He says: Slaves must be respectful and obedient to their masters, not only when they are kind and gentle, but also when they are unfair. You see, there is some merit in putting up with the pains of unearned punishment if it is done for the sake of God, but there is nothing meritorious in taking a beating patiently if you have done something wrong to deserve it. The merit, in the sight of God, is in bearing it patiently when you are punished after doing your duty.[81]

As with Paul, there is no questioning of the institution of slavery in Peter's letter. However, it should be remembered that, given the minority status of Christianity and for that matter Judaism within the empire, it is unlikely that any questioning of the system would have eventuated even if it had been thought desirable, and there is little evidence of that.

Summary
At its core then, the Christian story is one of God becoming incarnate and dying for a sinful people. The good news is that an act of disinterested love, made possible by a grace that is abundant, transforms and saves.[82] The implication is that human behaviour is not necessarily selfish; with grace building on nature, human beings may rise to a disinterested love of the other. That is what Christian love is about.[83] This disinterested love of the other and the idea of service to others gives impetus to the notion of justice and equity in the workplace.

McDowall postulates that Christianity held that, whilst not ceasing to be God's creature, humanity has now become His children. The practical implications of the new teaching were immense. If all were the sons and daughters of God, then all were equal, not of course in accidental quality such as health or talents or material riches, but in essentials: first of all, in the possession of the same glorious inheritance, now common to Jew and Gentile, equal in the new dignity of humanity derived from God's love and Christ's redemption, even if social institutions should make one a king and his fellow before God a slave or a commoner, equal in the rights to such a modicum of material goods as was necessary for the virtuous spending of this life; and beyond that modicum, riches might be unequally divided. The scope of social justice was extended, its foundation strengthened and ennobled. It obtained now, not between Israelite and Israelite, but between one person and another. It found a sanction in a common sonship and daughtership of God, but had previously failed to derive from a common dependence. The corollary of the fatherhood of God and of the brotherhood and sisterhood of men and women was more than a formula; it was the basis of the whole system of social rights and duties and it was given its sanction by Christ Himself.

He further suggests that in a society living in accordance with the precepts of the Gospels, human division between bondmen and freemen, slaves and masters becomes meaningless, as all live in the community of Christ. All its citizens are sons and daughters of the same Father, and therefore brothers and sisters living in the kingdom of God, a classless society in which all people are equal and free. Human distinction was achieved not in one's birthright, wealth or natural talent, but by self-sacrifice and service to one's brothers and sisters.

While the situation existed that a person's social status was thought to constitute their entire claim to consideration and worth, the institution of slavery could be seen as a logical and

The biblical worker

cruel consequence. Once, however, it came to be seen that under God men and women possess a worth and dignity which is intrinsic to them not only on the ground of their common nature but also and chiefly in virtue of the Father's love and design for them all, they then possess a moral claim to equal consideration and opportunity. The result in time was that under the doctrine of the fatherhood of God and the brotherhood and sisterhood of all people lay the basis and force of the socially regenerative work of Jesus. A consequence of this was that slavery came to be seen as monstrous and eventually disappeared. The later emergence of slavery in the countries of the New World was in effect a cameo development and relatively short lived.[84]

The Patristic Fathers, drawing upon the New Testament, were to advance these new concepts of work and the human person throughout the Roman world.

Notes

1 Psalm 15 from Good News Bible, Today's English Version, 1976.
2 Ps. 112:5.
3 Leviticus 19:18.
4 Deuteronomy 24:14, 15.
5 Ecclesiasticus 38:24–39.
6 Ibid., 34:21–2.
7 Goosen, p. 26.
8 Exodus 35:30-5.
9 Deuteronomy 4:7.
10 Goosen, p. 27.
11 Ibid. pp. 27, 28.
12 O'Donovan, p. 41.
13 Brown, Fitzmyer, Murphy, pp. 195, 196.
14 Ibid. p. 196.
15 Townsend, p. 19.
16 Ibid. pp. 15, 20.
17 Carpenter, pp. 231, 239.
18 Brown, Fitzmyer, Murphy, p.105.
19 Vermes, p. 143.
20 Goosen, p. 99.
21 Borne and Henry, p. 39.
22 Ibid. pp. 39, 43. Lucullus: a first-century Roman general famous for his lavish banquets.
23 Borne and Henry, p. 43.
24 Exodus 21:1–7.
25 Ibid., 22:1–4.
26 Nehemiah 5:1–5.

27 Byron, p. 44.
28 Ibid. p. 43.
29 1 Corinthians 9:16–19.
30 Martin, p. 132.
31 Exodus 21:1–11.
32 Leviticus 25:44–6.
33 Deuteronomy 15:12–15.
34 Exod. 21:26–7.
35 Davies, pp. 72, 73.
36 Rogerson, Davies and M. Daniel Carroll, p. 79.
37 Ibid. p. 79.
38 Ibid. pp. 80, 81.
39 Goosen, pp. 28, 29.
40 Eccles. 33:31–3.
41 Engerman, Drescher and Paquette, pp. 7–8.
42 Matthew 20:3.
43 Luke 16.
44 Mark 10:23.
45 Matthew 6:24.
46 Luke 14:33.
47 Matthew 16:24–5.
48 Matt. 5:14–30; Luke 19:11–26 (The Parable of the Pounds).
49 Ibid., 25:31–6.
50 James 1:22.
51 Ibid., 2:17.
52 Matt. 7:9.
53 Luke 11:5.
54 Matt. 13:55–6.
55 Eccl. 38:39.
56 Garriguet, p. 9.
57 Ibid. p. 11.
58 Ibid. p. 25.
59 Dowd, p.16.
60 Townsend, p. 29.
61 Ibid. p. 31.
62 Anderson-Scott, pp. 64, 65.
63 1 John 4:20–21.
64 Philippians 2:6–8.
65 2 Thessalonians 3:14–15.
66 Ibid., 3:7–9.
67 Goosen, p. 35.
68 Ephesians 4:1–6 (RSV).
69 Goosen, p. 36.
70 Townsend, p. 35.
71 Dowd, pp. 15, 16.
72 1 Cor. 7:21–4.
73 Rosner, p. 173.
74 Bartchy, p. 175.

75 Colossians 3:22–5 and Colossians 4:1.
76 Houlden, pp. 20, 21.
77 Galatians 3:26–9.
78 Houlden, p. 26.
79 Goosen, p. 36.
80 Anderson-Scott, p. 87.
81 1 Peter 2:18–20.
82 Matt. 10:17–27.
83 Neal, p. 102.
84 McDowall, pp. 18, 19.

Chapter 3

THE WORKER IN THE PATRISTIC ERA

The social teaching of the early Fathers

The writings of the early Fathers amplified the changes in attitude towards the person of a slave and *labor* which had begun with the proclamation of the Gospel. As in the New Testament, the institution of slavery per se was not questioned but the equality of all under God, the dignity and importance of the various manual crafts, the notion of *iustitia* and the development of the doctrine of the stewardship of the world's goods and the common ownership of property, as enunciated by the Church Fathers, was to form the framework of the social encyclicals dealing with the worker question from *Rerum Novarum* onwards. Justice and stewardship were important concepts in the development of later ideas which suggested that persons other than the rich, including the worker, had a right to share in God's provision for all humanity. Indeed, the importance of the concepts of stewardship and justice were acknowledged by Pius XI in *Quadragesimo Anno*.[1]

In their writings on the question of justice the Church Fathers, and Augustine in particular, drew heavily from Plato and Aristotle. It was Plato who said, 'Wherefore my counsel is, lest we hold fast ever to the heavenly way and follow after justice and virtue always, considering that the soul is immortal and able to endure every sort of good and every sort of evil.'[2] Plato also wrote on the function of the state and his thoughts are echoed by the stoics, particularly Cicero, and later by Augustine. Plato wrote of the legislator who did not aim at making any one class in the state happy above the rest. He held that happiness was to be in the whole state, and that the legislator held the citizens together by persuasion and necessity, making them benefactors of the state and therefore benefactors of one another.[3] Plato added that where the state sought the good of the whole, justice would most likely be found. He said that the aim in founding the state was not the disproportionate happiness of any one class but the greatest happiness of the whole. He opined that in a state which was ordered with a view to the good of the whole, justice would be most likely found, whereas in an ill-ordered state, injustice was most likely to be found.[4] Plato's reference to 'the good of the whole' is in many ways a foreshadowing of what Christians call 'the common good'.

Cicero questioned how the name 'human being' could rightly be given to any person who desired no community of justice or partnership in life with his fellow citizens. In the dialogue with Scippio in *De Republica*, Cicero seeks to demonstrate by practical examples that any government that is just is a good government, whereas without justice any form of government is bad. He says that nothing calling itself a commonwealth can exist without justice.[5]

Augustine tends to accept Cicero's statement that nothing is so inimical to a community as injustice, and that a country cannot be governed and cannot continue in being without a high degree of justice. In *The City of God* Augustine says that the one supreme God rules an obedient city according to his grace, and the soul rules the body in all men who belong to this city and so fully rules the vices in a lawful system of subordination. In consequence of this, just as the individual righteous man lives on the basis of faith which is active in love, so the associations, or people, of righteous men live in the same basis of faith, active in love, and love their neighbours as themselves. He is virtually saying here that where God is put first in the lives of men and women, justice in all things will flow from it.[6] Augustine was confident that there are norms shared between Christians and others, norms of justice and also norms of prudent and effective action. The framework for his thinking was Plato's doctrine of eternal norms, in this case *iustitia*, justice itself, according to which all temporal derivatives are to be judged.[7]

One may well ask the question as to whom *iustitia* applied and did it apply to tradespeople and servants? Given that the great majority of artisans and servants belonged to the class of slaves, the justice to which they were entitled was no more and no less than that accorded to slaves under Roman law. As we shall see, the Church Fathers, with one notable exception, did not question the institution of slavery. Their main contribution to social teaching lay in their formulation and enunciation of the doctrine of the stewardship of property, but the doctrine of stewardship of property did not imply that property was a social function only, or that the right to its use was merely conventional and conditional on its proper use. What it actually did mean was that God was the one owner with absolute rights. If God gives humanity possessions He can dictate the terms upon which humanity owns them. Divine will is set out in two principles. The first of them is that wealth is not an end in itself but must be subordinated to man's true end. The second is that wealth imposes a duty of almsgiving on its possessors. Both these doctrines occurred consistently in the patristic writings.[8]

The idea of the stewardship of property originates early in the patristic era. The *Didache* (AD 120–50), sometimes called the teaching of the twelve Apostles, stresses the necessity of hard work and condemns idleness. Work is seen as a means to earn the wherewithal to help others. It contains the famous statement 'Do not turn your back on the needy, but share everything with your brother and call nothing your own.' The *Didache*'s social teaching may be summarized as: praising hospitality, strongly urging almsgiving and a sharing of goods, and recommending kind treatment of slaves.[9]

The necessity of the crafts
Origen (AD 185–254), in a passage reminiscent of Ecclus 38:24–39, describes how the want of the necessities of life led to the invention of the arts, of husbandry, cultivation of the vine, of gardening and the arts of carpentry and smithwork. He says the want of covering introduced the art of weaving, woodcarving and spinning. The building of houses ascended to architecture, and sailing and pilotage developed to convey products to other places. He says that divine providence made the rational being subject to want in a far higher degree than the irrational animals. This was presumably to encourage humanity to develop the arts to its own advantage.[10]

All entitled to a livelihood

Irenaeus, Bishop of Lyons (*c.* AD 120–202) teaches that we should share what we have with others since what we have has come from God. He says that God knows that we would make good use of our substance because what we possess we ourselves have received from another. He also affirms the legitimacy of the acquisition of goods, of ownership and of profit in commerce when he says:

For who is there that sells and does not wish to make a profit from whom he buys, or who purchases anything and does not wish to obtain good value from the seller? Or who is there that carries on a trade and does not do so that he may obtain a livelihood thereby?[11]

In the second mandate of the Shepherd of Hermas, the shepherd says, 'Give to all from the fruit of your labour and from the rewards of your labours, which God gives you. Give to all the needy in simplicity, not hesitating as to whom you are to give or not give. Give to all, for God wishes his gifts to be shared amongst all. Those who receive will render an account to God why and for what they have received.' The idea of stewardship is strong here. In the first similitude the shepherd makes reference to not acquiring anything more than 'adequate sufficiency'. These words appear throughout the patristic writings. In the second similitude the shepherd speaks of a type of efficacious partnership between rich and poor. In the tenth similitude we see the image of the vine and the elm in which the shepherd is possibly drawing upon Jesus' reference to Himself as the true vine (John 15:1-5). He also recognizes the existence of rich and poor social classes and uses the image of the elm and the vine to show their mutual dependence.[12]

This implied partnership between rich and poor has a parallel in the partnership of labour and capital referred to by Leo XIII in his great social encyclical *Rerum Novarum*[13] and by Pius XI in *Quadragesimo Anno*.[14] In the teaching of Clement set out below, there is perhaps a presage of Leo XIII's concept of labour and capital.

Solidarity and subsidiarity
Clement of Rome defined 'sufficiency' as meaning that the owners of property or wealth should use for themselves only sufficient to meet their needs. What surpassed the measure of sufficiency was superfluous and should be shared with others whose primary needs were not being met. Clement and other patristic fathers developed the criterion of 'usefulness'. By this they meant that wealth should not be spent on useless things which were merely ostentatious. He uses the example of a knife, stating that an iron knife cuts better than one made out of gold or silver.[15]

In what is known as Clement's First Letter to the Corinthians, believed to have been written around the year AD 96, probably towards the end of the reign of Domitian, Clement, who was the third pope, developed the idea of social order and cooperation for the common good. He says:

> Really in the earnest then brothers, we must march under his irreproachable orders. Let us note with what discipline, readiness, and obedience those who serve under our generals carry out orders. Not everybody is a general, colonel, captain, sergeant and so on. But 'each in his own rank' (1 Cor. 15:23) carries out the orders of the emperor and of the generals. The great cannot exist without the small; neither can the small exist without the great. All are linked together, and this has an advantage. Take our body, for instance: the head cannot get along without the feet. Nor, similarly, can the feet get along without the head. 'The tiniest parts of the body are essential to it' (1 Cor. 12:21, 22) and are valuable to the total body. Yes, they all act in concord, and are united in a single obedience to preserve the whole body.[16]

Ignatius of Antioch, on his way to martyrdom in Rome around the year AD 107 wrote seven letters, six to different churches and one to Polycarp. In the letter to Polycarp, Ignatius exhorts masters to treat their slaves with respect and not to despise them. Ignatius was perhaps one of the first of the Church Fathers to expand upon St Paul's admonition on the treatment of slaves (1 Tim. 6:2).[17]

Basil the Great (AD 330–379) was noted as a reformer of liturgy and social activist. Like the other fathers he speaks of the necessity of the sharing of our possessions with others, as in his homily on Psalm 14. Likewise, in his homily entitled 'I will pull down my barns' he talks about the stewardship of God's goods. In Chapter 3 of the same homily he speaks of the social functions of riches.[18] In what is known as 'the Long Rules', Basil discusses the social nature of mankind and says that this sociability arises directly from humanity's nature. He says, 'Nothing indeed is so compatible with our nature as living in society and in dependence upon one another and loving our own kind.'[19] In these words of Basil can be seen the seeds of the concept of solidarity.

In Chapter 16, Book 5 of the *Divine Institutes* there is a passage in which the African Lactantius encapsulates the teaching of the Church Fathers on the dignity and equality of humanity when he says:

> Some will say, are there not among you some poor, and others rich; some servants and others masters? Is there not some difference between individuals? There is none; nor is there any other cause why we mutually bestow upon each other the name of brethren, except that we believe ourselves to be equal. Riches also do not

render men illustrious, except that they are able to make them more conspicuous by good works. For men are rich, not because they possess riches, but because they employ them on works of justice; and they who seem to be poor, on this account are rich because they are not in want, and desire nothing.[20]

Is this not the essence of stewardship?

In Homily 52 on St Matthew's Gospel, St John Chrysostom elaborates upon the interaction and interdependence of the various crafts and trades. He speaks of agriculture requiring the smith's art so that it may obtain from it spade and plough, shear and sickle, axe and other things. He says that a carpenter is required to provide the plough, the yoke and the cart. A currier is required to make the leather harness; a builder to build the stables for the cattle and houses for the farmers. The woodman is required to prepare the timbers and a baker is required to feed all of these people. Every one of the arts stands in need of the other.[21] Here again we see the development of the idea of solidarity amongst the workers of the various trades and crafts.

Stewardship

St John Chrysostom (AD 347–407) was a prolific writer on matters of social doctrine. He was so vehement in attacks upon the accumulation of riches and so passionate in exhorting charity and almsgiving and exalting the dignity of the poor that he was sometimes seen as a demagogue. In his treatize on wealth and poverty he says that the rich, by accumulating their wealth, have stolen from the poor. He goes on to say that the failure of the rich to realize that they hold their goods for the poor is 'to deprive the poor of their living' (Ecclus. 4:1). Like others of the Church Fathers he describes the rich man as a kind of steward of the money which is owned for distribution to the poor. He also refers to the term 'need' when he says that if the rich spend more on themselves than their need requires, they will pay the harshest penalty hereafter. Their goods are not their own but belong to their fellow servants.[22]

In Homily 12 on the First Letter of Paul to Timothy, St John Chrysostom says that it is virtually impossible to grow rich without injustice. He expands this to say that the root and origin of riches must have been injustice.[23] In Homily 10, one of his homilies on almsgiving, St John Chrysostom teaches of the solidarity between rich and poor when he says that the rich should know well and be assured that they enjoy a very great honour when they are made worthy to share in the hardships of the poor.[24]

In his thirty-sixth Homily on the Gospel of John, Chrysostom draws the distinction between 'work' and 'toil'. He postulates that in the earthly paradise, humanity had to work since it has been assigned the task of cultivating the earth, but not to toil. He says that toil is the consequence of sin. Chrysostom does not regard work as a shameful thing but as a means to discipline and correcting the deviations of sin and of obtaining the necessities required to assist others. He regards the primary purpose of work as the production of what is necessary and useful but not of what is luxurious and superfluous.[25]

In Homily 15 on the Gospel of John, Chrysostom develops the idea of the equality of humanity under God. He says:

> It is for this reason that God gave one house for all of us – this world; distributed all created things equally; kindled one sun for all; stretched above us one roof – the sky; set up one table – the earth. And he also gave another much greater table than this (Holy Eucharist) but this, too, is one – those who partake of the mysteries understand what I say. He has bestowed one manner of generation, the spiritual, for all; one fatherland for all – but in heaven; we all drink from the chalice. He has not bestowed more abundant and more honourable largesse upon the rich and meaner and less upon the poor, but has called all equally; he has furnished temporal as generously as spiritual.[26]

The writings of Gregory of Nazianzus (c. AD 330–390), Bishop of Constantinople, also pursued the idea of the common ownership of property. In his oration on the origin of wealth, poverty and avarice, Gregory refers to Jesus' words from Matthew 4:45 that God causes the rain to fall on the just and unjust alike and the sun to rise on all equally. Gregory says that God spreads out the earth for all the animals, with its fountains, rivers and forests; he gave air to winged animals, water to aquatic creatures, and to all the basic elements of life, not dominated by any power, not restricted by any law, not separated by any boundaries – all of these necessities of life God has put at the disposal of all, and abundantly so that no-one would lack anything.[27]

Lactantius (c. AD 250–317) is said to be the first patristic author to develop – in social matters – a relatively complete, organic and coherent doctrine based upon the dignity of the human person and on man's social consciousness, which he calls humanity. For Lactantius the dignity of the human person lay in the fact that he is made in the image of God, and God created a whole universe and placed man at the head of all creatures because humanity alone is able to admire his works. The consequence of this dignity is the duty of humanity or social living. Whereas for Aristotle it was necessary for man to live with others because of his weakness and inability to survive by himself, Lactantius held that for man sociability was something intrinsic to humanity itself. We must live together because of our humanity. For Lactantius another consequence of man's dignity is the fundamental equality of mankind. This equality does not deny the existence of social classes or differences. The evil does not lie in the existence of these classes or in material inequalities, but in the lack of social spirit or consequences amongst men and women.[28]

The development of the doctrine of stewardship is important for our time as there are those who maintain that helping the needy is always an act of voluntary charity without firm obligation. For the Church Fathers, on the contrary, the obligation was one of justice and therefore of duty.[29]

A variation on the golden rule

In Chapter 10, Book 6 of the *Divine Institutes* Lactantius developed further his ideas of the dignity of the human person and of humanity's social consciousness. He says that the first office of justice is to be united with God, the second is to be united with man. He calls the former 'religion' and the second 'mercy' or 'kindness', which virtue is peculiar to the just and to worshippers of God because this alone comprises the principle of common life. He says that God did not give wisdom to the lower animals but made them safer from attacking danger by natural defences. He says that God made humans naked and defenceless so that he might furnish them with wisdom and give them, besides other things, the feeling of kindness; so that humans should protect love and cherish each other and both receive and afford assistance against all dangers. He says that the greatest bond of human society is therefore kindness; and that anyone who has broken this is deemed impious and a parricide. Lactantius expressed his agreement with the Roman philosopher Lucretius who said, 'In short, we are all sprung from a heavenly seal; all have the same fathers.' Lactantius says that God, in his kindness, wished us to be a social animal. Therefore, he says, that in dealings with other men we ought to think of ourselves also. He says that we do not deserve to be set free in our own dangers if we do not assist others; we do not deserve assistance if we refuse to render it.[30]

Lactantius then, in the *Divine Institutes*, postulated that justice could not exist without religion and the worship of the true God. Much of what he said was particularly pertinent to the modern discussion as to the possibility of divorcing economics from ethics, and, as McDowell comments, we find in what he said nearly 1,700 years ago the refutation of an error which claims to mark a new advance in our progressive civilization.[31]

Gregory of Nyssa (c. AD 335–394), the younger brother of Basil, was the only Church Father to condemn slavery as a condition opposed to the freedom and dignity of mankind. In his fourth homily on Ecclesiastes, his abhorrence for the practice of slavery is evident. Referring to the buying and selling of slaves Gregory said:

> Tell me, how much is your life worth? What have you found among the creatures that is as valuable as your human nature? How many cents did you pay for reason? How many pence did you think God's image is worth? How many coins were you charged for the creature that God has made? 'Let us make', God said, 'man in our image and likeness' (John 1:26). Now, tell me, who is the one who buys, who is the one who sells, the one who is God's image? Who must rule over the whole earth? Who has received from God the dominion over all that exists on earth as heritage?[32]

In his treatise on the beatitudes he says that if men and women practised the virtue of mercy there would no longer be superiority or want. He says that life would no longer be lived in diametrically opposite ways, and that humanity would no longer be distressed by want or humiliated by slavery. He says that all things would be common to all and, as a citizen, everyone would be equal before the law, since the person responsible for government would of their own free will be on the same level as the rest. Gregory goes on to say that if such a state of affairs existed there would be no room left for enmity, envy would be futile, and hatred would die out. Remembrance of injuries would be banished along with lies, fraud and war, all of which are offspring of covetousness. With the departure of these evils there would enter in a whole array of good things: peace and justice with all their train of virtues. He concludes by saying that mercy is therefore the tenet of kindness and pledge of charity. It is the bond of all loving disposition.[33]

The common good

For Ambrose of Milan (*c.* AD 337–397) the idea of the common good was based upon nature itself. In Book 5 of the *Hexameron*, Ambrose says that in the primitive communities humanity established a political system based on nature, with the birds as models. As a result there was an equal participation in both labour and office. Each person in their turn learnt to set up a division of responsibility whereby they took turns in doing service and in supervising it. No one was devoid of office and no one was without their allotment of work. In this ideal state, no one became accustomed to unlimited power. In the same way no one was intimidated by long periods of servitude because, due to the interchange of office, advancement appeared all the more supportable in that it resulted in establishing that each person would have a share in the task of government. Here Ambrose is drawing upon Virgil, *Georgics*, 4:149–196.[34]

In his work on Naboth, Ambrose develops the theme of natural law in delineating the relationships between rich and poor. He says that the earth is established in common for all, rich and poor. He then asks why the rich demand special treatment. He continues that nature, which begets everyone poor, does not acknowledge wealth, for we are not born with clothing or begotten with gold and silver. Naked we are brought into life (Job 1:21), wanting food, clothing and drink, and naked the earth receives us whom it brought forth. The narrow sod is equally spacious for poor and rich. Nature, then, knows no distinction when we are born, and it knows none when we die. It creates all alike, and all alike it encloses in the bowels of the tomb.[35]

In his sermon on the duties of the clergy Ambrose says that nothing graces the Christian soul so much as mercy shown to the poor. They are to be treated as sharers in common in the produce of nature which brings forth the fruits of the earth for the use of all. In giving freely to the poor man, one is helping someone who is both your companion and brother.[36]

In Book 1 of the *Hexameron*, Ambrose says that a community rests upon justice and goodwill. Justice is concerned with the society of the human race and the community at large. Society is held together by justice and goodwill, which he also calls 'liberality' and 'kindness'. God has ordered all things to be produced so that there should be food in common to all; and that the earth should be a common possession of all. Nature has therefore produced a common right which greed has made the right of a few.[37]

In Book 3 of the *Hexameron* Ambrose says:

> It is clear, then, that we should consider and admit that what benefits the individual is the common good, and we should judge nothing as useful unless it benefits all. For how can one be benefited alone? What is useless to all is harmful. I certainly cannot conceive that what is useless to all can be of use to anyone at all. For if there is but one law of nature for all, there is also but one state of usefulness for all. And we are bound by the law of nature to act for the good of all. It is not, therefore, right for the person who wishes the interests of another to be considered according to nature to injure him against the law of nature.[38]

If we draw together all of Ambrose's thoughts in respect of justice, it can be said they bear a close resemblance to the modern day notion of 'social justice'.

In their teaching on the use of property the Church Fathers speak time and again of a person using for themselves only what is sufficient. The Greek word *autarkeia* denotes a standard of living sufficient to live life with a degree of human dignity. *Autarkeia* implies that ownership be subordinated to use, and not be for the sake of retaining or show.[39] However, in tandem with *autarkeia* is the idea of *koinōnia*. The *koinōnia* is the equality of fellowship that abolishes the differentiation between the rich few and the many who are poor. It is because of the patristic notion of *koinōnia* that patristic thought rejected private property. Private property essentially attacked the social nature of humanity and the personalized character of social relations. Thus in order to establish *koinōnia*, people must renounce their private ownership of the natural productive elements so that all could partake of them in common. Monopoly was no longer to be permitted. The owners should help restore the true essence of ownership under God, the one absolute owner and lord.[40]

Summary

It can be seen then that the early Church Fathers, whilst not directly developing a body of teaching in respect of the worker, developed a philosophical platform for its later development from the late nineteenth century onwards. The ideas of justice and fellowship of humanity, and kindness and charity to our brothers and sisters under God contributed to the recognition of the social nature of labour, an important concept in the development of the Catholic social thought in the nineteenth century. The Fathers of the Church did not consider work as an *opus servile*, although the culture of their day maintained precisely that such was the case. They always regarded it an *opus humanum*, and they tended to hold all its various expressions in honour.[41] This was to have a bearing on the amelioration of the conditions of slaves within the empire which occurred during the patristic era.

Slavery in the patristic era

Slavery in the Roman Empire was part and parcel of the economic institution. As Oliver O'Donovan points out, the ancient household not only served as a unit of economic consumption devoted to child rearing, mutual protection and emotional satisfaction, but was also the most important unit of economic production. O'Donovan says that the presence of slaves in the household allowed it to expand its functions out beyond its biological capacity, especially for tasks which required training or education, both of which had to be provided within the household if they were to be provided at all. In his view the slave market compensated for the absence of what, with unconscious irony, we may call a 'labour market'.

In O'Donovan's view slavery absorbed into society floating and property-less populations and those dislocated by being captured in war, exploiting their capacities to better effect than if they were day labourers. For the ancient world the idea of the 'abolition' of slavery as a social reform was inconceivable. That would have required the establishment of economic structures which had not at that time been even dreamed of. [42]

The legal defencelessness of the slave in ancient society was a function of the autonomy of the household. The division between the private and the public realms was so sharply delineated that those whose roles confined them to the former held little or no standing in the latter. He says that the analogy often drawn in the ancient world between slaves and children had a precise legal point as well as a moral one. The wise understood that within the family, good relations of loyalty and affection could, and should, be cultivated. The Greco-Roman philosophers inculcated the idea that a shared human nature was enough to ground the duties of ordinary humanity and to provide a possible basis for friendship; the point was simply that these relations belonged within the domestic rules and had no reflection in legal or political relations outside.[43]

In the later empire, as a result of the permeation of Christianity throughout Roman society, changes which had already been slowly taking place accelerated. The independence of the household was already being eroded by the encroachments of law, and restrictions began to be set around the freedom of the *paterfamilias* in respect of his dependants. Of the various philosophies existing in the Greco-Roman world, the stoic philosophy found the institution of slavery contrary to nature. However, the tendency of the philosophers was not to issue a general critique of social structures, nor to propose alternative structures, so much as to encourage philosophic distance from them and to encourage the cultivation of freely humane relationships in private. O'Donovan says that it is with these changes and evolutions that the Church was naturally associated. Christian thinkers such as Gregory of Nyssa (see p. 50) and the various Christian emperors ameliorated the condition of the slaves albeit to a limited degree. The Church also assumed a positive role in the manumission of slaves.

In an empire becoming increasingly Christian it was perhaps inevitable that the Christian teaching of the equality of all humanity before God would begin to blur the distinctions between citizen and slave. In the fourth century, Constantine decreed that when slaves were sold, husband and wife, parents and children had to be sold together.[44] Constantine in effect provided that when an estate was broken up, slave families were not to be separated. Further, by his provisions that manumission of slaves could take place in a church, he facilitated the ease with which manumission could be effected.[45] After Constantine, the Church developed its own form of informal Roman manumission called *manumission in ecclesia*.[46]

However, in spite of these developments, the word of St Paul remained the law of the Church. In AD 324 a canon of the Council of Granges stated that if anyone, under a pretext of pity, leads a slave to despise their master, and to remove themself from slavery, and not serve the master with goodwill and respect, that person was to be anathematized.[47] In 916 the Council of Altheim drew a parallel between the slave who fled his or her master and the churchman who abandoned the Church.[48] The institution of slavery was never questioned.

Towards the end of the fourth century Theodosius I tried to legislate for agricultural slaves, *coloni*, to be regarded as slaves to the land to which they were born. His intention was to provide a degree of stability to the family lives of the agricultural slaves.[49]

The manumission before a bishop in a church, as regulated by Constantine did, in certain circumstances, confer citizenship on the manumitted slave. The eastern emperor Justinian took this further. He provided that the appointing of a slave as one's heir, even if unaccompanied by an express gift of freedom, automatically effected manumission. The same can be said of adopting a slave as one's son or appointing him by will as tutor to one's son. Also in the later empire the slaves of pagans, heretics and Jews became free on adopting Christianity. In some cases the magistrates manumitted or compelled the master to do so; in others freedom was acquired automatically.[50]

To the question as to whether a Roman slave was a person or a thing, the answer is that he was both. He could be owned and as such was a *res*. However, the slave was a human being and as such a person. But the idea that personality implies 'a being or a group capable of legal rights and duties' developed slowly, and took shape only in the Byzantine period under the influence of Christian thought.

As far as the laws pertaining to slaves were concerned, the Church, even in the later empire, was able to change relatively little. The Christians protected slave marriages, urged non-Christians to set their slaves free or let them buy their freedom because they thought that the religious welfare of the slaves was in peril. They encouraged the manumission of slaves as a good work involving self-denial and the renunciation of one's possessions. The Church granted to slaves the principle of religious equality in its fullest extent.[51]

The main effect of Christianity upon the institution of slavery was a moral one. Lecky says:

> Christianity broke down the contempt with which the master regarded his slaves and planted among the slaves themselves a principle of moral regeneration which expanded in no other sphere with equal perfection. Its action in procuring the freedom of slaves was unceasing.[52]

The Church reproved the false idea that manual work was degrading, and insisted on the duty and the necessity of labour for all and on the self-respect which the practice of labour gives. The Church preached the equality of all in natural dignity, in personal responsibility, in the participation of heavenly graces and in the predestination to eternal happiness. While preaching to the slaves the duty of obedience to the master's just commands, the Church also insisted strongly on the duties of masters towards their slaves and had her teaching sanctioned by canonical enactments containing severe penalties.

The Church acknowledged no distinction between slave and freeman other than what was essential for the needs of existing society. All had the same sacraments. The marriage of slaves among themselves had the same sanction as that of the free. Clerics of servile origin were numerous; and so levelling was the Christian principle of personal equality that the See of Peter was sometimes filled by men born of slaves, such as Pius in the second century and Callistus in the third. In the Christian cemeteries there was no distinction between the tombs of slaves and those of the free.

The Church thus prepared the way for the eventual abolition of slavery. The emancipation of slaves was endowed with special ecclesiastical favour. It was usual to perform the ceremony of manumission in the church; and a bishop was accorded by civil law special powers to facilitate it. The Church also took liberated slaves under her special protection and strictly forbade that they should be in any way again reduced to servitude. Under the influence of the Church, the state made many other enactments to facilitate the manumission of slaves. The movement was further supported by the example of Christian masters who frequently set free their whole households of slaves. Besides all this, the general attitude of the Christians towards their slaves and towards the poor set an example which profoundly affected the whole tone of Roman society.[53]

Summary

In summary it can be said that the services of Christianity towards the breakdown of slavery in the later empire were threefold. Firstly, it supplied a new order of relations in which the distinction of classes was unknown. Secondly, it imparted a moral dignity to the servile classes. Thirdly, it gave an unexampled impetus to the movement of enfranchizement.[54] This impetus, as we shall see, would culminate in the evolution of slavery into the peasantry and craft guilds of the medieval period.

Notes

1 *Quadragesimo Anno*, pp. 26, 27.
2 Jowett, p. 416.
3 Ibid. p. 272.

The worker in the patristic era

4 Ibid. pp. 133, 134.
5 Keyes, pp. 42–8.
6 *Augustine*, pp. 890.
7 Babcock, p. 149.
8 McDowell, p. 30.
9 Richardson, p. 161.
10 *Translations of the Writing of the Fathers*, pp. 242–3.
11 Roberts and Robertson, pp. 503–4.
12 Phan, pp. 31, 32.
13 *Rerum Novarum*, para. 28.
14 *Quadragesimo Anno*, p. 52.
15 González, p. 228.
16 Phan, pp. 60–1.
17 Richardson, p. 119.
18 Phan, pp.110, 113, 115.
19 Ragner, p. 239.
20 McDonald, p. 326.
21 Parker Prest, pp. 710, 711.
22 Roth, pp. 49, 50.
23 Aquinas, Sr Thomas, pp. 149, 150.
24 Christo, p. 134.
25 Phan, p. 137.
26 Christo, pp.149–50.
27 Phan, p. 125.
28 McDonald, pp. 223, 224.
29 Harries, p. 40.
30 McDonald, pp. 374, 375.
31 McDowell, p. 45.
32 Phan, p. 128.
33 Graef, pp. 132, 134.
34 Savage, p. 201.
35 Ibid. p. 118.
36 *On the Duties of the Clergy*, Book 1, Chapter 2.
37 *Hexameron*, paras 130, 132 of Book 1, Chapter 28.
38 Phan, p. 179.
39 González, p. 228.
40 Avila, pp. 145, 146.
41 *Compendium of the Social Doctrine of the Church*, p. 154.
42 O'Donovan, p. 264.
43 Ibid. p. 265.
44 Wiedemann, p. 179.
45 Pohlsander, p. 69.
46 Harrill, p.189.
47 Bloch, p. 13.
48 Ibid. p. 13.
49 Turley, p. 141.
50 Lee, p. 4.
51 Troeltsch, p. 133.

52 Lecky, p. 69.
53 Cahill, E., pp. 12, 13.
54 Lecky, p. 66.

Chapter 4

THE MEDIEVAL WORKER

The decline of slavery

The extinguishment of the empire in the west temporarily checked the growth of Christian civilization in western Europe although in the eastern empire, which still considered itself Roman, the movement continued. However, the Teutonic chieftains, many of whom were Christians, who assumed power in the greater part of the western empire, gradually adopted the fabric of Roman law which had already been permeated with Christian principles. This law later became the basis of the legal systems of the various Teutonic kingdoms which emerged from the chaos of the decades which followed the decline of imperial authority in the West. This chapter shows how during the medieval period the status of the worker evolved from being that of a slave to that of an independent tradesman or peasant. The advent of the guild system and the Church's role in these events is considered.

The influence of the monks

Lecky speaks of how the stream of missionaries which at first flowed from Palestine and Italy now began to flow from the West. The Irish monasteries furnished the earliest and probably the most numerous in the field: St Columbanus evangelized in Gaul, St Gall in Switzerland. During the sixth, seventh and eighth centuries a constant stream of missionaries went forth from the Irish monasteries to every land from Lombardy to Sweden.[1]

In the sixth century the various Teutonic nations were gradually evangelized by the Church through the medium of her monastic institutions. Monasteries of the Benedictine Order became established throughout Italy and much of southern Gaul and Germania. In Gaul, Fresia and Germania the evangelization was largely carried out by Irish monks. It should be remembered that Hibernia never fell under the sway of the Romans. The first-century Roman military commander and governor of Britain, Gnaeus Julius Agricola, standing on the north-west shore of Britannia and gazing across the Irish Sea to the distant shores of Hibernia, is reported to have commented to his entourage that he believed he could conquer the island with two legions. Such a conquest, though contemplated by Agricola, never eventuated, and expansion of the empire ceased under the Emperor Hadrian AD 76–138, who had adopted a policy of consolidation. As a result the Irish were largely unaffected by the barbarian invasions of Roman Britain in the fifth century. In the years following the conversion of Ireland to Christianity by that redoubtable Roman Briton St Patrick and his followers, monasteries sprang up throughout the country. Inspired by monks such as Columcille, Columbanus, Aidan and others, the monks set off in every direction bent on glorious and heroic exile for the sake of Christ.[2]

The first monasteries were established by Columbanus in Gaul around the year 590. Other monks pushed eastward and north into Germania. *The Catholic Encyclopedia* estimates the number of Benedictine monasteries in Europe at the end of the thirteenth century at approximately 37,000.[3] The effect of the monasteries upon the history of western Europe cannot be underestimated. It was the monks who re-introduced to Europe the art of agriculture and encouraged the bringing of the land back into cultivation. The monasteries became centres of learning. The great classics of the Greco-Roman world were preserved and studied, as were the writings of the Greek and Roman philosophers. Gradually the condition of the slaves, particularly those on the ecclesiastical estates, improved as the principles of Christianity were brought to bear on the institution of slavery and work in general.

Documents of the fifth, sixth and seventh centuries contain numerous records of captives who had been reduced to slavery being redeemed by bishops, priests, monks and laymen. Such redeemed captives were reportedly sent back in their thousands to their home countries. At the same time, enactments were constantly being made in the national and provincial councils of the Church in the interests of slaves, providing for the protection of maltreated slaves and for the help and patronage of those who were liberated. Such provisions included the securing of the validity of slave managers, compelling rest on Sundays and feast days, forbidding or limiting the traffic in slaves, and forbidding that freemen should be reduced to slavery.[4]

In his work on medieval slavery and liberation Pierre Dockès says that the Church did not condemn slavery in itself any more than it condemned private property, and expressed the view that the Church accepted and propagated the idea that slaves were collectively responsible for their fate, as had they been free of all guilt, God would not have kept them in so frightful a situation.[5] In this writer's view Dockès underestimates the influence of the Church in the decline of the institution of slavery. Marc Bloch says that nobody doubted that slavery in itself was against divine law. Were not all men equal in Christ? In this primordial thesis, pagans converted to Christianity could recognize an idea that their own philosophies and legalists had made familiar to them, and that, at any rate, had not been without influence on Christian thought itself – except that where the Church talked of divine law, paganism had said 'natural law'. The parallel was so close that from the Carolingian era onwards, theologians tended to identify the two notions with one another.

Bloch stated that one must avoid underestimating the practical value of the principle of equality thus proclaimed. He said that even if it could lead to the better treatment of individuals – even to their treatment in a fashion that contrasts with the classic use of slave labour – of course, it must not attack the institution itself at its foundations. Taken literally, the entire social edifice would have crumbled. He said that doubtless, before God, the slave was the equal of his master – just as, in full conformity with the lessons of the Church, the Emperor Louis the Pious said in a capitulary that he was the equal of his subjects. However, no masters thought of abdicating their authority any more than the sovereign, and no-one asked it of them.[6]

Within the Church itself, slave birth was no disqualification for entering into the priesthood. From the later empire onwards an emancipated slave regarded as the dispenser of spiritual life and death often saw the greatest and the most wealthy kneeling humbly at his feet imploring his absolution or his benediction.[7]

From the fifth century onwards the Church, owing to various causes, found itself in the possession of immense estates in every country of western Europe. The immediate owners of these estates were the pope himself, the bishops, the cathedral or collegiate chapters, and the monasteries. By virtue of a fourth-century statute of Roman law, implemented due to the urging of the Church, rural slaves could not be removed from the lands on which they worked even when the lands passed to another owner. Following the barbarian migrations this law was abrogated, except for slaves attached to the ecclesiastical estates. The immense number of these slaves had the privilege of fixed work and permanent homes. By a series of canonical enactments the position of these slaves was gradually improved. In time, the privileges enjoyed by the slaves on the ecclesiastical estates were gradually extended to those belonging to the lay lords. The result was that, by about the tenth century, European slavery as it had hitherto been known had in practice given way to serfdom.

The way of life in the monasteries had a far-reaching influence upon the social customs of the societies around them. The austere self-denying lifestyle of the monks, the democratic spirit of their institutions, the notion of cooperation embodied in their corporate structure, their charitable works, their attitude towards their dependants and the poor, were all influences. In their working life they accorded a prestige to manual labour, which, among the barbarians, as previously in the empire, was esteemed unworthy of a freeman. Every Benedictine and Columban monk, including the abbot, was required by a rule of the congregation to spend many hours a day in manual labour either in the fields or in his workshop. This example contributed to the development of a lay artisan class of freeman which in turn prepared the way for the subsequent guild organizations.

The evolution of slavery into serfdom, whilst facilitated by the Church, had, according to Marc Bloch, been taking place since the days of the empire. Bloch states that the Germanic chieftains, into whose hands so many great domains had fallen, were prepared to adopt the tenant farming system as it was a part of their people's traditions. In ancient Germany, general economic conditions were not favourable for any kind of large-scale enterprize. The noble and rich had many lands, many of which lay fallow, and had many slaves often captured in warfare. He says that to make use of these vast resources as well as they could, there was nothing for them to do but divide them up. To feed so many people, it was absolutely necessary to allot to each one a plot of land, since it would not have been convenient to maintain them in the household of the master. Bloch, referring to the Roman historian Tacitus, who wrote in the first century AD, said that Tacitus noted the frequency of the slave–tenant arrangement on the far side of the Rhine at a time when such an arrangement was a rarity in Italy.[8]

During the Carolingian period (*c*.800) the position of the slave evolved to the extent that his position was a different one from what the word 'slavery' normally implies. The slave paid to his master only a part of the fruits of his labour and gave him only a part of his work time. This was because, even though his duties were theoretically limited, a necessity that obliged the master to allow the villein enough free time to extract his livelihood from the holding, and to pay his rents, also prevented those tasks from taking up all his time. It eventuated that he did not live out every moment under the orders of another. As Marc Bloch states, he had his home and hearth and he managed the cultivation of his fields himself. If he was particularly hardworking or particularly shrewd, he ate better than his neighbour and, insofar as there was a market, he could sell his surplus produce.

There further developed during this period a distinction between slaves who were provided with a house and adjoining lands and those who were not. The former were called *chasès* and were, under Carolingian law, regarded as part of the real estate. Other slaves were regarded as part of the furniture. The laws governing their disposal were therefore different in that those slaves who were not *chasès* could be sold outside the estate. Further, in the latter half of the ninth century, the custom of the manor, which had long served to regulate the relations between the lord and his free tenants, extended his protection to the slave tenant. Thus, during the latter half of the ninth century, even regarding strict law, the condition of *servus casatus*, another term for *chasès*, differed considerably from pure slavery. From an economic standpoint, the use that was made of his work did not correspond at all to the ordinary definition of slave labour. It is Bloch's opinion that by the end of the eleventh century there were practically no more slaves to be found on the European continent,[9] and he places the radical transformation experienced in the Middle Ages with regard to servitude firmly in the tenth and eleventh centuries.[10]

Pierre Bonnassie says that the decline of the slave system came about for a number of reasons, one of the most important of which was the practice of settling slaves on holdings. This took the form of enfranchizement *cum obsequio* motivated by economic factors. In the ninth century manumissions were having such an effect that slaves constituted a minority amongst the tenants of the great estates.[11] Although rural slavery in the ancient tradition still survived, it had become increasingly vestigial at the end of the tenth and beginning of the eleventh centuries.[12]

Ernst Troeltsch says that the Christian Church allowed slavery to endure without question right into the Middle Ages. He says that it was only largely modified by the process of economic evolution. Yet the Church was fully conscious of the inconsistency between this institution and the inner freedom and equality which was the Christian ideal. For Troeltsch this forms a most typical illustration of the attitude of Christians towards the world: they renounce the world, yet they compromise with it; and they did not, and could not, dream of making any changes in the social system.[13]

Yet is there not a certain wisdom in this attitude of the Church? If the kingdom of God is not of this world, any transformation of the social order will be wrought by the transformation of the hearts of men and women. Could it not be said that, on the question of slavery, this is exactly what occurred over a period of some eight centuries from the patristic era onwards?

Slavery to serfdom
Thus, the serf of the early Middle Ages, of the eleventh and early twelfth centuries, of the Crusades and Norman Conquest, is virtually a peasant. He is indeed bound in legal theory to the soil upon which he was born. In social practice all that is required of him is that his family should fill its quota of servile land, and that the dues to the lord shall not fail from absence of labour. That duty fulfilled, it is easy and common for members of the serf class to enter the professions and the Church, or, as Belloc says, 'to go wild' – that is, to become men practically free in the growing industries of the towns.[14]

Cahill says that whatever theory one may hold as to the origin and development of serfdom in the various nations of Europe, the main facts are certain. He states that three-quarters of the whole population of feudal Europe in the eleventh century were serfs. Almost all the territory was divided out into large manors or villas, varying in extent, each ruled by a feudal lord. The lord dwelt in the baronial castle and was supported by the labour of the serfs, whose dwellings were usually gathered together in a village on the manor lands. These lands were partly domain lands, in the immediate ownership (dominium) of the lord himself, and partly allotments held and cultivated by the serfs.

According to Cahill the amount held by each serf varied in different manors, or in accordance with the hereditary grade of the holder. In Britain the average amount was about thirty statute acres. Each holding consisted of numerous strips scattered about the great open fields of the manor, intermingled with the strips of the other serfs and of the lord himself. Of the whole manor land, the domain land usually amounted to about one-third or two-fifths, while the remaining two-thirds or three-fifths were held in villeinage by the serfs. Besides the divided lands there were usually some pasture and forest and different kinds of waste lands shared in common by all.

The serf was bound to the soil. He could not, without the lord's consent, migrate from the land he cultivated. Neither could he marry a wife from outside the manor without the lord's consent. Further, he usually could not, in default of a direct heir, dispose of his property at his death. It passed to the lord. The serf's rent was paid partly in kind and partly in personal services. Principal among the latter was a certain number of days work on the domain, usually two or three in the week, with additional days at special seasons such as ploughing time and harvest. The rent was paid in kind and usually consisted of part of the produce of the serf's holding. All the produce of the domain lands belonged to the lord, though a daily wage in kind was allowed to the serf for his days of service. In many cases the lord had claims also to what was called the 'heriot'. This was a certain portion of the serf's property such as the best animal or the best implement on the farm, which had to be handed over to the lord at the serf's decease before his son succeeded to the holding.

The medieval manor was almost wholly self-sufficient, everything needed being produced on the estate. Besides ordinary agricultural workers, the serf population included artisans in all the necessary crafts. Each of these had certain specified duties and clearly defined rights, all of which were determined by immemorial custom.[15]

Hence, even though the serf was in legal theory a slave, his actual position and privileges were far removed from those of slavery. All his essential family rights were secure. Given that the due services were fulfilled, he was his own master and, within limitations already implied, he was the complete owner of his own farm and of whatever other property he might acquire. The rent or the services due to the lord could not be increased by the latter with the increased value of the holding, even though the enhanced value was in no way due to the serf's labour. Besides all this, the serf's right to the lands held by him were indefeasible. He could not be evicted; nor could his land or his working capital be distrained for debt. In addition to his land he had several very important claims on the communal lands of the manor, such as free grazing rights, forest rights, fishing rights, turbary rights, the use of waterways, of water power, and so on. All these rights and the degree of each serf's and of the lord's own participation in them were regulated minutely by custom, and could not be altered by the lord. Hence, although in legal fiction, the lord was considered the owner of the whole manor and of all the property upon it, his rights were in practice strictly limited; and he was compelled to respect the privileges even of the lowest serf of the manor.

Cahill states that the treatment of the serfs on the ecclesiastical estates was particularly liberal in the matter of rights and services. He says that this fact gradually influenced the status of the whole serf population; so that for this reason, owing to the general tendency of Christian influence in favour of the poorer classes, the position of the serfs continued to improve steadily as long as the Church's influence prevailed.[16]

In a similar vein, Belloc writes that with the passing of every generation the ancient servile concept of the labourer's status grows more and more dim, and the practice of the courts and of society was to treat him more and more as a man strictly bound to certain dues and certain periodic labour within his industrial unit but in all other respects free. Belloc says that as the civilization of the Middle Ages developed, the character of his freedom became more marked.[17]

By the thirteenth century in England under the reign of Edward I, most of the serfs – who at the time of the Doomsday Survey of 1086 comprised nearly four-fifths of the total recorded population – obtained the privilege of commuting, for a yearly money payment, the burden of their personal services to the lords. By the fourteenth century the condition further improved, to the extent that serfdom had practically disappeared from England by the end of the fifteenth century. The same could be said on the Continent, where in France serfdom had practically disappeared in Normandy during the twelfth century, and in the northern provinces and rest of the country by the end of the thirteenth century. In Spain and Italy serfdom had been reduced by the end of the fourteenth century. However, Cahill says that the process of enfranchizement in Germany, Denmark and Sweden was checked in the sixteenth century by the rise of Protestantism, with the effect that by the end of the sixteenth century the position of the serfs was worse than it had been previously. Serfdom was not finally abolished in Barden until 1783, nor in Prussia until 1809. It lingered in Saxony and in other parts of Germany until 1832 and in Denmark until 1804.[18]

On the European continent, and particularly in France, there developed during the Middle Ages something akin to the modern-day cooperative. These associations were called *copani*, a term from which the modern word 'company' is derived. In the *copanis*, a certain number of serfs, generally from the same village, formed a group or corporation, holding and tilling their lands in common. They also held a great deal of their moveable property such as cattle, agricultural implements and so on in common. All services due to the lord were shared by them in common and they supported themselves and their families from the common store of produce. Besides the rights in the communal property, each one also had his own private property. This consisted of the property he possessed prior to joining the *copani* and the personal gains that later accrued to him. Each member retained his independent responsibility for his own family. The association had a chief, usually elected, who was the head of the corporative administration. The chief regulated the laws of purchase and sale, and decided each family's proper share in the common profits. From all accounts these communities were amongst the most prosperous of the French communities.[19]

A philosophy of work and the evolution of the guilds

In the Middle Ages the emphasis was laid almost exclusively on the value of redemption by labour, and this value is itself envisaged under the somewhat negative act of penitence. Work was suffering from which one profited as a step in the winning of paradise. This pessimism is cured from without by religious optimism and transcendent hope. It is even possible for us to argue that this pessimism continues to exist today and that labour continues to retain the taint of a fallen state attributed to it by the philosophers of antiquity such as Hesiod and Lucretius.

Etienne Borne and Francois Henry make the point that the doctrine of original sin seemed to lend the justification of theology to the psychology of despair. Generally speaking work was regarded as the punishment for original sin; but the distinction was not always clear, at any rate in the consciousness of the multitude, between work, which was a natural activity, and the pains of work which are the consequences of sin.[20]

Aquinas in some ways echoes these sentiments in his dissertation of the active life in comparison with the contemplative life. Drawing upon Aristotle he argues for the superiority of the contemplative life over the active life.[21] For Aquinas the concept of work is of something less transfigured and elaborative than the idea of contemplation and appears to be treated as something incidental. Borne and Henry pose that it was a grievous fact that the community which understood how to revalue in thought and to transform the pagan idea of contemplation according to the spirit of Christianity did not know how, or was unable, to revalue and transform the concept of work in the light of Christianity. It was, according to them, a society too often contented with a psychology which was vulgar, coarse and unconsciously penetrated with the ideas and prejudices of the ancient world. They believed that if medieval Christianity had made this effort, it would have found fresh and unexpected harmonies between work and contemplation. Borne and Henry were of the opinion that the Middle Ages, by maintaining the concept of the superiority of contemplation over action, and by insisting upon the curse which lies heavily upon human labour, seem to have gone on repeating the ideas of the pagan thinkers and writers. Thus the Middle Ages usually proclaimed the inferiority of work.[22]

The concept of natural law had a considerable bearing upon the development of the idea of the necessity of labour and the division of labour which that involved. According to Troeltsch this assertion is something new. He said that the primitive Church had maintained the ancient ideal of the citizen living on his own income, looking down upon the artisan class, and had only required for the working classes the exercise of love and kindness; otherwise labour was only fully honoured in the cloister. Now, according to Troeltsch, the medieval civil order is reflected in the social ideal of work and property and a differentiation which is based solely upon labour. The corollary of this, according to natural law, is the organization of class groups and corporations engaged in the same kind of work and also the organization of the authority directing society. This task consists in the care and preservation of those groups and their food supply, and on the other hand the restriction of individuals to their own class and to their work, in order that the social organization of society may not be disturbed.[23] The development of the class groups and corporations engaged in

The medieval worker

similar work was to become what is sometimes termed 'the guild system'.

Aquinas held that the diversification of capacities amongst the different classes and crafts was a gift of nature and was but the execution of a decree of providence. He said :

> One man does not suffice to perform all those acts demanded by society, and therefore it is necessary that different persons be occupied in different pursuits. The diversification of men for diverse tasks is the result, primarily, of divine providence, which details the various compartments of man's life in such a way that nothing necessary to human existence is ever lacking; secondarily, this diversification proceeds from natural causes which bring it about that different men are born with aptitudes and tendencies for the different functions and the various ways of living.[24]

The class groups and corporations engaged in similar work were in effect banding together for their preservation and their common good in accordance with the precepts of natural law.

Borne and Henry were of the view that the insufficiency of the elaboration of the idea of work must not be allowed to hide the extent of the revolution accomplished in the Middle Ages. In this period, work assumed a religious value for men, and was of service in putting into the life of individuals values of self-sacrifice and detachment. The tiller of the soil and the artisan had their personal ends to achieve and were no longer mere instruments. Work no longer served the purposes of freeing from the anxieties of its existence a few men who were predestined to a life of contemplative thought or heroism. It had an anterior meaning and took its place in the subjective life of each individual. Labour, the manufacture of a useful thing, no longer sufficed to occupy a man's soul, and the life of contemplation no longer excluded a life of productive labour. Through work, lived and submitted to as a penance, the humblest person could enter into communion with the saints. Work was now no obstacle to the spiritual life; on the contrary, it can be seen as a means to its attainment.[25]

The guilds

The guilds were described by Belloc as that instrument whereby any form of human economic activity can work corporately and yet at the same time with the recognition of human economic activity – that is, human dignity and the function of human free will. He described the essential element of the guild idea as that of men pursuing the same form of activity, but only in cooperation limited to the end of preserving the economic freedom – that is, the property and livelihood of each member of the guild.[26]

The medieval guild was essentially local, and the guilds in a single town formed a separate system. This applied to both the merchant and craft guilds but particularly to the craft guilds. This is probably due to the comparative localization of markets which arose because of the paucity of transport facilities. The guild was an association of independent producers each of whom worked on his own with a small number of journeymen and apprentices.[27]

G. D. H. Cole describes the guild as more regulatory than controlling. The guild did not manage the industry, though it sometimes acted as a purchasing agent for materials. The actual management was left in the hands of the guild members, the master craftsmen. However, the guild laid down elaborate regulations governing the actions and professional code of its members. These regulations, which are the essence of the medieval guild system, had as their basis the double object of maintaining the liberties and rights of the craft and its tradition of good workmanship and faithful communal service as expressed in the idea of the 'just price' discussed later. The guilds offered their members a considerable degree of security and status. They held in medieval society a recognized position as economic organs of the body social, possessing a tradition of free service and, on the strength of that tradition, filling an honourable place in the public life of the medieval city.[28]

Cole draws a comparison between the guild system as a method of the organization of industry and that of industry in the modern time. He says that the former was imbued through and through with a spirit of free communal service, a spirit entirely lacking in modern industrialism, having been replaced by the motives of greed and fear. Cole's is an observation with which this writer concurs. He says that whilst there were undoubtedly sharp practices and profiteering in the Middle Ages, the guildsmen and the guild that committed or sanctioned them did so in violation of moral principles which he and the guild had explicitly accepted as the basis of the industrial order. He says that today, on the other hand, moral principles are regarded almost as intruders in the industrial sphere, and many forms of sharp practice and profiteering rank as the highest manifestations of commercial sagacity.[29]

The first known medieval European craft guilds appeared around 1100 in Italy, the Rhineland and the Low Countries, and proceeded to spread quickly over western Europe. The origin of their existence and organization has been disputed and remains obscure. Were they a continuation, or perhaps revival, of the craft colleges (*Collegia*) of the Roman Empire, or were they a specialization of the Germanic social guild? Antony Black, quoting Mickwitz, says that Mickwitz argued for the former proposition as being the most probable for Italy and suggested that the practice may have been borrowed from Constantinople.

Black says that whereas in imperial Rome numerous trades had their own colleges which functioned only in specified trades under state licence, the European crafts seemed in general to be characterized by a greater degree of independence and functioned in every artisan's calling. Like the European economy itself, the guilds underwent a process of continuous development. He says that there may even have been some continuity with the modern labour union under industrial capitalism, which may be seen as a response to needs in some way analogous to those experienced in the early Middle Ages.[30]

Lujo Brentano considered it unlikely that the craft guilds were a reincarnation of the Roman *Collegia Opificum*. He considered it more likely that the craft guilds descended from the companies into which, in episcopal and royal towns, the bond handicraftsmen of the same trade were ranged under the superintendence of an official, or that they took their origin from a common subjection to police control or from common obligations to pay certain imposts.[31]

The guilds in everyday practice

Belloc described the guild as a society partly cooperative, but in the main composed of private owners of capital whose corporation was self-governing, and was designed to check competition between its members in order to prevent the growth of one at the expense of the other. He says that above all, the guilds most jealously safeguarded the division of property so that there should not be formed within its ranks a proletariat on the one side and a monopolizing capitalism on the other.[32]

Black says that the craft guilds aimed typically at securing continuity of work and income for their members and to maintain a fixed number of small independent producing masters in each craft. To this end they sought to limit competition. While most guilds took for granted a certain spread in the scale of operation, the general aim was to prevent the expansion of one man's business at the expense of others. Recognition of the guild's economic status was a matter for the city council or lord. As crafts sprang up in various cities during the twelfth and thirteenth centuries, their position was usually established by mutual agreement with the town authorities. The guild was allotted a prescribed role in the city's economic life, often designated specifically as a duty or office (*officium*). Black says the attitude of city authorities to the creation of new guilds became more permissive during the economic expansion of the twelfth and thirteenth centuries. In granting the Magdeburg shoemakers the right to elect their own magistrate, the archbishop stated his desire that 'liberty be the mother of our action' and that 'the guilds (*officia*) of our city, large or small, should each exist in their dignity according to their integral right (*in suo honore secundum ius integrum*)'. It was, for the archbishop, a matter of 'freedom and right'.[33]

There is in this a recognition by both the Church and the civil authority of what we would today term 'the right of association'.

The craft fraternities grew in the shelter of the Church. Many town craftsmen were church employees, the richer monasteries employing craftsmen as did the secular barons; and monasteries had their lay brothers. Terms like 'brother', 'sister', 'Order' and 'chapter' were borrowed from the Church by the crafts. The early craft fraternities appeared under the name of their patron saint, with tailors under John the Baptist, the blacksmiths under St Loi, the shoemakers celebrated St Crispins, and the stonemasons the four crowned martyrs who, like St Crispin and his brother, were legendary Christians of old Rome.[34]

Leeson was of the opinion that the guilds were a source of democracy of a deeper and more popular kind than that represented more formally by the Magna Carta and de Montfort's Parliament. He says that at a time when the chivalry of western Europe was studying how to cut the next nobleman's throat, ravish his wife and seize his castle in accordance with the highest knightly conventions, guild members were fined for missing meetings, refusing to serve as officers, being foul-mouthed, dozing off during the annual dinner, keeping the ale cup standing, or slandering a brother or sister. He adds that violence was not absent from the way of life, but they made a study to avoid it.[35]

In medieval society the status of a man was of primary importance. As Belloc says, it was his established condition. In original Christian society – the society which reached its flower

The medieval worker

in the Middle Ages – status was omnipresent. It did not cover the whole ground of human activity by any means, but it covered a sufficient area to make status the determining character of all society. A man's position was known, the duties and burdens attaching to it were known, as were also the advantages, and they were largely fixed; for the spiritual force and motif underlying the whole business was an appetite for security: for making life tolerable on its material side so that there should be room and opportunity for men to lead the 'good life' as the Greeks put it, or as the Catholic Church puts it, to 'save their souls'.[36]

The guilds were usually wealthy and powerful corporations. Each guild had its own hall, its own hospital, its own chapel, its special emblems, its particular banner, its distinctive uniform. In the magnificent civic displays in which the medieval age delighted, the guilds took a leading part and spared no expense. The principal sources of their revenues were:

1. the annual subscriptions of the members;
2. the entrance fees paid by apprentices, assistants and masters;
3. fines;
4. donations and bequests which often included lands or houses given for the purposes of the guild or for some specific object within the guild's jurisdiction.

The members of a craft guild were divided into three grades or classes: apprentices, journeymen and masters. To each grade belonged rights and duties peculiar to itself. Heading the guild administration was the governing council which usually consisted of four persons chosen annually from among the oldest and most trustworthy of the masters.

The period of apprenticeship was usually seven years, during which time the apprentice lived in the master's house as a member of the family and on terms of social equality. The master was responsible for the apprentice's moral and religious training as well as for his professional training. The term of apprenticeship completed, the apprentice became a journeyman. A journeyman served as an assistant for some years to the master. On the conclusion of this period the journeyman became a master craftsman in his own right, with his right to the establishment of his own workshop and employment of his own apprentices.[37]

The master was at the pinnacle of the craft guild. The master had his own establishment, either as his father's successor or otherwise. At that time it required no great capital to start an independent business, and the guild was usually ready to advance money for the purpose on easy terms to a deserving member. But to be enrolled as a master other conditions were required. The candidate had to be a practising Catholic. He was required to present satisfactory testimonials from the masters under whom he served as apprentice and journeyman. It was also necessary to pass a satisfactory professional test. This usually took the shape of presenting what was termed 'a masterpiece' of his own handiwork. Lastly, he was required to pay a fee and in the presence of the guild council swear an oath promising fidelity to all the obligations of the association.

The religious character of the guild is highlighted by Cahill in an extract from a guild document quoted by Janssen in his work *History of the German people at the close of the Middle Ages*. The document says:

> No trade or profession can succeed honorably unless the apprentice is early taught to fear God and be obedient to his master, as if he were his father. He must, morning and evening every day of the week, thank God for help and protection, for without God he can do nothing ... Every Sunday and holy day he must hear Mass and a sermon and read good books. He must be industrious and seek not his own glory but God. The honour of his master and of his trade he must also seek, for this is holy, and he may one day be a master himself, if God wills he is worthy of it ... When the apprentice fails in obedience and the fear of God, he shall be punished, so that through pain of the body, the soul may benefit.[38]

It is perhaps a sign of the secularism of the present age that much of the modern scholarship on the medieval guilds plays down the significance of their religious character. This is unfortunate as the guilds recognized in practice the intimate connection of religion with commercial relations and of all the activities of life. Although the primary object of the associations was economic, the guilds made every effort to secure good conduct and fidelity to religious duties on the part of their members. Individuals were punished or sometimes expelled from the guilds for immoral or irreligious conduct. Every guild was under the protection of a patron saint or was especially dedicated to the Holy Trinity or to the Virgin Mother of God under one of her titles. The portrait of the guild patron was painted on the banner of the guild, which was borne in public processions. The association of the patron saint with the trade that belonged to the guild intensified the craftsmen's pride in their work and the men's esteem for the nobility of manual labour. The church feast of the patron saint of the guild was always the occasion of the great annual guild banquet.

Each guild was associated with a church whose name it bore. Inside the church burned a candle in honour of the guild's patron saint. The Church gave spiritual aid and medical care, and certainly helped in writing and drafting the guild documents.[39]

The doctrine of the 'just price' (justum pretium)

The concept of a just price is an important development in Catholic social thought as it has a direct bearing upon the notion of the 'just wage' in its application to the rights of workers. It is a concept derived from the natural law. It is a precept of natural law, that it is a duty both to oneself and to one's relations, to gain a sufficient measure of property which will ensure maintenance of the family according to the standards of one's class. This is based upon the requirements of natural law – that is, with consideration for its suitability for production and the actual conditions of economic life which are to be taken into consideration. Troeltsch contrasts this approach, which he terms 'the traditionalist spirit', with the capitalistic spirit. It is expressed in the differentiation, according to its rank, of the way of life, and in the injunction to the political societies for a policy of protection of the food supply, and for the regulation of prices, to maintain for each individual the income according to his rank. It is the standpoint of the conservation of food supplies, which is closely connected with the maintenance of permanent professional groups, in which the same trade or calling is handed on without variation from father to son through many generations. It is further expressed in the doctrine of the *justum pretium* regulating trade and barter which objectively corresponds exactly to the value of the wares, and which may include in addition only that which is necessary for the life of the trader. Thus Troeltsch sums up the traditionalist thinking on economic matters:

> Property and gain are based on the personal performance of works; goods are exchanged only where necessary, and then only according to the principles of a just price which does not give an undue advantage to anyone;[40]

Aside from the craft guilds being concerned with maintaining a steady volume of business for their members, their chief aims were ensuring a satisfactory standard of workmanship and obtaining a fair price for its product. They were particularly concerned that a good product should be sold at a fair price.[41]

In Aquinas' view, fees for services were (like salaries and wages) a kind of price (*pretium*); they should be moderate, and the measure of their fairness take into account the situation of both provider and recipient, the nature of the transactions and the work (labour) involved, and the custom of the country. In any sale, buyer and seller would act justly if the price received by the seller and paid by the purchaser was neither more nor less than what the thing sold was worth. For them, the transaction represented the requirement of equality in mutual benefit (*communis utilitas*); sellers are recompensed for what they have given up (their costs, including fair wages for their labour, expenses incurred in transportation, and so on), and buyers are likewise compensated for the price they have paid by the value of what they acquire.[42]

If the equality and mutual benefit referred to above was not present in a transaction, the transaction was reckoned as unlawful to divine law. Aquinas says of such a dealing:

> Hence, according to the divine law, it is reckoned unlawful if the equality of justice is not observed in buying and selling and he who has received more than he ought must make compensation to him that has suffered loss, if the loss be considerable.[43]

In his doctrine of the 'just price', Aquinas is possibly giving expression to his view that the common good was undoubtedly more important than that of the individual (*majus set divinus est bonum multitudinis quam bonum unius*).[44] It is also perhaps an extension of his view that:

> Whatever is for an end should be proportionate to that end. Now the end of law is the common good; because as Isidore says, 'Law should be framed, not for any private benefit, but for the common good of all the citizens'.[45]

Thus, the laws of the just price had to be observed in wages, buying and selling, and in every contract of exchange, otherwise the contract was deemed to be unjust and invalid in conscience. In what can be seen as a stark contrast with many practices of modern twenty-first century capitalism, the fifteenth-century author Trithemius writes:

> Whoever buys up corn, meat and wine in order to drive up their prices, and amass money at the cost of others, is, according to the laws of the church, no better than a common criminal. In a well governed community all arbitrary raising of prices in the case of articles of food and clothing is peremptorily stopped. In times of scarcity merchants who have supplies of such commodities can be compelled to sell them at fair prices; for in every community care should be taken that all the members should be provided for, lest a small number be allowed to grow rich, and revel in luxury to the hurt and prejudice of the many.[46]

What a contrast this is with the practice of modern liberal capitalism where the masters of the financial system have, by the concentration of economic power, enriched themselves beyond the wildest dreams of their imagination, but at the expense of the many.

The objective value of a commodity was calculated mainly and primarily upon the cost of its production. This included the cost of materials and the value of labour. The cost of production was accounted the first charge upon the product and was itself determined on the basis of a reasonable standard of living for the producers. In the case of most commodities, the just price was usually fixed by the guilds, but often by the municipality or even by the state. However, even when the price was not legally determined, it was not left to the arbitrary decision of the buyer or seller, but was supposed to be fixed by what was known as the 'common estimation of the community'. Although prices may vary within certain limits, it was understood that to pass these limits for accidental causes, such as scarcity or the special needs of the buyer or seller, would be unjust.[47]

Just wage
Derived from the notion of the just price is the principle of the just wage. The recompense of labour or the rate of wages was determined in accordance with the general rules relating to just price. Labour is the ordinary means by which, according to the law of nature, man supplies the needs of human life. Labour was regarded as possessed of an intrinsic minimum value. This value was calculated on the principle that the worker should have the wherewithal to support life in reasonable human conditions according to his capacity and state. The price of the labour expended in the production of an article or the worker's wage was regarded as the first consideration in fixing the price of a commodity. The actual rate of wages was usually fixed by the guilds.

The obligation of paying a just wage was so universally accepted that the matter is little discussed by the medieval writers. Aquinas, according to Cahill, refers to the just wage only accidentally here and there in the *Summa*, where he takes for granted that the rate of wages comes under the laws of just price, and implies that just wages are to be measured not arithmetically, but proportionately. Albertus Magnus alludes to the same matter in his *Ethica*, where he implies that the human needs of the producer of the article or, in other words, the amount of the labour expended on its production, is the main element to be considered in estimating its exchange value.[48]

The principle of a just wage or a living wage, derived from and enunciated by the doctrine of the just price, was later to be set in stone by the great social encyclicals of the late nineteenth century and twentieth century: *Rerum Novarum*, *Quadragesimo Anno* and *Mater et Magistra*, the encyclicals which were to be the cornerstones of the development of Catholic social thought in respect of the rights of working men and women from that time to the present.

Thus the guild authority fixed the prices of labour as well as of products. The contingent object was the securing of a proper wage for the manufacturer and at the same time safeguarding the interests of the consumer. Thus every guildman, which generally meant every worker in the town, was enabled to earn a fair living; and the weak were protected from the effects of unfettered competition, in which they might be so disadvantaged as to be deprived of the means of supporting life. The guild regulations also aimed at securing the common good of the town. In medieval times there was a high standard of public spirit due partly to the precepts of Christian doctrine, which then dominated social relations, and partly to the democratic nature of the guild structure. The power of one guild was kept in due check by the others, who could retaliate against any association that acted unfairly. Hence the guilds legislated to prevent scarcity on the one hand, and overproduction on the other.

Summary

The medieval period saw the decline of slavery and the evolution of the peasantry. At the same time a new dignity was given to work and, through the guilds, artisans and craftsmen experienced pride in their workmanship and were accorded a status and recognition denied to them under the institution of slavery. The dignity of labour and of the craftsmen was to be largely

The medieval worker

destroyed by the onset of liberal capitalism in the seventeenth century, and the rise of two antagonistic classes, the capitalist class and the proletarian class. The decline of the guilds, and the reduction of those engaged in the various crafts, trades and the peasantry to a new relatively powerless and impoverished status, which came to be known as the proletariat, was a direct consequence of the onset of liberal capitalism. Subsequently society would be divided into two mutually antagonistic classes: the capitalist class and the proletarian class. These phenomena are discussed in the following chapter.

Notes
1 Lecky, pp. 246, 247.
2 Cahill, Thomas, p. 187.
3 Cahill, E., p. 27.
4 Cahill, E., p. 21.
5 Ibid. p. 53.
6 Bloch, p. 11.
7 Lecky, p. 67.
8 Bloch, p. 7.
9 Ibid. pp. 8, 9.
10 Ibid. p. 75.
11 Bonnassie, p. 315.
12 Ibid. p. 294.
13 Troeltsch, p. 133.
14 Belloc, *The Servile State*, p. 47.
15 Cahill, E., pp. 63, 64.
16 Ibid. p. 65.
17 Belloc, *The Servile State*, pp. 47, 48.
18 Cahill, E., pp. 68, 69.
19 Ibid. pp. 65, 66.
20 Borne and Henry, p. 45.
21 *The Summa Theologica of St Thomas Aquinas*, pp. 620–5.
22 Borne and Henry, pp. 50, 51.
23 Troeltsch, p. 317.
24 Vigongiari, p. ix.
25 Borne and Henry, pp. 45, 46.
26 Belloc, *The Crisis of Civilisation,* p. 218.
27 Cole, p. 43.
28 Ibid. pp. 44, 45.
29 Ibid.
30 Black, pp. 6, 7.
31 Brentano, p. cxiv.
32 Belloc, *The Servile State*, p. 4.
33 Black, p.18.

34 Leeson, p. 27.
35 Ibid. p. 26.
36 Belloc, *The Crisis of Civilisation*, p. 137.
37 Cahill, E., pp. 74, 75, 76.
38 Ibid. p. 76.
39 Leeson, p. 26.
40 Troeltsch, p. 320.
41 Black, p. 8.
42 Finnis, pp. 200, 201.
43 *Aquinas, Summa Theologica* quoted in *The Political Ideas of St Thomas Aquinas* ed. Dino Bigongiári, Hafner Press, New York, 1973, p. 145.
44 d'Entrevès, p. 27.
45 Bigongiari, p. 66.
46 Cahill, E., p. 43.
47 Ibid. p. 44.
48 Ibid. p. 46.

Chapter 5

THE RISE OF THE PROLETARIAT

The Reformation

Hilaire Belloc argued that just as the institution of slavery and the old pagan servile state slowly approached a distributive state under the influence of the Catholic Church and slowly disappeared as Catholic civilization developed, so it was that the servile state began to return where Catholic civilization receded.[1]

Referring to the decline of the guilds and the dissolution of the peasantry, the Irish–American Cardinal James Gibbons of Baltimore, who was the pastor of a largely working-class immigrant Catholic community, wrote in his famous 1887 *Memorial*, which he presented to Rome, that ever since the Reformation the democratic and cooperative institutions of medieval Europe had been on their deathbed. He said that in the year 1500 most Englishmen owned their own homes, but by 1600 only between two-thirds and three-quarters were still in possession of their own lands. By the year 1700 approximately fifty per cent had the economic buttress of a home behind them, but by the year 1900 less than one-tenth of the population possessed all of the land in the country. He said that what was true of real property was true also of the means of production. Trade and business in the Middle Ages were conducted on the principles of mutual help and assistance, and unlimited competition was never thought of. But with the breaking down of the corporate feeling of united Christendom, methods of business were introduced which Gibbons thought would have seemed deeply immoral one hundred years before.[2]

It has been argued that the rise of contract as against status was a major factor in the demise of the guilds and the rise of liberal capitalism. Belloc, for example, argued that where contract gained in importance, status diminished. With the decline of status, a person's position became less clear. Belloc believed that the overtaking of status by contract was a result of the revival of Roman law which modified and ousted the traditional popular law of the Middle Ages. Roman law gave sanction to contract and not to custom. Under Roman law a person did not hold their land feudally as an inherited right but rather by purchase or by will. The whole point of being an owner in Roman law was that the person held the right to contract as an absolute owner. In time this came to weaken the position of the peasantry as their economic position deteriorated and they were forced to alienate their land.[3]

He further argued that while the guilds flourished they were ruled by the concept of the just price and the idea of the guild worked through village life by making land tenure fixed and hereditary. He said that when the guild decayed as the result of the Reformation, when controlled industry proved unable to compete with the competitive industry, contract rapidly took the place of status. Belloc argued that in England, as the peasant lost status he fell into the condition of a mere wage labourer. On the other hand, on the Continent, particularly in France, the peasant, by becoming completely independent of local rules and of a lord, also got rid of status, and his functions became purely functions of contract. But instead of falling by loss of status into a condition of wage slavery, he rose into a condition of ownership.

John Tropman, speaking of contemporary United States society in words which are applicable to western society generally, says that whereas at the present time the Protestant work ethic is virtually synonymous with work itself, in the mediaeval Catholic world before the Reformation work was simply work. It was something which you did to provide the resources for you to eat and live. He says that after the Reformation, work was sacred and the money that work produced was a sign of moral worth. Elaborating on this he said that in pre-Reformation times, the purpose of work was to accomplish activities that provided goods and services, transformed materials and gleaned resources for oneself, one's community and one's society. The work process was instrumental, not transcendental. There was, he said, less sense than there would be later on of self-validation through work. Thus, in the Catholic ethic, work is a less powerful cradle of self-esteem than it is in the Protestant ethic. It is important, but one has no sense of being 'spoiled goods' if one does not have a job.[4]

Tropman is of the view that the Protestants' view of work was an inversion of the Catholic view. He said that in the traditional Catholic view work was a productive activity and even a community effort. He said the process was straightforward and was important because people were doing it. The resulting products were available to the whole community. One produced what one needed, consumed it, and shared the rest if others needed it. On the other hand, the Protestant view was that work, per se, was sacred and the process a cleansing one. Work became separated from the worker; work achieved predominance, and the worker was subordinated.[5]

The doctrine of the Communion of Saints taught that the Church was composed not merely of the living faithful but also of the departed, whether in Purgatory or in Heaven; and, further, that all the different classes or members of the Church could help each other by their prayers. The teaching on superogatory works and indulgences also tended to foster a strong sense of solidarity. On the other hand, as O'Brien points out, the Reformation was intentionally individualist. The doctrine of private judgement naturally led to a strongly individualistic character, which the leaders of the movement were unable to keep within the bounds they would have desired. He was of the opinion that the individualistic spirit of the Reformation neutralized where it did not mould the teaching of the reformers.[6] O'Brien stated that it was only natural that men who have been taught to rely on their own private judgement in matters of faith and on their own lonely efforts to attain salvation, should resent dictation and hindrances in their political and economic life. One's standpoint towards religion naturally colours one's standpoint towards every other human activity.[7]

Dr Cunningham was of the opinion that it was not necessary to labour a point that Calvinism was a form of Christianity which gave its sanction to the free existence of the commercial spirit and to the capitalist organization of industry.[8] H. G. Wood thought that it would have been unfair to criticize the Puritan outlook because it failed to anticipate the social evils of the Industrial Revolution, although it would deserve censure if, by its concentration on individual duty, it rendered man blind to the necessity of common action, and perhaps a little callous towards the evils in question. He believed it was undoubted that later Puritanism had this latter effect, although other evils of eighteenth-century life also cooperated to produce it. He thought that many good men of the Puritan style were, and perhaps still were today, attached obstinately to the principle of laissez-faire, because a deep-rooted trust in individual responsibility and self-help is part of their religious inheritance. He said that in this, Puritanism displayed the defects of its qualities and that the close connection between the Puritan ethic of prudence and the spirit of capital was undeniable.[9]

The rise of a proletarian class was both the corollary and antithesis of the spirit of capital which resulted in the emergence of a society in which there existed a new spirit for the making of money for its own sake, with the inevitable tendency for the rich to become richer and the poor poorer, and the division of society into two classes of possessors and proletariat, or the 'haves' and 'have-nots' of popular parlance.[10]

The evolution and development of the Protestant view of work with its emphasis upon the work and its products, rather than on the worker himself, was a significant factor in Britain and Ireland in the weakening of the status of workers and the rise of the proletarian class. The social problems which arose from this development were products of the spirit of individualism. Individualism was, according to Howell, a product of the Reformation. The new theology taught that redemption was based on individual faith; it ruled out the saving power of the Church by which men joined to the Church are saved by her; it refused to see that what is saved by the head is the body of Christ – that the salvation and sanctification of men is corporate. In time, this spirit of individualism overflowed into civil society at large and eventually led to unbridled competition, the economic doctrine of laissez-faire capitalism, and the exploitation of the worker in the absence of collective bargaining and any concept of justice in the workplace.[11]

Belloc also believed that Calvin was the spiritual father of what he termed 'the modern gospel of wealth'. The tenets of this belief were that a man's value, even his spiritual value, was connected with his power to accumulate money. Belloc argued that in denying the efficacy of good deeds and of the human will, by abnegations of doctrine, and in leaving aside as useless all the doctrine and tradition of holy poverty, Calvin opened the door to the domination of the mind by money. Aquinas had, centuries before, said that if men abandoned the idea of God as the supreme good, they would tend to replace Him with the idea that material wealth is the supreme good. Calvin never advocated in so many words, and indeed never thought, that men should principally pursue the accumulation of wealth, but he broke down the barriers which Catholicism had erected against that tendency, and, following on his teachings, Christendom began to turn to the idea of wealth as at least the only certain good, and therefore the main thing to be aimed at.[12]

Dissolution of the monasteries

The dissolution of the monasteries, with the resulting confiscation of their property, immediately produced considerable distress among the multitudes who had been maintained by the resources that the religious bodies had administered. It proved to be particularly hard on the tenants of the monastic lands, which were probably more than 2,000,000 statute acres in extent. The tenants had been accustomed to an easy and sympathetic mode of treatment at the hands of the monks. This now ceased as the ownership passed under the power of harsh and exacting landlords. Rack-rents were frequently exacted, and numerous exemptions and privileges to which the tenants had been accustomed were withdrawn. Another blow was the confiscation of the property of the guilds, of hospitals and alms houses. Destruction of the religious schools and colleges, in which so many children were educated free of cost, was further injurious to the poor.[13]

The English Protestant writer and social reformer William Cobbett, writing on the social effects of the dissolution of the monasteries and the seizure of church properties, said:

> The Catholic church included in itself a great deal more than the business of teaching religion and of practising worship and administering the sacraments. It had a great deal to do with the temporal concerns of the people. It provided, and amply provided, for all the wants of the poor and distressed. It received back, in many instances, what the miser and extortioner had taken unfairly away, and applied it to works of beneficence. It contained a great body of land proprietors, whose revenues were distributed, in various ways, amongst the people at large, upon terms always singularly advantageous to the latter. It was a great and powerful estate, independent both of the aristocracy and the crown, and naturally siding with the people. But, above all things, it was a provider for the poor and a keeper of hospitality. By its charity, and by its benevolence towards its tenants, and dependants, it mitigated the rigour of providorship and held society together by the ties of religion rather than by the trammels and terrors of the law.[14]

Belloc was of the view that had the new industrial development come upon a people who were economically free, it would have taken a cooperative form rather than the capitalist form it did. He said that coming as it did upon a people which had already lost its economic freedom, the new industrial development assumed at its very origin a capitalist form which it retained, expanded and perfected during the nineteenth and twentieth centuries. He said that it was in England that the industrial system arose, and that it was in England that all its traditions and habits were formed. Because the England in which the industrial system arose was already a capitalist England, modern industrialism, having spread from England, has proceeded upon the capitalist model.[15]

In England, the birthplace of industrial capitalism, there followed upon the dissolution of the monasteries by Henry VIII a concentration of the ownership of land in the hands of a powerful oligarchy of larger landowners. The monastic lands which had comprised at least one-fifth of the wealth of the country had been transferred to the great landowners, and this transference had tipped the scale entirely in their favour vis-à-vis the peasantry. This trend continued through the decades, so that by the year 1700 fewer than half the population inhabited a house of which they were the secure possessor or tilled lands from which they could not be evicted. Thus, with land and therefore wealth increasingly concentrated in the hands of a few large landowners, the dispossessed peasantry were evolving into an impoverished proletariat which was to provide a large pool of cheap labour for the impending Industrial Revolution. The large landowners, as the possessors of land and wealth, had become the emerging capitalist class.[16]

The vast growth of the proletariat and the concentrated ownership in the hands of a few, with the resultant exploitation by those owners of the great mass of the people, was not necessarily connected with the new improved methods of production beginning to emerge during the eighteenth century. The industrial system developed along capitalist lines, as it was regarded as normal and natural that those who produced the new wealth with the new machinery should be the dispossessed peasantry and newly arisen proletariat. This was because the England upon which the new industrial developments had come was already an England owned, through its landholdings and accumulations of wealth, by a small minority. It was already an England in which perhaps half of the whole population was proletarian and was therefore a readily available medium for exploitation.[17]

With the advent of the Industrial Revolution and the new methods of production, to whom could new industry turn for capitalization? Belloc cogently argues that the small landowner had already largely disappeared. The corporate life and mutual obligations which had supported him and confirmed him in his property had been broken to pieces by the deliberate action of the rich. He was ignorant because his skills had been taken from him and the universities closed to him. He was the more ignorant because the common life which had nourished his social sense and the cooperative arrangements which had once been his defence had disappeared. When you sought an accumulation of clothing, of corn, of housing, of fuel as the indispensable preliminary to the launching of your new industry, when you've looked around for someone who could find the accumulated wealth necessary for these considerable experiments, you had to turn to the class which had already monopolized the bulk of the means of production in England. The rich men alone could furnish you with a supply. These supplies, once found and the venture capitalized, that form of human energy lay best to hand which was the existing proletariat, which the new plutocracy had created by thrusting out the mass of Englishmen from the possession of implements, of houses, and of land, thereby cornering the wealth of the country after the Reformation. This resource was indefinitely exploitable, weak, ignorant and desperately necessitous, ready to produce for you upon almost any terms and glad enough if you would only keep it alive.

Belloc argues that this rich class, adopting some new processes of production for its private gain, worked it upon those lines of competition which its analysts had already established. Cooperative tradition was dead. Where would the new rich class find its cheapest labour? Obviously among the proletariat, not among the remaining small landowners. What class would increase under the new wealth? Obviously the proletariat again, without responsibilities, with nothing to leave to its progeny; and as they swelled the capitalists' gain, they enabled him with increasing power to buy out the small owner and send him to swell, by another tributary, the proletarian mass. Thereafter developed a snowballing effect. The rich, already possessed of the accumulations by which that industrial change could alone be nourished, inherited all succeeding accumulations of implements and all its increasing accumulations of subsistence. The factory system, starting upon a basis of capitalist and proletariat, grew in the mould which had determined its origins. With every new advance the capitalist looked for proletariat grist to feed the productive mill. To quote Belloc:

> Every circumstance of that society the form in which the laws that governed ownership and profit were cast, the obligations of partners, the relations between 'master' and 'man', directly made for the indefinite expansion of a subject, formless, wage-earning class controlled by a small body of owners, which body would tend to become smaller and richer still, and to be possessed of power ever greater and greater as the bad business unfolded.[18]

The rise of the proletariat and capitalist classes cannot be attributed solely to the Reformation, as there had already been developing in the latter Middle Ages an aggressive spirit of capitalism. McCarthy and Rhodes state that there was at this time an uneasy spirit, perhaps aggravated by tension between the newer entrepreneurial values and the traditional religious and cultural values. They say that life at that time was marked by an obsession with luck at the unpredictable wheel of fortune in the economic, political and social life of Europe. They are of the opinion that this tension deeply affected the practice of religion, and religious institutions in turn were transformed to serve this new world of traders and merchants.[19]

Rodger Charles believed that it was the 'Enlightenment' of the eighteenth century which freed the capitalists from moral restraint. *'Laissez-faire',* 'let them get on with it', was the cry. The market was a moral force; all would be well if the capitalists were free from moral restraints. The invisible hand of the economy would bring justice through selfishness. This principle, according to Charles, revolutionized economics and economic organization; it also tore both from links with objective finality. The Judaeo-Christian tradition of objective moral law knew that defrauding the labourer of his just rewards was a sin crying out to Heaven for vengeance. Now the Enlightenment canonized the selfishness of the rich. The labourer, who had helped to create wealth beyond previous imagining, was rewarded with whatever pittance his master offered him, according to the law of supply and demand in a market hopelessly tilted in favour of the master. An increasingly godless age found in Marx, an atheist prophet against this evil. His cure was worse than the disease, as experience would ultimately demonstrate; but the resultant sufferings imposed on humanity by the various derivatives of Marxism are to be laid at the door of those who produced so violent a reaction in Marx and Engels – the materialistic economism of the liberal capitalists.[20]

The Catholic social movement and the proletariat

The Catholic social movement in Germany and France
Social Catholicism, or Christian socialism as it was sometimes called, developed in Europe following the political and social changes which swept across Europe in 1848. The generic term 'Christian socialism' was first employed by a Frenchman, Francis Huet, in a book entitled *Le Regné Social du Christianisme,* published in 1853. However, two other French writers, the Abbé de Lamennais (1848) and Philippe Buchez, who wrote between the years 1838 and 1840 in terms couched in a similar vein to Huet, may lay considerable claims to priority in this matter.[21]

All of the three above-mentioned were republicans who sought to reconcile the Church and the revolution. Perhaps, because of this, Catholicism has unfortunately shown no great desire to honour any of them. This is unfortunate, as they wrote on the social question at a time when it was most unfashionable to do so.

Following the social and political convulsions in 1848, the French bishops attempted to respond to the ferment by calling attention to the insensitivity of owners to the needs of their employees. They called for a sense of partnership in which both the owners and the employees would be given due respect. This was a moral appeal and did not advocate any overhaul of systems. These bishops explicitly rejected the developing socialist interpretations of 'the proletariat'.[22]

The German Catholic Congresses, the first of which was the notable Congress at Mainz in 1848, had their origin in the society called the *Piusverein,* which had been founded by Kaspar Riffel for the defence of religious liberties from the perceived threat of Bismarck's *Kulturkampf.* The congress of 1858 was significant in that not only did representatives of *Piusverein* branches attend, but also representatives of other Catholic associations as well as prominent Catholics from the media and other professions. Henceforward, these congresses assumed the character of a Catholic parliament, with the social question featuring prominently.

Murphy argues that a significant shift occurred during the ministries of two bishops, Affre of Paris and, more importantly, Ketteler of Mainz. Bishop Affre addressed the situation by looking not only at the suffering of the worker but also at the situation which produced it. He asked a very pertinent question. Was it always to be that the integral laws of the economic system demanded the constant diminution of the worker, or could in fact certain virtues check this development?

If it can be said that any one person was the founder of social Catholicism, it is Bishop Wilhelm Emmanuel von Ketteler (1811–1877). Ketteler recognized the danger to the Church from the apathy of the wealthier Catholics, and even of large numbers of the clergy, in face of the misery and material degradation of working men and women. The appearance in 1848 of the *Communist Manifesto* of Karl Marx and Friedrich Engels heralded the birth of the socialist movement. At the time of its publication few appreciated its significance. Ketteler was one of the few who did. In 1848, two years before his consecration as Bishop of Mainz, Ketteler, who was then serving as a priest in Frankfurt, was requested by the then Bishop of Mainz to attend and participate in a series of Advent services at Mainz Cathedral. Ketteler delivered a series of lectures dealing with such social questions as property, moral freedom, the destiny of man, church authority and the family. It was during one of his lectures that he said:

> The task of religion, the task of the Catholic societies in the immediate future, has to do with social conditions. The most difficult question – one which no legislation, no form of government, has been able to solve – is the *social question*. The difficulty, the vastness, the urgency of this question fills me with the greatest joy! . . . It must now become evident which church bears within it the power of divine truth. The world will see that to the Catholic Church is reserved, the definite solution of the social question; for the state, with all its legislative machinery, has not the power to solve it.[23]

It was largely as the result of Ketteler's labours and incessant exhortations over a period of some thirty years that European and German Catholics in particular were stirred into vigorous action on the social question. Ketteler's papers delivered at the Catholic Congress in Mainz were seen as a significant church response to Marxist philosophy. Referring to Ketteler, another prominent Catholic leader of the time, Gaspard Decurtins, said of Ketteler's submissions to the Mainz Conference that it was to Ketteler that went 'the undying honour of having met the manifesto of the communists with a program of Christian social reform that stands unsurpassed to this day'.[24]

William Murphy lists three significant reasons for Ketteler's importance as a founding father of the Catholic social movement. He says that firstly, Ketteler saw clearly that social organization depended upon underlying philosophical and ideological presuppositions. In Ketteler's view, social organization must be mediated by doctrinal principles that uphold the value of the person and the equal dignity of all human beings. Secondly, he realized that the transformation of society is tied to the transformation of souls. Prior to Ketteler it seemed that the only goal for the encouragement of virtue was to transform individual souls. Ketteler saw that the encouragement of virtue must also unleash the potential virtue into the social situation. Thirdly, Ketteler argued that social actions spring intrinsically from Christian concern. People could not be Christian, Ketteler insisted, if their convictions did not flow into social action, and if their social action was not guided by the Christian principles that shaped their personal lives.

After the Mainz lectures, Ketteler not only challenged the socialist and capitalist mindsets of his day, but also its specific remedies. At an assembly of German bishops on 5 September 1869 he listed the following which he maintained eliminated or at any rate diminished the evils of the industrial system of that time:

- the prohibition of child labour in factories
- the limitation of working hours of factory workers
- the separation of the sexes in the workshops
- the closing of unsanitary workshops
- Sunday rest
- the obligation to care for workers who are temporarily or permanently disabled
- the appointment by the state of factory inspectors.[25]

The document issued by this assembly of German bishops in 1869 became known as a Christian Labour Catechism. The document stated inter alia that:

> The object of the labour movement must not be antagonism between the working man and the employer, but peace on equitable terms between both.

The document further said:

> The impiety of capital, which would treat the working man like a machine, must be broken. It is a crime against the working class; it degrades them.[26]

In western Europe and particularly in France, the development of social Catholicism had its roots in the conservative aristocratic classes. Joe Holland is of the view that the concern of social Catholics in France at that time reflected a romantic vision of the Middle Ages; a family-centred agricultural system with urban craft guilds and communal corporations. This romantic conservative approach became dominant among Catholics vocal and active on the social question at the local level. According to Holland they challenged all of liberalism, including its economic doctrine. These conservatives assumed that the Enlightenment's mechanistic paradigm needed to be resisted and the old organic-hierarchical paradigm defended, with a special role in society for the Catholic religion and for the aristocracy. Two prominent advocates of social Catholicism at this time in France were the Viscount de Bonald and his son, the Cardinal Archbishop of Lyon, Louis de Bonald. Viscount de Bonald attacked the bourgeoisie class whose interests he said were served at the expense of the moral and physical health of the working class. In the 1830s Cardinal Louis de Bonald accused the employers of the city of Lyon of exploiting the workers by treating them as nothing more than a machine.

One of the main reasons for the leadership of social Catholicism in France remaining aristocratic was that the organization of workers in France was illegal at that time. For example, the workers' clubs and workshops set up for the unemployed were organized and directed by members of the aristocratic class, such as Armand de Melun.[27]

Philippe Buchez, referred to previously, produced a Christian socialist periodical named *L'Atelier*. The Christian democracy of Buchez predated the advent of Marxism. He was an advocate of producer cooperatives as well as profit sharing in capitalist enterprises. At the time, he was regarded as being quite radical, but much of what he said has been adopted by mainstream social Catholicism. His producer cooperatives may perhaps be a forerunner of today's worker cooperatives, examples of which are seen in the Basque country of Spain, France, Germany, North America and elsewhere in the world.

There were other Catholic publicists and economists of different political views who spoke strongly in favour of social reform and advocated Catholic organizations to combat what they saw as the evils resulting from industrial liberalism. Among these may be mentioned Chateau Briand, Louis Veuillot, Lacordaire (the great Dominican preacher), Viscomte Ville-neuve-Burgemont and Frederick Ozanam. Ozanam, who is perhaps

The rise of the proletariat 93

best remembered as the founder of the Society of St Vincent de Paul, wrote a good deal on the social question and on the role to be played by Christianity in the formation of social wellbeing.

Lacordaire, Ozanam, de Coux and the Abbé Henri Marget established a Catholic daily newspaper, *L'Ere Nouvelle*, in the years following the revolutions of 1848. Ozanam insisted in the pages of this publication that 'behind the social revolution was a political revolution . . . the arrival of the working class'.

One of the associates of Lacordaire was Abbé Félicité de Lamennais. Lamennais founded the journal *L'Avenir* in 1830. The journal proclaimed on its masthead 'God and Liberty'. Lacordaire in an article in *L'Avenir* described laissez-faire capitalism as the abandonment of the weak to the hands of the strong. He said that whenever laws have been made they have been made for the protection of the weakest. The working man is weaker than the master and therefore should be protected by law. Another writer with *L'Avenir* was Charles de Coux, a Catholic professor in political economy. He wrote in *L'Avenir* that Catholicism in its practical consequences presented the most admirable system of social economy that had ever been given to the world. He argued that the combat at that time was essentially the same as it was in the Middle Ages. Catholicism, he said, was now at grips with the aristocracy of capital as formerly it had been with the aristocracy of the land.

L'Avenir was far too progressive for its time and aroused the hostility of Louis Philippe's government (1830–48) and of certain of the hierarchy. Under pressure exerted upon Rome by French, English and Austrian members of the hierarchy, *L'Avenir* was indirectly denounced by Gregory XVI in his encyclical *Mirari Vos*. Following the decline of *L'Avenir*, both Lamennais and de Coux continued their activities through other publications and journals.[28]

Under Marget's editorship *L'Avenir* became a bold advocate for the working class, but the Catholic reaction against the revolution worked against them, and the journal lacked wider support in the French Church. As a result the journal folded within twelve months.[29]

The two men who made the most significant contribution to the development of the Catholic social movement in France were two young Catholic noblemen, officers in the French Army, who made each other's acquaintance while prisoners of war during the Franco-Prussian War of 1870. These were Count Albert de Mun and the Marquis Réné de la Tour du Pin. Both de Mun and Tour du Pin witnessed the dreadful scenes of the Paris commune insurrection of 1871, and were involved in operations against the insurgents. Both men were shocked by the ruthlessness of the measures adopted against the defeated communists and came to appreciate that it was the excesses of the rich and noble and not the proletarian insurgents that were fundamentally responsible for the death and ruination which had occurred during the insurrection. Towards the end of 1871 these men and other leading gentlemen of Paris outlined a social programme which included the establishment of Catholic working men's clubs on a large scale. Although these clubs relied heavily on the patronage of the educated classes, and were not made up exclusively of members of the working class, they continued to expand to the extent that by 1884 there were over 400 committees with 50,000 members in France. However, their real significance was that they initiated a national movement which aroused the Catholic upper classes to a sense of their social obligations.[30]

From Germany and France the Catholic social movement gradually spread into all countries of western and central Europe including Switzerland, Belgium, Holland and later on Italy, Spain and England. The beginnings of the movement in Switzerland are associated with the names of Cardinal Mermillod and Gaspar Decurtins. Mermillod filled in Switzerland somewhat the same position as Ketteler had in Germany. Decurtins was a disciple of Ketteler and a friend of Cardinal Manning. He, like de Mun in France, believed in political agitation for social reform.

The Fribourg Union
It was under Decurtins' auspices that the first International Federation of Catholic Social Workers was formed in 1884 at Fribourg under the presidency of Cardinal Mermillod. This conference came to be known as the Fribourg Union and met in October of each year from 1885 to 1891. The initial members of the Fribourg Union were Cardinal Mermillod, La Tour du Pin, Louis Millicent, Prince Karl von Lowenstein of Germany, Count Fraz Kuefstein, a representative of the Austrian Corporatavist School of Vogelsang, and delegates from Italy and Switzerland. The deliberations of the Fribourg Union were intense. Krier Mich says that they frequently commenced deliberations at 9.30 a.m. and concluded at 6.30 p.m. They divided into small groups which presented a conclusion to a general meeting of the union. This generally comprised between twenty and thirty-two persons, including theologians, political leaders and aristocracy.[31]

The Fribourg Union, mainly through the writing of Jesuit theologian August Lehmkuhl, set forth two basic principles of work and wages that marked a significant Catholic social reform. Firstly, the conference stated that a worker must not be seen only as a commodity but as a person. Secondly, a just wage is determined by double criteria, namely

1. the value of human work must prevail over discussions of wage contracts, and
2. the just wage is determined by the minimum necessary to maintain a family in ordinary circumstances.

In what must have been seen as a radical move, the conference advocated the intervention of the state when wage contracts entered into between labour and capital were deemed to be oppressive to the worker.

In these circumstances the state intervened to ensure the workers received what was necessary for their subsistence. The state's duties were to correct abuses and harmonize the activities of private enterprises with the common good whilst leaving the greatest possible freedom to private initiative. This position allowed for greater state intervention than did the position of the laissez-faire capitalist, but less state intervention than was demanded by the socialists.[32]

As a result of the deliberations of the Fribourg Union over a period of some six years, a social code and programme was drawn up and presented to Leo XIII by Cardinal Mermillod during a special visit to Rome for that purpose in 1888. This document was probably one of the causes of the publication of *Rerum Novarum* some three years later. It is perhaps of some significance that the Fribourg Union discontinued its sittings following the publication of *Rerum Novarum* in 1891.

The Catholic social movement in England and the United States

In England Cardinal Manning was a strong advocate of social reform. He was the author of numerous letters to the press and of articles and periodicals in which he supported the workers and their demands for protective legislation. He played a key role in the support of the just demands of the London dockers and in the eventual settlement of the great dockers strike of 1889. He was ably supported in his stand on the social question by Bishop Bagshawe of Nottingham. Cardinal Manning, who was a convert to Catholicism, was an ultramontanist who strongly believed that the Church and the pope in particular must speak out strongly on the social question and the rights of the workers in particular. In one of his notable speeches he declared that in the future the Church would have a new role to play. He said:

> A new task is before us. The church has no longer to deal with parliaments and princes, but with the masses and with the people. Whether we will or no, this is our work; we need a new spirit and a new law of life.[33]

Cardinal Manning's role in the British dock strike and his numerous articles on the social question received prominence not only in England but also on the Continent. In England, his standing and prominence was extraordinary given the minority status of Catholicism in England. However, the industrial working class in both England and the United States contained a significant Irish immigrant population.

It was the British dock strike more than any other factor which brought Manning into focus as a social reformer, a character which Protestants had never associated with the Church, which they were inclined to dismiss as reactionary. Indeed, at this time Manning's views seemed odd even to his co-religionists, who, to his regret, continued to display little interest in social questions. Manning recognized the ideals of the working classes, and perhaps because the religious tradition of Catholicism into which he had entered still seemed eccentric to English life, he had a ready sympathy for trade union activists. During the dock strike he was able to address the directors with some authority because his brother had been a former chairman of the docks. He warned the dock owners that revolution was imminent, although he apparently also confided to the strikers that he had never 'preached to so impenitent a congregation'. Trade union leader Thomas Mann said of him:

> I shall ever remember him as the finest example of genuine devotion to the down-trodden. He was never too busy to be consulted, or too occupied with church affairs to admit of his giving detailed attention to any group of men, whom kindly influence could help, and he was equally keen to understand any plans of ours to improve the lot of these men.[34]

Holland says of this Irish working class that, coming from a church historically unified as an impoverished peasantry oppressed by a foreign and Protestant conqueror, and so used to resisting economic oppression from English imperialism, the Irish immigrants carried a model of evangelization that never lost its working-class character. Holland was of the opinion that the Vatican ultramontanists strongly supported this Irish model for English- speaking countries.[35] It is perhaps because of this that the Irish Catholic working class played a significant role in the development of the labour movements in Britain but, perhaps more particularly, in the United States and Australia.

In the United States Cardinal James Gibbons and Archbishop Ireland had, along with Cardinal Manning in Britain and Count Albert de Mun in France, been outspoken critics of laissez-faire capitalism. Cardinal Gibbons was the leader of a largely Irish immigrant working class community. He vigorously defended the early union movement in the United States known as the Knights of Labour against papal condemnation as a secret society, and he subsequently presented his arguments in a famous 1887 'Memorial' presented to Rome, in which he cited Manning's words on the necessity for the Church to deal with the masses and with the people, quoted earlier, and then added his own: 'To lose the heart of the people would be a misfortune for which the friendship of the few rich and powerful would be no compensation'.

Gibbons was candid. He spoke directly and sincerely to Rome on the plight of the great mass of people which he described as: 'The struggle of the great masses of the people against the iron-clad mail power which ... often refuses them the simple rights of humanity and justice'. He also spoke of: 'Being alarmed at the prospect of the Church being presented before our age as the friend of the powerful rich and the enemy of the helpless poor'. He warned that: 'Such an alliance or even apparent alliance, (would) have done the Church untold harm'.[36]

Conclusion

The nineteenth century had been a century of revolution. It was also the century which witnessed the consolidation of western society into two classes: the capitalist class and the proletariat. Since the publication of the Communist Manifesto in 1848, Catholics had in the main shown themselves more concerned with resisting the spread of Marx's doctrine than with changing the social conditions which provided a fertile field for the acceptance of Marx's ideology by the proletarian class. It is perhaps surprising that church leaders took so long to formulate a Catholic response to the Communist Manifesto. And it is perhaps also surprising that the momentum towards a church response was driven equally by the laity and the clergy.

The Church's response, when it did come in the form of *Rerum Novarum*, was both comprehensive and revolutionary and would be the cornerstone of all future social teaching on the worker question. Marx, though a false prophet, had successfully read the signs of the times and is to be credited with having stirred the consciences of Christians, though unintentionally, by inspiring fear of the class war he preached.

Notes
1 Belloc, *The Servile State*, p. xii.
2 Holland, p. 141.
3 Belloc, *The Crisis of our Civilization*, p. 140.
4 Tropman, pp. 49, 50.
5 Ibid. p. 53.
6 O'Brien, p. 77.
7 Ibid. p. 79.
8 Ibid. p. 101.
9 Ibid.
10 Ibid. p. 65.
11 Howell, pp. 182, 183.
12 Belloc, *The Crisis of our Civilization*, pp. 117, 118.
13 Cahill, E., p. 99.
14 Cobbett, p. 115.
15 Belloc, *The Servile State*, p. 69.
16 Ibid. pp. 66, 67, 68.
17 Ibid. p. 72.
18 Ibid. pp. 75, 76.
19 McCarthy and Rhodes, p. 185.
20 Charles, p. 71.
21 Gide and Rist, p. 526.
22 Murphy, p. 8.
23 Cahill, pp. 255, 256.
24 Ibid. p. 255
25 Krier Mich, p. 7.
26 Metlake, pp. 162, 163.
27 Holland, pp. 132, 133.
28 Cronin, and Flannery, pp. 106, 107.
29 Holland, p. 137.
30 Cahill, E., p. 259.
31 Krier Mich, p. 9.
32 Ibid. pp. 9, 10, 11.
33 Townsend, p. 76.
34 Mayor, p. 111.
35 Holland, p. 140.
36 Ibid. p. 141.

Chapter 6

RERUM NOVARUM
The Magna Carta of the social order

The decade before 1891

The years prior to *Rerum Novarum* had seen the formulation and tendering to Rome of a number of submissions pertaining to the social question and the relationship between labour and capital. The deliberations of the German Catholic Congresses and of Archbishop Ketteler who, according to William Murphy, Leo XIII spoke of as 'my great predecessor, the man from whom I learned' [1] in particular had been noted in Rome, as had the conclusions of the Fribourg Union delivered to Pope Leo XIII by Bishop Mermillod. There was also the famous 'Memorial' on the social question presented to Rome by Cardinal Gibbons of Baltimore and the writings of Cardinal Manning, whose support of the British dockers during the British dockers strike and the significant role played by him in the settlement of the dispute had not gone unnoticed in Rome.

Significantly, in 1888 Cardinals Manning and Gibbons had intervened jointly with the Vatican to prevent the placing on the Index of Henry George's work *Progress and Poverty*. Henry George had stood as a candidate for the mayoralty of New York City, and in the course of his campaign had urged the imposition of a capital gains tax on increases in the value of property as a means of addressing the social problems of the United States – a suggestion which roused the ire of the capitalist classes both in the United States and Europe. In 1887 Cardinal Gibbons travelled to Rome to make submissions to Leo XIII on behalf of the Knights of Labour, the first American trade union. Whilst making submissions to Leo XIII on behalf of Henry George and the Knights of Labour, Gibbons urged the Pope to issue an encyclical on the rights and duties of both labour and capital. Up until this point the prevalent view in the west was to the effect that it was improper for the Pope and bishops to intervene in the marketplace. These men and others were able to persuade Leo XIII to accept a different point of view.

Although Catholic social thought did not commence with the proclamation of *Rerum Novarum*, prior encyclicals contained no direct reference to the rights and obligations of labour and capital. In *Quanto Conficiamur Moerore,* promulgated on 18 August 1863, Pius IX condemned what he saw as the errors of avarice and the insatiable passion for power and possessions that overrides all rules of justice and honesty and that seeks profit with clearly no regard for one's neighbour, and the wrongful placing of happiness in the procuring of riches and money.[2]

In the encyclical *Quanta Cura,* promulgated on 8 December 1864, Pius IX says that human society, when set loose from the bonds of religion and true justice, can have no other end than the purpose of obtaining and amassing wealth.[3] In *Qui Pluribus* Pius IX expressed the view that self-interest and avarice were at the core of what he termed 'the unspeakable doctrine of communism'.[4] In *Nostis et Nobiscum,* promulgated on 8 December 1849 and in *Quod Apostolici Muneris,* promulgated on 28 December 1878, Pius IX accused the ideologies of socialism and communism of deluding the 'lower class' with the promise of happier conditions in the future.[5] Michael Schuck considers that the pre-Leonine popes considered socialism and communism as a derivation of the social contract theory of political liberalism. He also believed that Pius IX linked the social contract theory of political authority with the rise of economic avarice.[6] Pope Clement XIV, in the encyclical *Cum Summi,* promulgated on 12 December 1769, says that human rights include the individual citizen's right to educate and care for children, possess property and receive necessary material goods from the superfluity of society.[7] Whilst the expectation is that justice will prevail, there is no direct 'coming to grips' with the imbalance of relationship between labour and capital. *Rerum Novarum* was to be the first such reference.

An encyclical on the social order had become a necessity. Cuthbert was of the view that the socialists, in insisting upon the solidarity of society, had become to an increasing number of men the exponents of a deep moral truth. It was a truth to which Catholicism had borne evidence throughout the long ages of its history; but the socialists, by preaching the doctrine of solidarity with a loud voice and perpetual insistence, had made themselves in popular estimation its proper exponents.[8] It was also difficult at that time to remove from the mind of Catholics the notion that the Church was on its defence against universal anarchy and revolt. This notion had become so ingrained that the ordinary Catholic was apt to see a conscious attack on Catholic teaching and sentiment in every new development of secular life.

Leo XIII

Vincenzo Gioacchino Pecci was born on 2 March 1810 in Carpineto, south of Rome. He was ordained to the priesthood in December 1837 on the completion of his studies at the Gregorian University. He served in the Vatican diplomatic corps as the governor of Benevento and Perugia. He was later sent as the papal nuncio to Belgium in 1843. On the death of Pius IX he was elected pope on 20 February 1878, a few days before his sixty-eighth birthday. In the same year as his election to the pontificate he published his first encyclical, *Quod Apostolici Muneris,* which was in the main an attack upon the socialist movement. However, in a similar vein to Pius IX, he expressed certain concerns about the social question, but in the general terms of justice, charity and the duty of the rich to provide for the needs of the poor but made no specific reference to the rights and obligations of labour and capital.

Early in his pontificate, Leo XIII demonstrated a concern for the social question by encouraging the formation of the Roman Committee of Social Studies, and placed at its head Cardinal Jacobini, the Vatican prefect of propaganda. The committee included prominent civilian leaders as well as Bishop Mermillod, the president of the Fribourg Union founded a few years later. Towards the end of 1889, Leo XIII requested the Jesuit priest Matteo Liberatore, who had written a series of articles on the morals of political economy, to write the first draft of an encyclical on the social question of the working class. Liberatore was assisted by Cardinal Tommaso Zigliara. The final draft was completed early in 1891, with a final critical review being carried out by Cardinal Mazzella.

On the condition of the working classes

Leo XIII's encyclical on the condition of the working classes was entitled *Rerum Novarum* and was published on 15 May 1891 in the fourteenth year of his pontificate. From the viewpoint of the worker the encyclical was a milestone and has earned Leo XIII the title of 'The Workers' Pope'. The encyclical goes straight to the point in issue. In paragraph 6 the Pope says:

> The present age handed over the workers, each alone and defenceless, to the inhumanity of employers and the unbridled greed of competitors. A devouring usury, although often condemned by the Church, but practised nevertheless under another form by avaricious and grasping men, has increased the evil; and in addition the whole process of production as well as trade in every kind of goods has been brought almost entirely under the power of a few, so that a very few rich and exceedingly rich men have laid a yoke almost of slavery on the unnumbered masses of non-owning workers.[9]

As well as dealing extensively with the relationship between labour and capital, the encyclical also deals with private property and the importance of the family. The encyclical's teaching on the family leads directly into the expounding of the idea of a just and living wage for the worker. The encyclical also deals with the role of the state in ensuring the protection of the working classes. It is in the context of these matters that this encyclical will be discussed.

Labour and capital

In paragraph 27 of *Rerum Novarum* Leo XIII says that work is one of those conditions of the human existence which will accompany men to the end of their lives. He refers to Gen. 3:17: 'Cursed is the ground because of you; in toil you shall eat of it all the days of your life'.[10] He then goes on to say that those who claim they can banish the tribulation of work from human life perpetuate a fraud. The best course is to view human affairs as they are and seek the appropriate redress.

In paragraph 28 he says that it is abhorrent to accept the view that one class of society is of itself hostile to the other. Using the analysis of the human body, he says that just as the various parts of the body harmonize with one another, so it should be that its two classes (labour and capital) should agree harmoniously and should properly form balanced counterparts to each other:

> Each needs the other completely; neither capital can do without labour, nor labour without capital. Concord begets beauty and order in things, conversely, from perpetual strife there must arise disorder accompanied by bestial cruelty. But for putting an end to conflict and for cutting away its very roots, there is wondrous and multiple power in Christian institutions.[11]

Paragraphs 30 to 32 detail the duties and obligations existing between capital and labour. Paragraph 30 calls upon the workers to perform entirely and conscientiously whatever work has been voluntarily and equitably agreed upon. The key word here is 'equitably'. This paragraph also contained exhortations to refrain from violence, rioting, and the injuring of the property of the employer.

Paragraph 31 on the other hand stated that workers were not to be treated as slaves and that the dignity of the human personality was to be respected in them as it had been ennobled through the Christian character. Gainful occupation is not to be viewed as a mark of shame, but of respect. In unequivocal language, the encyclical says that it is shameful and inhuman to use men as things for gain and to put no more value on them than what they are worth in muscle and energy.[12]

Leo XIII said that the Church, with Jesus Christ as teacher and leader, sought the joining of the two social classes to each other 'in closest neighbourliness and friendship'.[13]

Leo XIII emphasizes the empathy which Jesus had for the worker and the poor. In paragraph 37 of *Rerum Novarum* he says that no one should be ashamed because they made their living by toil. This was confirmed by the fact that Jesus who, being rich, for the salvation of men, became poor, and willed Himself to be thought the son of a carpenter, not disdaining to spend the greater part of His life at the work of a carpenter. 'Is not this the carpenter, the son of Mary?'[14]

Leo XIII goes on to say that the favour of God Himself seems to incline more toward the unfortunate as a class, for He calls the poor blessed[15] and invites most lovingly all those who are in labour and sorrow[16] to come to Him for solace.[17]

In paragraph 38 Leo XIII, in language reminiscent of the patristic idea of stewardship, argues for the reconciliation of the differences between the capitalist and working classes by saying that all have equally been redeemed by the grace of Jesus Christ and restored to the dignity of the sons of God, with the result that they are clearly united by the bonds of brotherhood not only with one another but with Christ the Lord. The goods of nature and the gifts of divine grace belong in common and without distinction to all humanity and that no one, unless they be unworthy, will be deprived of the inheritance of Heaven. Referring to Romans 8:29 he says that we are all heirs of God and joint heirs with Christ [*sic*].[18]

Solidarity

It is stated in Ecclesiastes: 'Two are better than one, because they have a good reward for their toil. For if they fall, one will lift up his fellow; but woe to him who is alone when he falls and has not another to lift him up.'[19] In *Rerum Novarum* Leo XIII says that experience shows that the inadequacy of one's own strength impels and urges mankind to enlist the help of others. Again, referring to Prov. 18:19: 'A brother helped is like a strong city'.

Just as a man is drawn by his natural propensity into civil union and association, so he also seeks for his fellow citizens to form other societies, admittedly small and not perfect but societies nonetheless.[20] This idea of 'solidarity' as expressed by Leo XIII provides a justification and support for the establishment and existence of trade unions and the general right of workers to combine for their common good.

John Paul II provided an excellent definition of solidarity which he described as 'virtue'. Solidarity was not a feeling of vague compassion or shallow distress at the misfortunes of so many people, both near and far; on the contrary, it was a firm and persevering determination to commit oneself to the common good – that is to say, to the good of all and of each individual, because we are all really responsible for all.[21]

Trade unions

The Pope gave support to the establishment of trade unions, albeit a qualified one. Some confusion arose as to whether Catholics could join secular unions. It should be borne in mind that the encyclical was addressed to a Catholic audience. In actual practice, Catholics participated extensively in secular unions from their inception, and later encyclicals, particularly *Quadragesimo Anno,* clarified the position.[22]

He argued that humanity was permitted by a right of nature to form private societies. The state had been instituted to protect, not to destroy natural right, and if it should forbid its citizens to enter into those associations it would clearly be doing something contradictory to itself because both the state and private associations were begotten of one and the same principle, namely that men are by nature inclined to associate. Whilst stating that there may be circumstances in which the state could oppose the establishment of certain associations whose objectives were clearly at variance with good morals, justice, or the welfare of the state, Leo XIII cautioned against any move by the state against private societies that sound reason would not support. Quoting from Thomas Aquinas he said that laws were to be obeyed only insofar as they conformed with right reason and thus with the eternal law of God.[23]

Leo XIII said that the state should protect these lawful associations and should not interfere with their private concerns and order of life, as vital activity was set in motion by an inner principle which was very easily destroyed by intrusion from without. He goes on to say that if citizens have the free right to associate, as in fact they did, they also must have the right freely to adopt the organization and the rules which they judged most appropriate to achieve their purposes. Workers' associations ought to be so constituted and so governed as to furnish the most suitable and most convenient means to attain the object proposed, namely that the individual members of the association secure, so far as possible, an increase in the goods of body and of soul and of prosperity.[24]

At a period in history in which the right of association of workers was severely curtailed by the state in the greater part of Europe and in the United States, these words of Leo XIII were a significant and radical development.

The confusion and controversy which arose over the issue of Catholics joining secular trade unions arose largely from Leo XIII's concern that many of the existing trade unions were under the control of secret leaders who applied principles which were not in harmony with either Christianity or the welfare of the state. He feared that the participation of Catholics in such associations may be detrimental to their faith, and for this reason he advocated the formation of Christian trade unions. Having said this, however, it must be emphasized that *Rerum Novarum* contained no direct prohibition on Catholic participation in secular trade unions, and indeed such participation was the norm. Leo XIII believed that the principal goal of trade unions should be the moral and religious perfection of its members. There was a danger that if this were not so they would degenerate in nature and would be little better than those associations in which no account was ordinarily taken of religion. He believed that when the regulations upon which the workers' associations were founded were based upon religion, the way was easy towards establishing the mutual relations of the members so that peaceful living together and prosperity would result.[25]

A living wage

Rerum Novarum challenges the notion that free consent fixes the amount of a wage. It was a tenet of liberal capitalism that a worker was entitled to whatever sum he had agreed to accept as a wage. The fact that his bargaining position vis-à-vis the employer was greatly inferior was of little consequence. The employer, after paying the agreed wage, was deemed to have discharged his obligations. It was only proper for the state to intervene to protect the rights of an aggrieved party in the event of a breach by the other party. Leo XIII argued that work was both personal and necessary. It was personal because the energy utilized in work inheres in the person and belongs completely to him or her by whom it is expended, and for those whose use it is destined by nature. It is necessary because humanity has need of the fruit of its labours to preserve life; and nature itself, which must be most strictly obeyed, commands humanity to preserve it. Hence, by combining the personal and necessary aspects of work, Leo argued that the preservation of one's life was a duty common to all individuals and that to neglect this duty was a crime. There arose therefore the right of securing things to sustain life, and only a wage earned by one's labour gives a poor person the means to acquire these things.[26]

Leo argued that whilst it may be accepted that worker and employer may enter freely into agreements concerning the amount of the wage, an element of natural justice should always underlie such agreements. He added that a more ancient and greater principle than the free consent of contracting parties was that the wage should not be less than enough to support a worker who is thrifty and upright. He condemns a situation which arises where a worker is compelled by necessity or moved by fear of a worse evil to accept a harder condition which he must accept against his will because the employer or contractor imposes it. In such a circumstance the worker is submitting to force against which justice cries out in protest. To establish real pay in accord with justice, many factors had to be taken into account, but in general the rich and employers should remember no laws, either human or divine, permitted them to oppress the needy and the wretched for their own profit or to seek gain from another's want. As to what constitutes a just wage, Leo XIII said:

> If a worker receives a wage sufficiently large to enable him to provide comfortably for himself, his wife, and his children, he will, if

prudent, gladly strive to practise thrift; and the result will be, as nature itself seems to counsel, that after expenditures are deducted there will remain something over and above through which he can come into the possession of a little wealth.[27]

This criterion for a worker's wage has come to be referred to with the passage of time as a 'just wage' or 'living wage' and would be further developed by later encyclicals.

Writing on the determination of a just wage some thirty years after *Rerum Novarum*, Joseph Husslein, SJ said that the Church will not admit that wages are just, simply because they were determined by a 'free' contract between the employer and employed. On this principle the stronger in wealth or the more cunning in wit could always take advantage of his weaker and more innocent brother. Such was the theory of liberalism and modern commercialism, but not the doctrine of the Church of Christ.[28]

Working conditions

Leo XIII had no illusions as to the scope of the exploitation and misery of the working classes whom he described as the oppressed workers who ought above all to be liberated from the savagery of greedy men who inordinately used human beings as things for gain.[29] Leo refers to scripture: 'Remember thou keep holy the Sabbath day'[30] and 'He rested on the seventh day from all his work which he had done'[31] and says that neither justice nor humanity can countenance the exaction of so much work that the spirit is dull from excessive toil. The working energy of a man is circumscribed by definite limits beyond which it cannot go. It is developed by exercise and use, but only on condition that a man seeks rest from work at regular intervals. He says that with respect to daily work, care ought to be taken not to extend it beyond the hours that human strength warrants. The lengths of rest intervals ought to be decided on the basis of the varying nature of the work, of the circumstances of time and place, and of the physical condition of the workers themselves.[32]

To summarize, Leo said of working conditions that it should be the rule everywhere that workers be given as much leisure as will compensate for the energy consumed by toil, as rest from work was necessary to restore strength consumed by use. In clear and precise language he said:

> In every obligation which is mutually contracted between employers and workers, this condition, either written or tacit, is always

present, that both kinds of rest be provided for; nor would it be equitable to make an agreement otherwise, because no one has the right to demand of, or to make an agreement with anyone to neglect those duties which bind a man to God or to himself.[33]

In an age in which liberal capitalism had no difficulty with working young children and women for excessively long hours in abominable working conditions, especially in coal mines, Leo XIII takes issue with these practices. Speaking of the exploitation of children, he said that special care ought to be taken that the factory does not get hold of them before age has sufficiently matured their physical, intellectual and moral powers. The budding strength of childhood, like greening verdure in spring, is crushed by premature harsh treatment, and in such circumstances the educational needs of the child are forgone. It was not right to demand of a woman or a child what a strong adult man was capable of doing or would be willing to do.[34]

Private property and the worker

Leo XIII regarded property as a right natural to humanity. He said that the exercise of this right, especially in the life of society, was not only lawful but clearly necessary. He refers to Aquinas, who said, 'It is lawful for man to own his own things. It is even necessary for human life'. [35]

As mentioned earlier, the Pope implied that a worker's wage be sufficiently large to enable him to provide comfortably for himself, his wife and his children and 'come into the possession of a little wealth'.[36] Leo saw that the inequitable division of property between 'two classes of citizens with an immense gulf lying between them'[37] was inimical to society in that the rich and powerful class diverted to its own advantage and interest all productive sources of wealth and exerted no little power in the administration of the state. On the other hand, he saw the needy and helpless masses, who possessed little, as a ready source of disorder.[38] This situation could be rectified if the working classes were enabled to possess sufficient wealth to acquire property. In this we see the seeds of the idea of 'distributism', an economic idea which encourages the distribution of property to as many as possible rather than its concentration in the hands of a few.

The worker and the state

In stating what he believed the role of the state should be vis-à-vis the worker, Leo XIII draws upon the principles of distributive justice. Distributive justice may be defined as 'the law of nature by which the state is bound to secure for each of the citizens his or her due and proportionate share of the advantages and helps which are the end and purpose of civil society; and to allot the public burdens in due and equitable proportion'. The duties of distributive justice are those of the state towards its members.[39]

Leo XIII said that as those governing the state ought primarily to devote themselves to the service of various groups within the state and the whole of the commonwealth; and as it has in fact done so with respect to industry and trade, agriculture and other such matters, so it should also be conscious of the welfare of the workers. He said, 'Therefore, . . . it is within the competence of the rulers of the State that, as they benefit other groups, they also improve in particular the condition of the workers'.[40]

In drawing upon principles of distributive justice, the Pope quotes Aquinas, who said, 'Even as part and whole are in a certain way the same, so too that which pertains to the whole pertains in a certain way to the part also'.[41] Consequently, Leo said that among the numerous and weighty duties of rulers who would serve their people well, it is first and foremost that they protect equitably each and every class of citizens, maintaining inviolate that justice especially which is called distributive.[42]

Leo XIII said it would be quite absurd for the state to look out for the interests of one portion of its citizens and to neglect another. Public authority ought to exercize due care in safeguarding the well-being and interests of non-owning workers. Unless this were done, justice which commanded that everyone be given his or her own would be violated. In words radical for their time, he said that if the energy and effectiveness of workers was so important, it was incontestable 'that the wealth of nations originates from no other source than from the labour of workers, equity therefore commands that public authority show proper concern for the worker so that from what he contributes to the common good, he may receive what will enable him, housed, clothed and secure, to live his life without hardship. Whence, it follows that all those measures ought to be favoured which seem in any way capable of benefiting the condition of the workers'.[43]

Leo XIII said that because workers were numbered among the great masses of the needy, the state should accord them special care and foresight. If any injury had been done or threatened the common good or the interests of individual groups, if that injury could not be repaired or prevented in any other way, it was necessary for public authority to intervene. If the employer class should oppress the working class with unjust burdens or should degrade them with conditions inimical to human personality or human dignity, or if health should be injured by immoderate work practices, the power and authority of the law manifestly ought to be employed. State intervention, however, was qualified to the extent that such intervention should only be such as was required to rectify the situation.[44]

In paragraph 56 Leo XIII makes reference to the intervention of the state in the matter of workers' wages. He says that onerous working conditions and the belief that pay is inadequate frequently give workers cause to strike. Because such interruption of work inflicts damage upon employers and the workers themselves, and injures trade and commerce and the general interests of the state, the conditions which give rise to strikes ought to be remedied by public authority. The authority of the law should anticipate and prevent the evil from breaking out by removing early the causes from which conflict between employers and workers in respect of wages was bound to arise. It would seem from this, although it is not precisely clear, that Leo XIII is possibly anticipating the creation of some form of state tribunal possessing the authority to determine wages and salaries. Such tribunals now exist widely throughout the world.

Biblical references
In *Rerum Novarum*, Leo XIII makes frequent references to Scripture. These references – some thirty of them – are used to support the positions which he takes in various issues of the encyclical. He draws upon Aquinas on nine separate occasions and upon Gregory the Great on one occasion.

The legacy
Rerum Novarum is the cornerstone of Catholic social teaching, particularly teaching in respect of the rights of the worker. It is significant that the encyclicals of subsequent pontiffs dealing with the social question are generally promulgated on the anniversary of *Rerum Novarum*. It has also become the reference point of the various national bishops' conferences of the

world and their pronouncements on social matters. Virtually all subsequent encyclicals and announcements dealing with the social question have been elaborations upon, or refinements of, this first great social encyclical.

Leo XIII plotted a course between the Scylla and Charybdis of extreme capitalism and extreme socialism. He condemned the laissez-faire doctrine that economic life should be subject only to the rule of supply and demand by insisting that, like every other area of life, economics should be regulated by considerations of social justice and Christian charity. He rejected as false the Marxist contention that private ownership of the means of production and profit inevitably resulted in the exploitation of labour by capital and the misery of the proletariat. Contrary to this belief he held that the cause of the pitiful condition of the working classes was not the profit motive itself but its exemption from proper control. Its unregulated operation resulted in the concentration of economic power in the hands of a few magnates who were able to use it for their own self-interests.

Henry Townsend was of the opinion that Leo XIII recalled Catholic thought from a cul-de-sac to the main road. In doing so he gave it a direction and impulse which initiated a fruitful development. He believed that Catholics were encouraged to abandon their attachment to the past with what he termed its romantic idealization of the Middle Ages, and to devote their zeal to a social reconstruction based on a conception of justice, traditional in principle but contemporary in application. He said that concern for the poor was translated into concern for the industrial proletariat; exhortation to charity into an appeal for economic justice; and negative protest into a demand for legislation designed to protect the masses of workers from exploitation, and give them economic security and opportunity as their due by natural right.[45]

David Hollenbach said that Leo XIII had a vision of the mutuality of the relationships between persons or groups which shape and influence the life and action of that person or group. Human dignity, namely the fact that human beings are not things or mere means, always exists within these various concrete relationships. The justice or injustice of these relationships is to be judged in terms of the way they promote human dignity by enhancing mutuality and genuine participation in the community, or, put negatively, by the way they abuse human dignity by reifying persons and excluding or marginalizing them from the relationships without which humanity withers. This vision of mutuality and participation was, according to Haughey, the basis of Leo XIII's moral protest against an industrial economy in which a small number of very rich men were able to lay upon the working masses of the poor a yoke little better than slavery.[46]

Neuhaus believes that what the Church has to say about social, political and economic questions is authoritative to the degree that it is implicated in the revealed story of salvation. He says that Catholic social doctrine is directed against both utopianism and deep despair. The Church's distinctive contribution is not to remove all uncertainties, but to sustain people in a world where, short of the kingdom come, uncertainty is a certainty. Their Christian faith enables them to act in the carriage of their uncertainties.[47]

This writer shares the view of Holland that on the political side *Rerum Novarum* confirmed the principle of the interventionist or regulatory state as rooted in the classical Catholic-Aristotelian understanding of politics in service of the common good, although it advocated a limitation of the state's role. On the economic side it affirmed the correlative rights and duties of both capital and labour, which is rooted in the classical Catholic understanding of an organic-hierarchical society.[48] It could be said of the encyclical that it marked the first major confrontation of the Church with the prevailing liberal capitalist ideology existing in Europe and North America and pinpointed liberal capitalism as the cause of the pitiful status of the working classes.

There were those Catholics who held to the view that the Church should not concern itself with matters other than the spiritual. They believed that the Church and civil society should remain distinct. It is in this writer's view unreal and dangerous to accept such a separation as a concept of any real value. It is dangerous for the faith, for it can be the faith of the poor only if civilization makes it easily accessible to them and does not make it a privilege for a chosen group of spiritually minded people. It is dangerous for the civil society, for it leaves that society to shape itself in an incomplete and inhuman manner.[49]

Although *Rerum Novarum* condemned the ideology of socialism, it contained much to endear itself to the working classes and their leaders. One such was the British labour leader and Congregationalist Ben Tillett, who wrote to Cardinal Manning following the publication of *Rerum Novarum* saying:

> I have just been reading the Pope's letter – a very courageous one indeed, one that will test good Catholics much more effectively than

any exhortation to public worship. As you know, some of us would disagree very strongly with many of the strictures laid upon socialists. These are minor matters. The Catholic sympathy abounds in a generous strength. I hardly think our Protestant prelates would dare utter such wholesome doctrine.[50]

Certainly since the publication of *Rerum Novarum* the consideration of the moral dimension in political economy has been insisted upon by the various popes and other church leaders. As McCarthy and Rhodes point out, there is a necessary and appropriate role for theological reflection that does not presume the Pope's competency over the technical economic or political ingredients. But they reject as irrational the disguised neoplatonic idea that religion and piety are other worldly, purely individual, and exclusively interior states. What the popes and other church leaders insist upon is a person-centred definition of any system: social, economic or political. The human has priority. Thus the religious teachings concerning the nature and destiny of human life and human relations are an essential, not tangential, element in every aspect of society.[51]

In 1992 the Universities of Oxford, Boston and Melbourne sponsored an international conference at Boston University entitled The Worth of Nations. The conference was held to mark the centenary of *Rerum Novarum*. One of the speakers at the conference was the then Archbishop of Melbourne, Archbishop George Pell, presently Cardinal Archbishop of Sydney. In the course of his address, the Archbishop said that Leo XIII's sanctioning of trade unions was a decisive factor in their becoming an integral part of western society. He added that the success of trade unions was, in turn, an important reason behind the failure of Marxist predictions about the increasing misery of the working class in capitalist society. The communist collapse has been a massive blow to the Enlightenment myth that progress is inevitable, that traditions can be ignored, or should be denied, and that human reason is all powerful. If the collapse of communism is the denouement of the French Revolution, the beginning of that end may well have been marked by the promulgation of *Rerum Novarum* in 1891.[52]

Included in the closing speeches and messages delivered at the Second Vatican Council was a message from the council to workers. The message was read by Cardinals Zoungoana, Quintero and Monreale. It said in part:

> The church is your friend, have confidence in her. In the past, regretful misunderstandings have, over too long a period, maintained a

spirit of mistrust and lack of understanding between us, and both the church and the working class have suffered from this.

This statement was a significant admission of the situation which had existed prior to *Rerum Novarum*. *Rerum Novarum* was the first, and a most significant, step in effecting the reconciliation of the Church and working class.[53] In *Centesimus Annus,* promulgated on the hundredth anniversary of *Rerum Novarum*, John Paul II said prior to *Rerum Novarum* a twofold approach prevailed in the Church. One was directed to this world and this life to which faith ought to remain extraneous; the other was directed towards a purely other-worldly salvation, which neither enlightened nor directed existence on earth. He said that Leo XIII's approach in publishing *Rerum Novarum* gave the Church 'citizenship status' as it were, amid the changing realities of public life, and this standing would be more fully confirmed later on. Leo XIII created a lasting paradigm for the Church. The Church, in fact, had something to say about specific human situations, both individual and communal, national and international. She formulates a genuine doctrine for these situations, a corpus which enables her to analyse social realities, to make judgements about them and to indicate directions to be taken for the just resolution of the problems involved.[54]

The import of *Rerum Novarum* and its significance in the fabric of Catholic social thought is stated by Pius XI in *Quadragesimo Anno* when he said that *Rerum Novarum* had become in truth a memorable document to which may well be applied the words of the prophet Isaiah: 'A standard set up unto the nations!'[55]

Notes
1 Weigel and Royal, p. 9.
2 *Quanto Conficiamur Moerore.*
3 *Quanta Cura.*
4 *Qui Pluribus.*
5 *Nostis et Nobiscum; Quod Apostolici Muneris.*
6 Schuck, pp. 18, 19.
7 *Cum Summi.*
8 Father Cuthbert, OSFC, *Catholic Ideals in social life*, R. & T. Washbourne Ltd, London, 1911, p. 78.
9 *Encyclical letter of His Holiness Pope Leo XIII on the condition of the working classes, Rerum Novarum.*
10 RSV Catholic Edition, Ignatius Press, San Francisco, 1952.

11 *Rerum Novarum*, para. 28.
12 Ibid., paras 30, 31.
13 Ibid., para. 33.
14 (RSV) Mark 6:3.
15 (RSV) Matthew 5:3.
16 Ibid., 11:28.
17 *Rerum Novarum*, para. 37.
18 Ibid., para. 38.
19 (RSV) Ecclesiastes 5:9,10.
20 *Rerum Novarum*, para. 70.
21 *Solicitudo Rei Socialis*, para. 38.
22 *Quadragesimo Anno*.
23 *Rerum Novarum*, para.72.
24 Ibid., para. 76.
25 Ibid., paras 74, 77, 78.
26 Ibid., paras 61, 62.
27 Ibid., para. 65.
28 Joseph Husslein, SJ, *The World Problem: Capital, labor and the Church*, P. J. Kennedy & Sons, New York, 1919, p. 47.
29 *Rerum Novarum*, para. 59.
30 Exodus 20:8.
31 Genesis 2:2.
32 *Rerum Novarum*, paras 58, 59.
33 Ibid., para. 60.
34 Ibid., paras 59, 60.
35 *Rerum Novarum*, para. 36.
36 *Rerum Novarum*, para. 65.
37 Ibid.
38 Ibid.
39 Cahill, E., SJ, p. 514.
40 *Rerum Novarum*, para. 48.
41 *Rerum Novarum*, para. 49.
42 Ibid.
43 Ibid., para. 51.
44 *Rerum Novarum*, paras 52, 53, 54.
45 Townsend, p. 77.
46 Hollenbach, p. 213.
47 Neuhaus, p. 119.
48 Holland, p. 144.
49 Danielou, pp. 21–2.
50 Mayor, p. 253.
51 McCarthy and Rhodes, p. 182.
52 Livingstone, pp. 208, 209, 210.
53 *Vatican Council II, Closing Speeches and Messages*, 22630.
54 *Centesimus Annus*, para 5.
55 *Quadragesimo Anno*, p. 12.

Chapter 7

THE CHESTERBELLOC ERA

Background

In the years following *Rerum Novarum* and until the promulgation of Pius XI's encyclical entitled *On Social Reconstruction, Quadragesimo Anno,* on 15 May 1931, few people had greater influence upon Catholic thinking in respect of the social order than did Hilaire Belloc and Gilbert Keith Chesterton. Their numerous writings and dissertations on the social order, which tend to reach the same conclusions although expressed in different styles, have led to their works being frequently fused together under the title of 'The Chesterbelloc'. Belloc's style was one of logical analysis, with one argument leading in turn to another. On the other hand, Chesterton was a frequent user of allegory to paint a picture of what society and people were really like.

Belloc and Chesterton wrote at a time when, in spite of *Rerum Novarum*, many in Europe still associated Catholic political views with opposition to freedom, equality and revolution and as somewhat reactionary. The writings of Belloc and Chesterton bear no resemblance to that kind of conservative Catholicism. They were rather in empathy with the Thomist traditions of natural law, popular sovereignty, the stewardship of riches, concern for the poor and right to oppose bad governments – ideas which underwent a revival in the latter part of the nineteenth century and which were reflected to a large degree in *Rerum Novarum*. Their views, particularly in relation to distributism, and division of society into the capitalist and proletarian classes, are as much a source of scholarship and interest in the early years of the twenty-first century as they were when written. Like the great social encyclicals, the writings of Belloc and Chesterton on the social question possess an aura of timelessness. Although not possessing the authority of papal pronouncements, their works have had a significant and lasting impact upon the *corpus* of Catholic social thought.

Capitalism

Chesterton's writing on the subject of capitalism evidences a distinct dislike for industrial capitalist society, which he described in typical Chestertonian manner as an 'animated muck-heap'.[1]

Chesterton defined capitalism in terms of people rather than philosophy. He defined it as an economic condition in which there was a class of capitalist, roughly recognizable and relatively small, in whose possession so much of the capital is concentrated as to necessitate a very large majority of the citizens serving those capitalists for a wage. Chesterton leaned heavily on the arguments of Ruskin, stressing the deleterious effects which capitalism had on the good of the individual and society. He found his epoch ugly, and considered the division of labour a major source of the evils of the time. This led to what he termed 'specialism' and the specialization of the individual. This resulted in the individual being unable to aspire to a wide range of interests and to 'universality' of spirit because of preoccupation with perfecting himself in a trade that would uphold him in a more or less ruthless society.[2]

In one of his later works, *The Well and the Shallows* (1935), Chesterton took issue with the notion that capitalism was some form of eternal truth handed to Moses on Mount Sinai. He thought of it rather as the dispossession of the populace of all forms of real productive property; all instruments of production in the hands of the few; all the millions merely the servants of the rich few, working for a wage, always an insecure wage, generally a mean and inhuman wage.

Chesterton argued that under capitalism and the reign of employers, a pool of unemployed was deemed desirable, as the system seemed most effective when operating in this manner. He believed that unemployment acted as a pivot for the whole capitalist process.[3] Little has changed since Chesterton's time. There are those in industry today who, imbued with the tenets of neoliberal capitalism, argue that the existence of a sizeable pool of unemployed is necessary for the efficient functioning of the modern labour market. This idea is usually couched in terms of labour market flexibility.

The type of industrial capitalism so deplored by Chesterton could not, and did not, arise in places where there had hitherto been a distributive civilization like that of a peasantry. Capitalism was a monster that grew in deserts. Industrial servitude had, he said, almost everywhere arisen in those empty spaces where the older civilization was thin or absent. Thus, it grew up easily in the north of England rather than the south precisely because the north had been comparatively empty and barbarous through all the ages when the south had a civilization of guilds and peasantries. He said it grew up easily in the American continent rather than the European continent precisely because it had nothing to supplant in America but a few savages, while in Europe it had to supplant the culture of multitudinous times.[4] Chesterton also saw capitalism as an enemy of the family. He was of the opinion that what destroyed the family in the modern world was capitalism. It was the epoch and power of capitalism which had broken up households, encouraged divorces, and treated the old domestic virtues with more and more open contempt. Capitalism had forced a moral feud and a commercial competition between the sexes and had destroyed the influence of the parent in favour of the influence of the employer.[5]

Chesterton's assertion that certain aspects of capitalism are detrimental to the welfare of the family and marriage are worthy of note in the light of a recent Australian study by the Centre for Population and Urban Research at Monash University.[6] It is entitled *Men and Women Apart: partnering in Australia* and is to this writer's knowledge one of the few such studies in existence. The study examines in detail the relationship between full-time employment, remuneration and the level of partnering in Australia. The conclusion, although applicable to Australia only, may well have application in other industrial capitalist societies. The summary of the report reveals that there is a direct correlation between men with low incomes and de facto partnerships. Married men are now predominantly drawn from the ranks of the better off. The increase in the overall divorce rate in Australia during the period of the study is predominantly amongst men and the women who are less affluent. The study showed that full-time employment amongst males aged thirty to thirty-four had declined from 78 per cent in 1986 to 67 per cent in 2001. It further stated that there was a reluctance of these men to take on marriage and parenthood responsibilities, and this was probably a reflection of their financial circumstances as well as the concurrent increases in the cost of establishing a household. Marriage partnerships are being concentrated amongst the affluent, whereas broken marriages, lone-parent families and single persons rank amongst the economically disadvantaged.[7]

With the hollowing out of the middle classes in western industrial societies and the acceptance by current economic orthodoxy of the notion of a perpetual pool of unemployed, Chesterton's assertions in this regard are as relevant today in this age of that soulless entity 'corporate capitalism' as they were when he made them. Belloc defines the capitalist state as:

> A society in which the ownership of the means of production is confined to a body of free citizens not large enough to make up properly a general character of that society, while the rest are dispossessed of the means of production and are therefore proletarian, we call *capitalist*.[8]

His definition closely resembles that of Chesterton. Belloc sees the development of industrial capitalism as a situation in which society is rapidly coming nearer to the establishment of compulsory labour among an unfree majority of non-owners for the benefit of a free minority of owners.

Robert Nisbet, in his introduction to the 1977 Liberty Classics edition of *The Servile State,* said that Belloc was an admirer of William Cobbett, who had himself drawn upon the writings of Edmund Burke. He says that there is a strong element of Burke's philosophy in Belloc, as indeed there was in the writings of many nineteenth and early twentieth centuries social commentators, whose fundamental devotion to tradition and continuity did not preclude their hostility to all forms of large-scale organization, whether it be economic, religious or political, in which the liberty and security of individuals were sacrificed.[9]

Belloc viewed capitalism as an intermediary stage in the evolution of the servile state. Where a few possessed the means of production, perfectly free political conditions were impossible. Further, it was a feature of capitalism that it must keep alive by non-capitalist methods the great masses of the population who, because of their weak bargaining position and their inability to possess property, would otherwise starve to death. The unfettered capitalist system was moreover a system of waste. It comprised a mass of isolated, imperfectly instructed competing units whose clashing efforts resulted in enormous fluctuating waste of resources.[10]

Chesterton believed that the way of the future was communism but was of the opinion that it would be no worse than capitalism had been. Communism and capitalism were for him equal heresies. In *The Crime of the Communist*, one of the later Father Brown stories, a discourse takes place in which Father Brown says:

> Of course, communism is a heresy; but it isn't a heresy that you people take for granted. It is capitalism that you take for granted; or rather the vices of capitalism disguised as a dead Darwinism. Do you recall what you were all saying in the common room, about life being only a scramble and nature demanding the survival of the fittest, and how it doesn't matter whether the poor are paid justly or not? Why *that* is the heresy that you have grown accustomed to, my friends; and it's every bit as much a heresy as communism. That's the anti-Christian morality or immorality that you take quite naturally.[11]

Chesterton here makes a clear link between Darwinism and the evils of industrial capitalism.

The following satirical verse of G. K. Chesterton expresses the disdain with which both he and Belloc viewed the capitalist system and class:

> They have given us into the hand of new unhappy lords
> Lords without anger and honour, who dare not carry their swords.
> They fight by shuffling papers; they have bright dead alien eyes;
> They look at our labour and laughter as a tired man looks at flies,
> And the load of their loveless pity is worse than the ancient wrongs,
> Their doors are shut in the evening; and they know no songs.[12]

The proletariat and the servile state

For Chesterton, the calling of workmen was the noblest of all human functions. It was a source of ire to him that industrial capitalism did not accord the worker the dignified title he deserved. Instead the worker was regarded as a member of that vast anonymous mass titled 'workers' which was a vast, grey horde of people apparently all exactly alike, like ants, and who were always on the march somewhere, presumably to the ninth or tenth Internationale. He believed that this dehumanizing way of dealing with the people who do most of the practical work on which society depended, merely because they were unfortunate enough to have to do it for a wage, was quite as irritating to anybody with real popular sympathies as was the inward contempt of the classes that were established and ought to be educated. In true Chestertonian fashion he said that a workman was a man, a particular sort of biped; and that two of them were not a quadruplet, nor fifty of them a centipede.[13] His point here is that whilst it can be said that the sociology of industrial capitalism began with an identification with individualism, for the proletariat – which, according to Belloc, comprised nineteen-twentieths[14] of the population – its ultimate organization has corresponded to a complete loss of individuality.

There is an interesting essay of Chesterton, in which he says, somewhat tongue in cheek, that capitalism really ought to be called proletarianism. He says the point is not that some people have capital, but rather that most people only have wages because they do not have capital. Realizing the misunderstandings to which this definition would lead, he explained that what he complained of was that the current defence of existing capitalism was in reality a defence of keeping most men in wage dependence – that is, keeping most men without capital.[15] Chesterton's frequent reference to the idea of men being kept in wage dependence and without capital reflects his views on property and distributism, a subject referred to later in this chapter. Like Cobbett, Chesterton wanted to see working men have a sense of honour; and he was conscious that this sense of honour was everywhere being broken down by the cruel and ignoble industrialism of his time.

Belloc was somewhat saddened by his realization that the attitude of the proletariat in England towards property, and towards the freedom which alone was obtainable through property, was no longer an attitude of experience or even of expectation. He believed that they thought of themselves as wage-earners only, and were content if they attained increases of their weekly wage without aspiring to the acquisition of property. Belloc felt that the proletariat had lost the instinct, use and meaning of property and that this had two very powerful effects which strongly inclined modern wage-earners to ignore the old barriers which lay between a condition of servitude and a condition of freedom. The first effect was that property was no longer what the proletariat sought nor what they thought obtainable for themselves. The second was that they regarded the possessors of property as a class apart whom they always must ultimately obey, often envy, and sometimes hate; and whose moral right to so singular a position most of them would hesitate to concede and many of them would now strongly deny, but whose position they, at any rate, accepted as a known and permanent social fact, the origins of which they had forgotten, and the foundations of which they believed to be immemorial.[16]

Chesterton believed that socialism was an extension of the capitalist process of concentration. Just as capitalism concentrated ownership in the hands of the few members of the capitalist class, so socialism concentrated control of industry in the hands of the few members of boards of control appointed by the state. He maintained that the socialist ideal was fundamentally mistaken and that, while a utopia in which all private property was abolished would certainly be less unjust than the existing arrangement; regimentation for everyone was no more desirable than regimentation for the proletarian class.[17]

He found socialism a somewhat vague doctrine and described it as a system in which the corporate unity of society was responsible for all its economic processes, or all those processes affecting life and essential living. If anything important was sold, the government sold it; if anything important was given, it was the government that gave it; if anything important was even tolerated, the government was responsible for tolerating it. Because of these features of socialism, Chesterton viewed it as the very reverse of anarchy and as a system which exhibited an extreme enthusiasm for authority.[18]

Belloc believed that industrial society would develop in any or all of three directions. These were:

1. Re-establish a system in which the ownership of the means of production was in the hands of the political officers of the community.
2. There would be the re-establishment of the distributive state in which the mass of citizens would severally own the means of production.
3. There would eventuate the servile state in which those who did not own the means of production should be legally compelled to work for those who did and should receive in exchange a security of livelihood.

Belloc believed that it was the collective ideal which would emerge triumphant as it appealed the most naturally and easily to a society already capitalist on account of the difficulty which such a society had in discovering the energy, the will and the vision requisite for the establishment of a distributive state. However, he said that in actual practice the ideal collective state which was bred out of capitalism led men not towards the collective state or anything like it but to a third utterly different thing – the servile state.[19]

Belloc saw industrial capitalism as moving in the direction of the servile state. He described the servile state as an arrangement of society, in which so considerable a number of families and individuals were constrained by positive law to labour for the advantage of other families and individuals, as to stamp the whole community with the mark of such labour. This arrangement of society he called 'the servile state'. He said that a society was not servile in which men were intelligently constrained to labour by enthusiasm, by a religious tenet, or indirectly from fear of destitution, or directly from love of gain, or from the commonsense which teaches them that by their labour they may increase their wellbeing. A clear boundary existed between the servile and the non-servile condition of labour, and the conditions upon either side of that boundary utterly differed one from another. He said that where there was compulsion applicable by positive law to men of a certain status, and such compulsion enforced in the last resort by the powers at the disposal of the state, there is the institution of slavery; and if that institution be sufficiently expanded, the whole state may be said to repose upon a servile basis and is a servile state.[20]

If one were to remove the facade of twenty-first-century neoliberal capitalism, one could be excused for opining that there are indications that, having shown such promise in the 1950s, 1960s and 1970s of a desire to distribute the wealth of society more equitably, there is now once again an emerging pattern of behaviour bearing some of the hallmarks of Belloc's servile state. This is evidenced by the encouragement of pools of unemployed, the curtailment of the rights of trade unions in respect of industrial action in support of their claims, the growing power of the large corporations, particularly the transnationals, with the inherent concentration of ownership in the hands of fewer and fewer, the erosion of small proprietorship and consequent hollowing out of the middle class and the once-again growing numbers of the proletarian class.

Distributism, property and the worker
The Distributive League was founded in London in 1926. It comprised people from all walks of life and all religious denominations. The leading exponents of the distributist idea were Belloc, G. K. Chesterton and his brother Cecil Chesterton. Broadly speaking the aim of the league was to encourage governments to bring in measures which would restore property and the ability to acquire property to ordinary people – that

is, to the proletarian class. This was to be done by encouraging what may be called a distribution of ownership entailing smallholdings, small shops, individual craftsmen, as against corporations and large landowners. In the 1920s and 1930s distributism, as advocated by Belloc and Chesterton, was widely regarded as an exceedingly radical policy which, given the widespread acceptance of the tenets of liberal capitalism, it probably was at that time.

For both Belloc and Chesterton the fatherhood of God was paramount in their social thinking, particularly in the relationships of one person with another. Concomitant with that was the idea of the dignity of work and the relationship of the worker with the fruits of his toil. It was Chesterton who argued that the machine should not exist save as the servant of the man and that the things one produced were precious like one's own children.[21]

The idea of distributism went beyond the notion of property. It included such things as responsibilities and the powers of state. Chesterton believed that as much as possible of a human life should be given to every human being. He believed that there should be in the world a great mass of scattered powers, privileges, limits, points of resistance, so that the great mass of the common people would be enabled to resist tyranny. The distribution of power and authority was a bulwark against tyranny.[22]

The distributists saw themselves as revolutionary in the sense that a revolution meant a reversal of direction. They sought a world which was as far removed from the existing world as the existing world was from the world of socialism. They saw little difference between socialism and industrial capitalism. For distributists it was a tenet that, if one concluded property in itself was not evil but only a small number of its owners, then the remedy was to increase the number of those owners. They saw the re-establishment of a distributive state in which the mass of citizens should severally own the means of production and share in the profits in the modern mercantile sense of the word 'shares' – that is, something divided and not merely pooled. This wider distribution of property would evoke in men and women the most individual and the most interesting qualities. Chesterton's yearning for the dignity of the human person, the dignity of labour, and the development of the human personality through the ownership of property by the proletarian mass, was succinctly expressed in his words:

I sit amid droves of overdriven clerks and underpaid workmen in a tube or a tram; I read of the great conception of Men Like Gods and I wonder when men will be like men.[23]

Belloc held that the capitalist society was open to reform in two ways. There could be an attempt to achieve the collectivist state or a reaction towards a situation where there was an equitable division of property in a distributive state. The collectivist state was, in Belloc's view, the negation of private property and the management of the means of production by the political officers of the community. The distributive state was the one in which there existed a wider distribution of property until such time as the ownership of property became the mark of the whole state and free citizens were normally found to be the possessors of capital, land or both.[24]

With property being more equitably distributed amongst the members of society, the class war between the capitalist class and the proletarian mass would come to an end insofar as the theory of class war divided all people into either employers or employed. Chesterton thought, however, that any move to return the ownership of property to the great mass of people would be resisted by the property-owning class as, whilst they were willing to give the proletariat a vote, they had long ago discovered that giving him or her a vote did not necessarily give them any power. Speaking allegorically, Chesterton said they were not willing to give the proletariat a house, a wife, a child, or a dog, or a cow, or a piece of land, because possession of these things really did give him power.[25]

Prominent in the idea of proletarian ownership of property was the ownership of a home. Chesterton saw the home as a 'sphere of liberty for the ordinary mass of mankind'.[26]

Chesterton has a graphic and witty way of arguing that those who aspire to the accumulation of property at the expense of inevitable distribution are in effect the enemies of property. They are enemies of property because they are the enemies of their own limitations. They do not want their own land, but other people's. When they remove their neighbour's landmark, they also remove their own. A man who loves a little triangular field ought to love it because it is triangular; anyone who destroys the shape, by giving him more land, is a thief who has stolen a triangle. He said that a man with the true poetry of possession wishes to see the wall where his garden meets Smith's garden; the hedge where his farm touches Brown's. He cannot see the shape of his own land unless he sees the edges of his neighbour's. It is the negation of property that the Duke of Sutherland should have all the farms in one estate – just as it would be the negation of marriage if he had all our wives in one harem.[27]

In summary then, what the distributists sought to do was to strengthen and support shopkeepers, independent craftsmen and small farmers, and on the other hand work towards the formation of a new class of small proprietors by breaking up big estates and big enterprises. Chesterton was not a utopian; neither did he believe that distributism was a dream of an ideal society to be brought into being at some future date. He had a definite programme for the gradual breaking up of the larger enterprises and their replacement with smaller units. These involved changes to the law of succession to replace primogeniture by the Napoleonic law under which inherited property was divided amongst the children. Other changes involved legal aid to small proprietors wishing to defend their properties against the rich and to government subsidies aiding the establishment of small enterprises and the imposition of tariffs to protect them.

Although neither Chesterton nor Belloc drew upon the teaching authority of the Catholic Church for their political and social views, they believed that what they advocated was dependent upon Christian doctrine and the teaching of the Gospels. They both believed that the salient doctrines of Christianity were best represented within the Roman Catholic Church. They believed that insofar as modern men and women still had any political ideals, these were Christian ideals; and insofar as they became detached from a genuine Christian faith, they withered away. Chesterton argued that all the principles of the French Revolution and of modern reform movements – the creed of liberty, equality and fraternity, together with faith in the possibility of heroic action to make the world better – all derived from Christianity, and could not long survive away from it.

Margaret Canovan said that this point seemed the most obvious in the case of the political principle dearest to Chesterton's heart: equality. He remarked that, of his own generation of liberal and enlightened ex-Christians, the equal worth of all human beings had seemed an obvious truth that did not need religious mythology about the fatherhood of God to back it up. But in his own lifetime he had watched the spread of doctrines dividing men into superior and inferior races, or elites and masses, and was convinced that there was no basis for democracy except in a dogma about the divine origin of man.[28]

Belloc and Chesterton were in no sense defenders of the status quo. Their writings, like the writings of any Marxist, are full of the rhetoric of revolution. They were, however, equally opposed to both capitalism and socialism, taking the view that the problem with capitalism was not that there was too much respect for property, but rather too little. They viewed capitalism as a system in which small property and small businesses were ultimately swallowed up by more and more large monopolies, with the result that the vast majority of the population became dependent upon organizations which were socialist in their scale though not in their social conscience. Their influence upon Catholic social thought has been enormous. For decades the writings of Belloc and Chesterton were deemed compulsory reading along with the social encyclicals for all those engaged in the social apostolate and Catholic action, and continue to be of considerable relevance today.

If it can be said that Belloc and Chesterton wrote in the spirit of *Rerum Novarum,* it can also be said that the spirit of Belloc and Chesterton is present in Pius XI's encyclical *Quadragesimo Anno,* promulgated on 15 May 1931. Pius XI's references to property, profit sharing, families, worker participation and the ownership of the means of production bear a resemblance to the writings of Belloc and Chesterton and the distributist ideal, and mark a significant development of the principles laid down in *Rerum Novarum*.

The worker-priest experiment

During the Second World War and for several years thereafter there occurred in France the controversial experiment which came to be known as the 'worker-priests'. In March 1943, two Jocist chaplains in Paris, the Abbés Godin and Daniel, submitted to Cardinal Suhard a programme for the conquest of the proletariat for Christianity. They gave the cardinal an account of their ten years' experience working with the working classes and of what they termed as the almost complete de-Christianization of the working masses. They asserted that there was a division separating the parishes from the people and that there was no place for the workers in the Church of that time. They alleged that the traditional methods of preaching services and good works did not catch hold of the masses but turned those whom they did influence into members of the bourgeoisie. Their solution was the establishment of small Christian communities independent of the parish churches in the midst of the proletariat. Impressed by the submissions of Abbés Godin and Daniel, Cardinal Suhard commissioned Godin to establish a team of priests for that purpose.

Later that year Cardinal Suhard, with Abbés Godin and Daniel, together with Father Augros, superior of the Mission to France, decided on the foundation of what was known as the Mission to Paris, a team of priests relieved of their regular duty in order to devote themselves to evangelizing the common people of Paris and workers generally. The mission was to work with no preconceived plan of action, in close liaison with Christian laymen determined to give up their life to this task and under the direct control of the archbishop.[29]

In December 1943 and January 1944 the Mission to Paris was established in a small number of centres throughout France, and at the outset there were six priests available for this programme, which was not at that time referred to as a 'worker-priest' programme since those involved were not engaged full- time in the workforce. By late 1944 the programme had evolved to the extent that there were over 100 priests with full-time employment in the ranks of the proletariat. Other priests declined to commit themselves to full-time employment outside the parish, but did so on a part-time basis. The main centres of such activity were Paris, Combs-la-Ville, Lisieux, Givors and Marseilles. It was to be the role of the worker-priests to evangelize amongst the working people with whom they associated and worked. Generally speaking they were relieved from all parochial duties. It was customary for all the worker-priests in a particular diocese to meet weekly to review their progress and objectives. Many of them became active members of the trade union movement.

By the end of October 1953 it was becoming obvious that there was considerable disquiet in the assembly of cardinals and archbishops of France and indeed elsewhere in Europe as to the desirability of the concept of worker-priests and the direction in which the movement was seen to be heading in France. At the assembly of cardinals and archbishops of France in October 1953 the most important item on the agenda was the question of worker-priests. At the end of the assembly certain directives were issued in which a warning was given to those who claimed to give a political interpretation to the teaching and action of the Church. At the same time the conference praised the efforts of Catholic Action and other groups evangelizing the working classes. Of worker-priests as such there was no mention. From this time onwards there was a progressive and perceptible change of attitude in the French hierarchy and at the Vatican towards worker-priests. There appeared to be a fear that the worker-priests would either slip towards Protestantism or that they would deviate into communism. Pius XII was reported to have said that it would have been better for the work of the Apostles to be left undone than that the priesthood be prejudiced.[30]

In November 1953 Cardinals Feltin Liénart and Gerlier issued a statement in which they said that the worker-priest experiment as it had evolved to date could not be maintained in its current form. They demanded that henceforth:

- they be specially selected by their bishops
- they receive a sound doctrinal training
- the time they devoted to manual work be limited
- they leave temporal responsibilities to laymen
- they take part in the life of the parish church.

In late November 1953 the bishops decided to ask their worker-priests to hand in their temporal commitments and discreetly leave their trade unions. The practical reaction by various bishops to this directive was far from uniform.[31] It is also clear that there was at this time a growing doubt as to the effectiveness of the worker-priest experiment.

In September 1953 an article appeared in the Italian weekly *Oggi* by Father Rotondi, a man who was known to work closely with Pius XII, which said that the worker-priest experiment had all the characteristics of a frontal attack which took no account of losses if only it could carry the position. He went on to say that any leader, having reached a certain stage of the battle, begins to reckon his losses by reference to the ground gained. Moreover, with the passage of time, had not the worker-priests changed into the priest worker? Had not he, whose aim ought to be cooperation between the classes, slipped into the Marxist struggle? The worker-priests, he said, ought not to spread their false idea that the priest can become identified with particular classes of people to whom his services are directed.

In January 1954 Cardinal Liénart, one of the three French cardinals, issued a statement in which he said that the current worker-priest experiment could not be continued in its original form but must be followed up in a new form. He said that the Holy Father had taken this decision for doctrinal reasons. Being a priest and being a worker were two separate functions, two different states of life. They could not be joined in one and the same person without derogating from the idea of the priesthood. The business of the priest was to consecrate his life to God and to the service of souls. The worker accomplished a temporal task. Even if the method of apostolate as practised by the worker-priests had to some degree been effective, we have no right to trench on the priesthood as established by Christ.[32]

In February 1954 some seventy-eight worker-priests signed a memorandum of protest against the directives calling for an end to the experiment, and in Paris some 250 militant Catholic Actionists signed an appeal against the decision of the hierarchy and the Vatican. *L'Osservatore Romano* saw the declaration of the worker-priests as evidence of support for a class spirit. It saw its continuance as being in stark opposition to the paternal impulse by which the bishops were moved. The article went on to say that the Church could not accept such a struggle, either in theory or in practice. The following day, 22 February 1954, the Rome correspondent of *Le Figaro* said that in Rome the question of the worker-priest was out of date. There was only one question – obedience or disobedience.

In France, different dioceses reacted in different ways to the directives. Some bishops were reluctant to comply with the directives but did so grudgingly. Within twelve months, the worker-priest experiment had officially ended, although it is believed that some two-thirds of them defied the direction and continued to work.[33]

Notes
1. Chesterton, *A Miscellany of Men*, p. 43.
2. Klipper, p. 44.
3. Chesterton, *The Well and the Shallows*, pp. 131,132.
4. 'The Beginning of the Quarrel' in *Chesterton's Stories Essays & Poems*, introduction by Maisie Ward, p. 201.
5. Chesterton, *The Well and the Shallows*, p. 148.
6. 'Cobbett and Capitalism' in *G. K. Chesterton: a selection from his non-fictional prose,* selected by W. H. Auden, Faber & Faber, London, 1970, p. 37.
7. Birrell, Rapson and Hourigan, pp. vii, viii, ix.
8. Belloc, *The Servile State*, p. 81.
9. Belloc, *The Servile State*, Liberty Classics, Indianapolis 1977, pp. 20, 21.
10. Ibid. pp. 114, 115,116.
11. Chesterton, *The Father Brown Stories*, p. 672.
12. Conlon, p. 13.
13. Chesterton, *As I Was Saying: A Book of Essays*, pp. 170, 171.

14 Belloc, *The Servile State*, Liberty Classics, p. 153.
15 *Chesteron's Stories Essays & Poems*, 1965, pp. 196, 197.
16 Belloc, *The Servile State*, Liberty Classics, , p. 155.
17 Canovan, p. 47.
18 Chesterton, *The Outline of Sanity*, pp. 7, 8.
19 Belloc, *The Servile State*, Liberty Classics, pp. 41, 42.
20 Ibid. p. 51.
21 Chesterton, *The Outline of Sanity*, p. 87.
22 *Do We Agree?* p. 25.
23 Chesterton, *The Outline of Sanity*, p. 230.
24 Belloc, *The Servile State*, Liberty Classics, pp. 42, 125.
25 Chesterton, *The Outline of Sanity*, p. 229.
26 Canovan, p. 49.
27 Chesterton, p. 48.
28 Canovan, pp. 118, 119.
29 *The Worker-Priests: A Collective Documentation,* translated from the French by John Petrie, Routledge & Kegan Paul, London, 1956, pp. 6, 7.
30 Ibid. p. 39.
31 Ibid. pp. 38, 40.
32 Ibid. pp. 41, 42, 43.
33 Ibid. p. 48.

Chapter 8

PIUS XI

Quadragesimo Anno

Background

At the time of the publishing of *Quadragesimo Anno*, the world was in the grip of the Great Depression. In the industrialized nations of Europe and North America some 25 million workers had been forced into a state of unemployment. In Russia the Bolshevik revolution of October 1917 had brought a new dimension to the struggle between the classes and had provided the socialist movements of the world with an ideological and geographical homeland. The penetration of the working classes by Marxist ideology proceeded apace throughout the world. On the other hand, in Western Europe, forms of authoritarianism combining the cult of the state with socialist ideas were gaining prominence under the general nomenclature of fascism.

In Western Europe, particularly in France, Germany and Italy, the Christian Democratic movements which had earlier shown such promise stood seriously weakened and discredited. On the other hand, the various episcopal conferences of the Church had not been slow in enunciating within their respective nations the principles laid down in *Rerum Novarum*. A significant example was the pastoral letter of the United States bishops published on 26 September 1919. The bishops were cognisant of the fact that the recent war had sharpened the issues and intensified the conflict that was raging in the world of industry. They said that although the elements of the conflict in industry were unchanged, also unchanged were the principles which had to be applied if peace and order were to be restored. They said that it had to be realized that in industrial disputes there were more rights to be considered than simply those of capital and labour. The rights of the community must prevail. Referring to *Rerum Novarum* they said that the moral value of man and the dignity of human labour were cardinal points in the social question. It was a shameful and inhuman thing to treat men like chattels and as a means for making money or simply as machines for grinding out work. The employer, by treating the worker first of all as a man, will make him a better worker. The worker, by respecting his own dignity as a man, will compel the respect of his employer and of the community.

The United States Catholic bishops were, perhaps, the first episcopal conference to lend support to the idea of industrial arbitration courts. They said that 'Like the law court, the tribunal of industrial arbitration provides the nearest approach to justice that is practically attainable'. The bishops did however recognize that no human institutions, including industrial tribunals, were infallible.[1]

Pius XI

Pius XI was elected pope in 1922 following the death of Benedict XV. In his earlier life he had been a librarian at Milan and at the Vatican. He later became Cardinal Archbishop of Milan and held this office immediately prior to his election to the papacy. Pius XI strongly believed that the resolution of the world's problems lay not in the mere human institutions but in the establishment of the peace of Christ in the kingdom of Christ. Accordingly in 1925 he established the 'Feast of Christ the King'. This was his way of emphasizing the lordship of Christ over all human endeavours.

Following the disbandment of the Fribourg Union after the publication of *Rerum Novarum* another international union on a much wider basis was established in Malines in 1920 under the presidency of Cardinal Mercier. The union, which was officially called 'The International Union for Social Studies', included in its membership distinguished Catholic scholars in social and economic sciences from France, Germany, Holland, Belgium, Italy, Spain and England. When Cardinal Mercier died in 1924 he was replaced as president by Archbishop Van Roy, his successor in the See of Malines. One of the most important achievements of the Malines Union was the publication of the *Code Social* in 1927. This was a compendium of Catholic principles and conclusions applicable to the socio-economic conditions in Europe and America. Its conclusions and recommendations were later published as a *Code of Social Principles* and were to have a direct influence on *Quadragesimo Anno*.

Pius XI had long been concerned about the political, economic and social developments taking place in the industrialized world and expressed his concern in the first encyclical of his pontificate, *Ubi Arcano,* promulgated on 23 December 1922. In this encyclical he describes the war between the classes as a chronic and mortal disease of present-day society which was like a cancer eating away the vital social fabric of everything which contributed to public and private welfare and to national prosperity.[2] He accordingly charged his confidante, Father Wlodimir Ledochowski, Superior General of the Jesuits, to oversee the preparation of a new encyclical. In due course the writing of the encyclical was entrusted to the German Jesuit Father Oswald von Nell-Breuning, who had been a student of the German Jesuit Heinrich Pesch. Assisting Nell-Breuning was Gustav Gundlach, who had also been a student of Pesch. Heinrich Pesch was well known for his 3,900-page work entitled *Textbook of National Economics* and his shorter work, *Ethics and the National Economy*.

Both Nell-Breuning and Gustav Gundlach had been contributors to the deliberations of the Malines Union. According to Krier Mich, Nell-Breuning reportedly met Pius XI on one occasion only on the completion of the first draft. Subsequent communication was mediated through Ledochowski. Towards the end of the preparation of his draft Nell-Breuning received from Pius the controversial sections dealing with Italian Fascism which, according to Krier Mich, were written by Pius himself.[3]

Pius XI's concern and love for the working class was also demonstrated in his lesser known encyclical, *Nova Impendet,* promulgated on 2 October 1931, a few months after *Quadragesimo Anno*, which dealt primarily with the social dislocation caused by the depression. He said:

> A new scourge threatens, indeed, it has already in large measure smitten the flock entrusted to us. It strikes most heavily at those who are the most tender and are Our most dearly beloved; upon the children, the proletariat, the artisans and the 'have-nots'.[4]

Quadragesimo Anno is reported to have gone through eight drafts before the final document was agreed to by Pius XI. It was fitting that, in accordance with its title, it should be promulgated on 15 May 1931, the fortieth anniversary of the promulgation of *Rerum Novarum*.

The encyclical

In *Quadragesimo Anno*, Pius, as he states at the commencement of the encyclical, sought to clarify certain doubts which had arisen in connection with *Rerum Novarum* and to develop more fully some of the points raised by Leo XIII. It could be said that *Quadragesimo Anno* further developed certain of the matters raised by Leo XIII in *Rerum Novarum* and in addition raises certain new matters not covered by Leo XIII. As this work pertains to the Church's social teaching in respect of workers, those sections pertaining to matters other than the rights and duties of workers will be discussed only briefly and in general terms.

Labour and capital

Pius XI reiterated the words of Leo XIII in *Rerum Novarum*: 'It is only by the labour of working men that states were rich', and 'Capital cannot do without labour, nor labour without capital'.[5]

Like Leo, Pius XI advocated the cooperation of labour and capital in the spirit of Christian love and the brotherhood and sisterhood of the community under God. At the same time, like Leo, he saw the priority of labour in the fruits of the economic system. He said:

> Is it not indeed apparent that the huge possessions which constitute human wealth are begotten by and flow from the hands of the working man, toiling either unaided or with the assistance of tools and machinery which wonderfully intensify his efficiency?

He was highly critical of aspects of liberal capitalist ideology, some of which he associated with the Manchester School, which ascribed to capital alone, what was due to the combined efforts of labour and capital. This ideology assumed that the accumulation of riches must fall to the share of the wealthy, 'while the working man must remain perpetually in indigence or reduced to the minimum needed for existence'.[6]

He said, speaking of the processes of production, that it was entirely false to ascribe the results of the combined efforts of labour and capital to either party alone, and that it was flagrantly unjust that either should deny the efficacy of the other and seize all of the profits.[7] However, like Leo XIII, Pius condemned Marxist socialism, which sought to concentrate ownership in the hands of the state, and those workers who, incensed against the violation of justice by capitalists, went too far in vindicating the one right of which they were conscious, and sought to abolish all forms of ownership and all profits not obtained by labour for the sole reason that they were not acquired by toil.[8]

Pius described as inept and unfounded those who relied upon the words of St Paul 'If any one will not work, let him not eat,'[9] as a scriptural vindication of their argument that the fruits of production could be the property only of those whose manual labour produced it. What Paul was doing in this passage was admonishing those who refused to work though they could and ought to have done so, and admonishing us all to use our time diligently and our powers of body and mind so as not to become burdensome to others as long as we were able to provide for ourselves. He said that in no sense did Paul teach that labour was the sole title giving a right to a living or to profits.[10]

Pius was cognisant of the changes which had occurred in the relationship between labour and capital since *Rerum Novarum*. He held that the capitalist system itself was not to be condemned and was not vicious by its very nature, but it violated right order whenever it so employed the working or wage earning classes as to divert business and economic activity entirely to its arbitrary will and advantage without any regard to the human dignity of the workers, the social character of economic life, social justice and the common good. He said that since *Rerum Novarum*, with the worldwide diffusion of industry, the capitalist economic regime had penetrated everywhere and had invaded and pervaded the economic and social sphere even of those who lived outside its ambit, influencing them and intimately affecting them by its advantages, inconveniences and vices.[11]

The industrial capitalist system was becoming global.

Trade unions

In the years following *Rerum Novarum* some confusion arose as to whether the terms of the encyclical were such that Catholic workers were forbidden to join secular trade unions. *Rerum Novarum* had certainly encouraged the participation of Catholic workers in denominational unions, and the establishment of such unions was encouraged. Leo XIII saw such unions as a necessary part of the workers' spiritual development. He said:

Therefore, having taken their principles from God, let those associations provide ample opportunity for religious instruction so that individual members may understand their duties to God, that they may well know what to believe, what to hope for, and what to do for eternal salvation, and that with special care they may be fortified against erroneous opinions and various forms of corruption. Let the worker be exhorted to the worship of God and the pursuit of piety, especially to the religious observance of Sundays and Holy days.[12]

He believed that workers' associations ought to be so constituted and so governed as to furnish the most suitable, most convenient means of securing, as far as possible, an increase in the goods of body, soul, and of prosperity. He feared, however, that the secular trade unions were largely under the control of secret leaders who sought to apply principles which were neither in harmony with Christianity nor the welfare of states. Workers, he said, were faced with two choices: either to join associations in which it was feared that there was a danger to religion or to form their own associations. He asked the question: could anybody hesitate to affirm that the second course was the means to be followed?[13]

Quadragesimo Anno removed any doubt that existed and opened the way for Catholic workers to participate in secular trade unions or neutral trade unions. Pius XI recognized that the laws of various countries or peculiar economic conditions, or the existence of dissension in the minds and hearts of modern society, or the necessity of uniting forces to combat the growing ranks of revolutionaries, often made it impossible for Catholics to form Catholic unions. He said that under such circumstances they seemed to have no choice but to enrol themselves in neutral trade unions. He added the rider that such trade unions should always respect justice and equity, and leave to their Catholic members full freedom to follow the dictates of their conscience and to obey the precepts of the Church.[14]

In his commentary on the encyclical, Nell-Breuning, who is credited with the drafting of the greater part of *Quadragesimo Anno*, said that by mentioning labour unions in general, Leo XIII did not specify whether Catholic workers should form a unit organization that would realize all of their thoughts or a multitude of organizations to carry out various tasks. Nell-Breuning believed that Pius XI showed that *Rerum Novarum* was intended to be a skeleton law. Leo was not concerned with the form, but with the content. Consequently, Catholic workers were free in individual cases to follow different roads without deviating from the line prescribed by Leo XIII.[15]

Nell-Breuning believed that the non-denominational trade unions could not appropriate Catholic religious and moral doctrines and neither did Pius XI expect them to. He was satisfied if they observed the principles of natural morality, especially right and justice, principles which remained unaltered by Catholic moral doctrine. In non-denominational trade unions, the Catholic, like everyone else, had to follow his conscience, and for its true development obey the teachings of the Church which, in the name of God, also proclaimed and explained the natural moral code.[16]

Whatever uncertainty may have existed prior to *Quadragesimo Anno*, in practice, the various episcopal conferences of the industrialized nations of Europe and North America were generally supportive of Catholic worker participation in non-denominational or neutral trade unions, and regarded such participation as being in accordance with *Rerum Novarum*.

The individual and social character of labour – worker participation

Pius XI spoke of the features of labour as being both individual and social. Man's toil could not produce due fruit unless human society formed a truly social and organic body, unless labour be protected in the social and judicial order, unless the various forms of human endeavour dependent one upon the other were united in mutual harmony and mutual support and unless brains, capital and labour combined together for common effort. The reference to the combination of brains, capital and labour is one which Pius uses on a number of occasions. The overlooking of the social and individual character of labour results in labour being neither equitably appraised nor properly recompensed in accordance with principles of strict justice.[17]

It is in respect of Pius XI's advocacy of a form of worker participation in the ownership, management or profits of industry that *Quadragesimo Anno* is perhaps its most radical. Pius states that it is desirable that where possible the wage contract should be modified by a contract of partnership between capital and labour so that in this way wage earners were made sharers in the ownership, or the management, or the profits of the concern. This is in keeping with the concept of labour and capital being in partnership, as expressed both in *Rerum Novarum*[18] and *Quadragesimo Anno*.[19]

Worker participation is also a practical application of Pius XI's exhortation in *Quadragesimo Anno* that the principles of right reason and Christian social philosophy regarding capital, labour and their mutual cooperation must be accepted in theory and *reduced to practice.*[20] The idea is probably also an expression of *Quadragesimo Anno*'s abiding concern with the institutional arrangements that affect the development of human personality, and the potential for self-realisation which compelled its interest in the relationship between employer and employee.[21] Nell-Breuning said that the Pope did not intend to show a preference for partnership over the wage contract or to recommend its acceptance. He said that contracts were instruments which could be made to suit the situation. Wage and partnership were not therefore rigidly opposed to each other, and innumerable changes were possible between the straight wage contract and the straight partnership by combinations of the two forms of contract with one or the other predominating. He said that the Pope steered a middle course by stating that he deemed it 'advisable' that the wage contract should 'when possible' be modified somewhat by a contract of partnership.[22] This declaration of Pius was to result in some confusion on this question during the pontificate of Pius XII.

In post-Second World War Germany it was asserted by a number of Catholic writers that workers had a right to share in the management of industry as a natural right, arguing that this natural right gave effect to the sense of responsibility implanted in human nature by God.[23] The argument generated by this claim caused some controversy, and in a letter to the Catholic International Congresses for Social Study and Social Action on 3 June 1950 Pius XII stated that no right existed in respect of the joint management of economic enterprises.[24] Again on 14 September 1952 in a letter to Austrian Catholics, Pius XII said that he had declined to deduce directly or indirectly from the labour contract the right of the employee to participate in the ownership of the operating capital and its corollary, the right of the worker to participate in decisions concerning operations of the plant.[25]

However, ten years later on the sixtieth anniversary of *Rerum Novarum*, John XXIII apparently conceded what Pius XII had denied when he said:

> Attention is drawn to the fact that the greater amount of responsibility desired today by workers in productive enterprises, not merely accords with the nature of man, but also is in conformity

with historical developments in the economic, social, and political fields.[26]

John XXIII said that he had no doubt that employees should have an active part in the affairs of the enterprises where they worked, whether these enterprises be private or public.[27]

Wage determination

For both Pius and Leo XIII the centrepoint of wage determination is the concept of the just wage. For Pius the requisite condition for labour's economic value was the cooperation in mutual harmony of 'brains, capital and labour' referred to earlier. For Pius, justice to labour was only done when the social as well as the individual character of labour was recognized. For Pius a just wage was a wage determined in accordance with the principles of commutative justice, which the *Catechism of the Catholic Church* defines as that justice which regulates exchanges between persons in accordance with a strict respect for their rights. The catechism says that commutative justice obliges strictly; it requires safeguarding property rights, paying debts, and fulfilling obligations freely contracted.[28] In fact, for Pius, commutative justice and charity were the only determinants in the relation between capital and labour. He says:

> The mutual relations between capital and labour must be determined according to the laws of the strictest justice, called commutative justice, supported however by Christian charity.[29]

Pius's major addition to *Rerum Novarum* on the subject of wages was his enunciation of the factors to be taken into account in determining a just wage. The considerations were threefold. Firstly, consideration had to be given to the needs of the worker and his family. Secondly, consideration had to be given to the economic condition of the enterprise concerned. And thirdly, the common good of society must be taken into account.[30]

Pius reiterates *Rerum Novarum* in advocating a family wage sufficient for the support of the worker and his family. He could also refer to his previous encyclical *Casti Conubii*[31] in which he also referred to the need for a family wage. Pius did not advocate any greater wage for a married worker over a single worker. The family wage was one which should be guaranteed to every adult working man.[32] This is an addition to what is held in *Rerum Novarum* where reference is made to the wage paid to the worker as being sufficient to enable the head of every family to earn as much as is necessary for himself, his wife, and for the rearing of his children.[33] In receiving a just wage the single adult working man is enabled thereby to set aside a modest sum from his wages in contemplation of future marriage and the purchase of a dwelling.

This situation is in accordance with the principles of commutative justice which, according to Nell-Breuning, say that the value of work depends upon the position it holds in the structure of the economic system, in which commutative justice demands of both parties to the labour contract, that the one does not demand more than this value and that the other does not pay less than this value. He says that if the economic system was working properly and both parties gave labour a proper place in the system, thus enabling it to do its share, then the value of work performed would be equal to family needs and consequently a family wage would be paid in accordance with justice. If, however, economic structure was disturbed or if it proved to be impossible to give labour its proper place in the system, then the value of work done would fall short of family requirements. In this situation the employer would not be required, either on the basis of commutative justice or for any other reason, to pay family wages. On the contrary, in this instance he is unable to pay them. Any attempt to pay them in spite of it would merely result in further dislocation of the economic structure, and would endanger the employer himself.[34]

Contained within that section of *Quadragesimo Anno* which refers to the matter of wages - although, according to Nell-Breuning, intended to be a subject other than that of wages - is praise for that system whereby increased wages were paid in consequence of increased family burdens, and special provision was made for special needs.[35] This idea has found its way into the social security systems of most industrialized economies under the heading of family allowances. However, family allowances are threatened by the widespread acceptance of neo-liberal capitalist ideology.

In taking into account the economic condition of the enterprise, Pius was cognisant that the reasons why an enterprise was unable to stand wages of a certain level may differ widely, even apart from exaggerated wage demands which obviously exceeded the value of labour performed as well as any reasonable demands for a family wage. He recognized that the incapacity for paying appropriate wages may be the fault of the business itself. Therefore, he declared that indolence, lack of courageous and energetic enterprise and technical and economic stagnation resulting from it, could not be considered reasons for cutting wages. Whoever hires workers must first of all guarantee full and just compensation for their performance; only then could he begin to think about income from his enterprise. This is merely the inference from the fact that, as an independent capitalist, he must accept good as well as bad consequences. The alternative, if he does not wish to do this, is to become an employee and renounce the economic independence of the capitalist.

However, there may be other impersonal reasons for an employer's inability to pay proper wages, reasons that are beyond his control and which Pius enumerates. For instance, the enterprise may be suffering from unfair handicaps or may be unable to get the prices for its products for a variety of reasons. Under such conditions it will be impossible for him to pay full wages or a family wage respectively. However, the fact that an injustice may have been suffered by the employer does not entitle him to do injustice to others. But, without being unjust, the employer can give his employees the choice between the only two possibilities: either shut down and lay off, or continue work at lower wages. In this case, the employees may well choose the lesser evil. They will either accept well-paying employment that offers itself elsewhere, or, if such opportunity is lacking, they may elect to stay where they are at a lower rate of pay. In this situation the employer must waive his claim for profit and interest, although he has the right to demand a proper amount to enable him to live and perform his functions as an employer.[36]

In considering the exigencies of the common good, Pius deals with two considerations in the importance of the wage level to general welfare. First is his desire for the wage level being sufficient to enable the worker, by economizing, to apportion part of their wage after their necessities have been met to attain the possession of a certain modest fortune as was also advocated in *Rerum Novarum*. Writing of the acquisition of property by the worker, Pius said that, by thrift, the workers may increase their possessions and by the prudent management of the same may be enabled to bear the family burden with greater ease and security, being freed from that hand-to-mouth uncertainty which is the lot of the proletarian. They would then be in a position not only to support life's changing fortunes, but also have the reassuring confidence that, when their own lives are ended, some little provision would remain for those whom they leave behind.[37]

However, of equal importance in considering the level of wages and the common good, is the question of the availability of employment. *Quadragesimo Anno* was, of course, written at the time of the Great Depression, and the problems of unemployment would have been foremost in the mind of Pius XI and those involved with its drafting. The level of wages therefore had to be considered with a view to the effect upon the level of unemployment. Pius XI said:

> To lower or raise wages unduly with a view to private profit, and with no consideration for the common good, is contrary to social justice which demands that by union of effort and goodwill such a scale of wages be set up, if possible, as to offer to the greatest number opportunities of employment and of securing for themselves suitable means of livelihood.[38]

Implied in this part of the encyclical is an exhortation that wages can no longer be considered alone without reference to economic circumstances. We are required to make a broad and thorough study of the economic system as a whole and of the arrangement and interrelation of its members. Pius XI does not elaborate on this line of thought but is satisfied with opening up this avenue of thinking for our further investigation and conclusion.

Evolution of labour law
Pius XI was cognisant of the development of an entirely new branch of legal knowledge which had taken place since *Rerum Novarum*. This law, which has come to be called labour law, concerns such diverse fields as health, housing, wages, conditions of employment and all matters pertaining to workers. Pius comments that such laws as had been introduced since *Rerum Novarum* appear to draw strongly from that encyclical even though they did not always agree in every detail with the recommendations of Leo XIII. *Rerum Novarum* must be accredited with much of the improvement in the conditions of working men and women that had occurred since *Rerum Novarum*.

Pius implies that the legislative power of the state should be used where necessary for the common good. Referring to the fixing of the scale of wages, he said that the wage scale must be regulated with a view to the economic welfare of the whole people.[39] He later suggests the use of legislative powers for the re-establishment of vocational groups which were part of a corporative venture involving both labour and capital, a subject dealt with later.

Nell-Breuning held that in a certain sense labour law could be considered as part of the social policy, and obviously *Quadragesimo Anno* wanted to stress the close relationship between such enterprises and the development of the modern labour code. However, labour law means more than social politics; in a certain sense, labour law encroaches upon the realm of social reform. Labour law means more than the relationship between employer and employee as stipulated by contract and civil law and regulated in individual labour contracts. Nell-Breuning said that labour law includes the entire legal order within which the dependent hired labour of all grades is accomplished. He said that in this sense labour law was a vital and essential part of the legal constitution of the social economy.[40]

Worker and property

Pius XI deals with this subject in *Quadragesimo Anno* under the heading of The Uplifting of the Proletariat. In this section Pius advocates the acquisition of property by the working class as a means of alleviating their condition. He points to the necessity for measures which will facilitate such acquisition and condemns the inequitable distribution of the world's goods amongst the various classes. He said:

> The immense number of propertyless wage earners on the one hand, and the super-abundant riches of the fortunate few on the other, is an unanswerable argument that the earthly goods so abundantly produced in this age of industrialism are far from rightly distributed and equitably shared among the various classes of men.[41]

Vocational groups

As a way of reconciling the differences between the working and capitalist classes, Pius XI advocated the formation of what he called vocational groups. He said that society was in a strained and therefore unstable and uncertain state, being founded as it was on classes with contradictory interests and hence opposed to each other, and consequently prone to enmity and strife. He said that vocational groups would bind men together, not according to the position they occupied in the labour market, but according to diverse functions which they exercised in society. For as nature induced those who dealt in close proximity to unite into municipalities, so those who practised the same trade or profession, economic or otherwise, combined into vocational groups. These groups, he said, were considered by many to be, if not essential to civil society, at least its natural and spontaneous development. In these associations, he said, the common interest of the whole group must predominate, and among those interests the most important was the directing of the activities of the vocational group to the common good.[42]

Nell-Breuning, who had been entrusted with the writing of *Quadragesimo Anno*, asked the question: Why a corporate organization according to vocations? His answer to his own question was that the organization was corporate because these social groups, which formed themselves according to vocational relations, must be developed into true and real organs of the social body. He said that they were more than merely the total number of people who happened to apply themselves to a particular vocational activity at any one time. They had to be permanent corporate bodies, vocational groups not merely in a statistical sense, but vocational groups in the legal sense.[43]

According to Nell-Breuning, the Pope contemplated a twofold division: one according to territorial units, the other according to the nature of the vocation. In his view there would be public legal territorial sections and public legal vocational groups, both of which would penetrate each other. The division into vocational groups was in existence in communities and the country at large. The vocational groups would be territorially subdivided according to communities and provinces. This twofold organization would provide a double structure and increased security for the nation. Nell-Breuning likened the structure to horizontal and vertical girders, both of which combined to make the structure secure and safe against high winds.[44] This vocational group structure is often referred to as the principle of solidarism.

Although later social encyclicals make no direct reference to vocational groups, John Paul II in *Laborem Exercens* makes reference to each person being fully entitled to consider himself a part-owner of the great workbench at which he is working with everyone else. He says that a way towards that goal could be found by associating labour with the ownership of capital as far as possible, and by producing a wide range of intermediate bodies with economic, social and cultural purposes. These would be bodies which enjoyed real autonomy with regard to the public powers and pursued their specific aims in honest collaboration with each other and in subordination to the demands of the common good.[45] In this writer's view this is a clear reference to the solidarism of Pius XI in *Quadragesimo Anno*.[46]

The following year, in his encyclical *Caritate Christi Compulsi*, promulgated on 3 May 1932, Pius XI referred to what he termed the 'execrable hunger for gold' and excessive self-love which ordered and subordinated all things to its own advantage, and not only neglected but trampled upon the advantage of others and thereby brought about an iniquitous disturbance of affairs and the unequal division of possessions, as the result of which the wealth of nations was heaped up in the hands of a very few private men who, as he had warned the previous year in *Quadragesimo Anno*, controlled the trade of the whole world at their will, thereby doing immense harm to the people.[47]

The conclusion is that if the false distribution of the world's goods so abundantly produced has led to a tremendous number of workers confronting a minority of extremely rich, then it must become the objective of the well-ordered system to make good in the future the sins of the system in the past. The principles of distributive justice are applicable here.

By the acquisition of property in accordance with distributive justice we find a practical application to the benefit of the worker of the principles laid down by Pius XI in *Quadragesimo Anno*, where he said that the wealth which was constantly being augmented by social and economic progress must be so distributed amongst the various individuals and classes of society that the common good of all, of which Leo XIII spoke, was thereby promoted. The Pope said that every effort should be made to ensure that in the future a just share only of the fruits of production be permitted to accumulate in the hands of the wealthy and that an ample sufficiency be supplied to the worker.[48]

Conclusion

Quadragesimo Anno removed certain ambiguity that had arisen in respect of the application and construction of *Rerum Novarum*, which could be likened to a skeleton which was fleshed out by *Quadragesimo Anno*, and introduced the new concept of worker participation in the ownership and management of industry. The encyclical also dealt with subject matters beyond the scope of this work. These include the principle of subsidiarity, solidarism (also referred to as corporativism), individualism and Catholic action. *Rerum Novarum* and *Quadragesimo Anno* are frequently studied together, as *Quadragesimo Anno* complements *Rerum Novarum*.

Holland refers to *Quadragesimo Anno* as being Pius XI's response to the new corporate form of capitalism. He said that Pius boldly updated Leo XIII's historical encyclical *Rerum Novarum* and unequivocally condemned 'economic liberalism' while offering stronger support to workers and directly challenging the new national concentrations of capital. He highlighted the principle of subsidiarity and proposed a corporativist alternative to both liberal and socialist models of society. Holland says that Pius XI criticized national capitalism more boldly than had Leo XIII but did not reject it.[49]

Novak said that as a result of *Quadragesimo Anno*, the appeals that Pius XI had made for social justice encircled the globe, and advanced societies, after the Second World War, had reshaped themselves by democratic checks and balances, enterprise economics, and welfare systems barely imagined in 1931.[50]

Krier Mich, writing of the effects of the encyclical in the United States, said that in the broader sense the encyclical helped to energize those involved in social ministry, and in some areas of the country helped to shape the education of priests. He cites the Rector of St Mary of the Lake Seminary in the Archdiocese of Chicago, Reymold Hillenbrand, as having educated a generation of Chicago priests to a sense of liturgy, community and social involvement. President Roosevelt is said to have declared in Detroit on 2 October, 1932 that *Quadragesimo Anno* was as radical as he was and one of the greatest documents of modern times.[51] In an interview on the ABC programme 'Encounter' of 27 July 2003, Mary Ann Glendon, the Learned Hand Professor of Law at Harvard University who has represented the Vatican at various United Nation conferences, said that the United Nations Universal Declaration of Human Rights of 1948 contained certain verbal formulations which have a familiar ring to persons who were familiar with *Rerum Novarum* and *Quadragesimo Anno*. She said that the consistent use of the word 'person' rather than 'individual', the affirmation of a worker's right to just remuneration for himself and his family, the right of the family to protection by society and the state, and the right of parents to choose the education of their children, were such examples.[52]

Quadragesimo Anno was a radical encyclical which reinforced and expanded upon the principles set down by *Rerum Novarum*. Its provisions in suggesting a form of partnership agreement between labour and capital and those advocating worker participation in the management and profits of enterprises, and its definitive advice on determining what constituted a 'just wage', were seen as being somewhat radical at the time and still do not rest easily with some modern Catholic thinkers. However, *Quadragesimo Anno*, together with *Rerum Novarum*, constitutes one of the cornerstones of the *corpus* of Catholic social thinking.

Notes

1. Pastoral Letter, The Hierarchy of the United States, 26 September 1919.
2. *Ubi Arcano dei Consilio*.
3. Krier Mich, pp. 77, 78.
4. *Nova Impendet*, 22630.
5. *Rerum Novarum*, pp. 18, 31.
6. *Quadragesimo Anno*, p. 29.
7. Ibid. p. 28.
8. Ibid. p. 31.
9. 2 Thessolonians 3–10.
10. *Quadragesimo Anno*, p. 31.
11. Ibid. pp. 49, 50.
12. *Rerum Novarum*, para. 77.
13. Ibid., paras 73, 74.
14. *Quadragesimo Anno*, pp. 17, 18.
15. von Nell-Breuning, p. 56.
16. Ibid. p. 64.
17. *Quadragesimo Anno*, p. 35.
18. *Rerum Novarum*, p. 18.
19. *Quadragesimo Anno*, p. 28.
20. The italics are the writer's.
21. Thomas C. Kohler in Murphy, p. 39.
22. von Nell-Breuning, p. 163.
23. Townsend, p. 82.
24. 'Pius XII, Letter to Catholic International Congresses for Social Study and Social Action June 3, 1950' in Cronin, *Social Principles and Economic Life*, p. 146.
25. 'Pius XII Letter to Austrian Catholics September 14, 1952' in ibid. p. 147.
26. *Mater et Magistra,* para. 93, p. 29.
27. Ibid., para. 91, p. 28.
28. *Catechism of the Catholic Church*, para. 2411, 2579.
29. *Quadragesimo Anno*, p. 52.

30 Ibid. pp. 36, 37, 38.
31 *Casti Conubii*.
32 *Quadragesimo Anno*, p. 36.
33 *Rerum Novarum*, para. 65, p. 40.
34 von Nell-Breuning, pp.177, 178.
35 Ibid. p. 179.
36 Ibid. pp. 183,184.
37 *Quadragesimo Anno*, p. 33.
38 Ibid. p. 36.
39 Ibid. p. 37.
40 von Nell-Breuning, p. 46.
41 *Quadragesimo Anno*, pp. 32, 33.
42 Ibid. pp. 41, 42, 43.
43 von Nell-Breuning, p. 221.
44 Ibid. p. 222.
45 *Laborem Exercens*, para. 14, p. 63.
46 *Quadragesimo Anno*, pp. 41, 42, 43.
47 *Caritate Christi Compulsi*, 22630.
48 *Quadragesimo Anno*, pp. 30, 33.
49 Holland, p. 206.
50 Novak, *The Catholic Ethic and the Spirit of Capitalism*, p. 92.
51 Krier Mich, pp. 86, 87.
52 Transcript of 'Encounter', ABC, 27 July 2003.

Chapter 9

PIUS XII

and the national episcopal conferences

Background

Eugenio Pacelli was ordained to the priesthood in 1899. After his ordination he spent the greater part of his service in the Vatican Diplomatic Corps and was, immediately prior to his election as Pope, the Secretary of State under Pius XI. He was elected pope on 2 March 1939 by the conclave which followed the death of Pius XI in February of that year. He adopted the name of Pius XII.

Pius XII, although he did not promulgate any encyclicals specifically dealing with the social question, said a great deal on this subject through various allocutions and addresses. He exhibits in all of these a firm commitment to the principles laid down by *Rerum Novarum* and *Quadragesimo Anno*. Pius introduces no new thought on the social question and the rights and duties of capital and labour, other than to state that there was no pre-existing right for employees to participate in the ownership of the operating capital and in management.[1]

The earliest indication of Pius XII's concern for the condition of the worker was in an encyclical written to the United States bishops on 1 November 1939. In the encyclical entitled, *Sertum Laetitiae* Pius XII repeats the exhortation of Pius XI in *Quadragesimo Anno* for the payment of a family wage to workers on a scale sufficient to make decent provision for the common needs of their families. He repeats Pius XI's words that if the present conditions could not secure a living wage for the worker and his family, then social justice demanded that changes be introduced at the earliest possible moment so as to guarantee to the worker just such a wage.[2]

Pius XII added that if those who enjoyed power and wealth had a duty of supplying with ready compassion the needs of the destitute, they were bound by an even stronger title to give them what was their just due. He said that as a matter of right the wages of working people must be such that they are sufficient to maintain them and their families.³

In his Christmas radio broadcast of December 1942, Pius XII, speaking of the necessity for a just wage which covered the needs of the worker and his family, referred to the great social encyclicals of his predecessors and his own previous messages and said that the Church did not hesitate to draw the practical conclusions which were 'derived from the moral nobility of work and to give them all the support of her authority'.⁴

In the same letter, like *Rerum Novarum* and *Quadragesimo Anno*, he speaks of the conservation and perfection of the social order which would make possible and assured, even if in a modest way, the ownership of private property by all classes of society. He also spoke of a social order which promoted a social spirit which smoothed over the friction arising from privileges or class interests and which, through the assuring experience of a genuinely human and fraternally Christian solidarity, removed from the workers the sense of isolation.⁵

Pius XII was aware, however, of the shortcomings in the structure and machinery of the capitalist system. He said:

> The Church cannot ignore or overlook the fact that the worker, in his efforts to better his lot, is opposed by a machinery which is not only not in accordance with Nature, but is at variance with God's plan and with the purpose he had in creating the goods of earth.⁶

The community and the natural law

Pius XII taught that the community existed for the benefit of humanity. He said that it should be noted that in his personal being man is not finally ordered according to his usefulness to society. On the contrary, the community exists for man. The origin and the primary scope of social life was the conservation, development and perfection of the human person, helping him or her to realize accurately the demands and values of religion and culture set by the Creator for every person and for all of humanity.

The natural law was the foundation on which rested the social doctrine of the Church. It was the Church's perception of the world which inspired and sustained the Church in building up this social doctrine on such a foundation. He said that when the Church struggled to win and defend her own freedom, she was actually doing this for the true freedom and fundamental rights of humanity. In the Church's eyes these essential rights were so inviolable that no argument of the state and no pretext of common good could prevail against them. Pius XII believed that whatever changes occurred in the social order of society, the scope of every social life remained identical, sacred and obligatory. It was the development of the personal values of men and women as the image of God, and the obligation remained with every member of the human family to realize his or her unchangeable destiny, whomsoever was the legislator or whatever the authority whom he or she obeyed.[7]

The dignity of labour

Pius XII addresses the subject of the dignity of work on four separate occasions: his Christmas broadcast of 1942, an address to Italian workers in 1943, in a letter to Semaines Sociales of 1947, and in his Christmas message of 1955. In the 1942 address he said that all work had an inherent dignity and at the same time a close association with the perfection of the person. The noble dignity and privilege of work was not in any way cheapened by the fatigue and the burden associated with it, which had to be borne as a consequence of original sin and in obedience and submission to the will of God.[8]

In the 1955 Christmas address Pius XII said that man could consider his work as a true instrument of his sanctification because by working he makes perfect in himself the image of God, fulfils his duty and the right to gain for himself and his dependants the necessary sustenance, and makes himself a useful contributor to society. By bringing about this order the worker obtains security for himself and at the same time brings about the 'peace on earth' proclaimed by the angels.[9]

In an address to Italian workers Pius speaks of the labour of man as being a participation in God's work of creation, and he implies that because of this the workers obtained personal dignity which they should uphold and defend. He said that the material with which the workers toiled was created by God from the beginning of the world and in the laboratory of the ages. It was moulded by God on the earth and deep beneath the surface of the earth by various cataclysms, natural evolution, eruptions and transformations so as to prepare the best abode for mankind and his work. He said that this material with which the labourer toiled should be a continual reminder to the worker of the creative hand of God.[10]

In a letter to Semaines Sociales of 18 July 1947 Pius XII said that human labour itself was a factor over and above the distinction between employer and employee. He defined human labour as the work to be done, the job to which every man contributed something vital and personal, with a view to supplying society with goods and services adequate to its needs. Human labour, understood in this sense, drew men together in a genuine and intimate union and restored form and structure to a society which had become shapeless and unstable.[11]

A community of work

In a 1956 address to the International Conference on Human Relations in Industry, Pius XII foreshadowed the later idea of John XXIII of the production process as a community of work:

> The working community, which today is established on the basis of employer–employee contracts of large enterprises, constitutes on the employer's part a true commitment toward the employee, for they actually require from the latter the best part of their time and effort. It is not, therefore, simply a question of hiring a workman and buying from him so much labour – it is rather a man, a member of human society who brings his share of cooperation to the good of this same society in his respective industry.[12]

Worker participation

As noted earlier, Pius XII denied the existence of any right subsisting in employees to participate in either the capital of an enterprise or in the management of an enterprise. This denial was based on the right of an individual and of the family to own property, and therefore any right of an employee to participate either in the management and/or ownership of an enterprise would be in conflict with the right of ownership. However, this was not to say that Pius did not believe that worker participation either in the ownership or management of industry or both was not desirable. In fact his view was similar to that of Pius XI in *Quadragesimo Anno*. In an address to Catholic employers on 7 May 1949, Pius XII said that if both employers and workers had a common interest in the healthy prosperity of the national economy, why should it not be legitimate to give to the workers a just share of responsibility in the organization and development of that economy.[13]

In an indirect way Pius XII argues in favour of systems of production in which the worker is encouraged to take an active interest in his task, and which engages the attention of the worker to the extent that he obtains a feeling of putting his personal resources into his work and developing them. The opposite of this is a system in which the nature of the work distorts or degrades the worker's personality to almost vanishing point, with the result that his productive effort is slowed down.

On the other hand, when the worker is able to maintain an active interest in his task a feeling is generated that he is using not only his muscular power but also his very soul, and his labour is recompensed by pride in the work accomplished which grows within him, and a feeling that his work is not merely a means for making a living but something in which he finds a sense of life and a measure of his personal and social being. From the point of view of productivity alone, these factors merited the serious consideration of the managers of industry.[14]

The class struggle

In an address to Austrian Catholics on 13 September 1952 Pius XII spoke about two phases of the social dispute upon which the Church was entering at the time of his writing. Both of these questions are still very much in issue today. The first is the overcoming of the class struggle through an organic coordination of employer and employee, for class struggle can never be a goal of Catholic social ethics. He said that the Church was always aware of its duties toward all classes and layers of the people.

The second issue with which the Church is concerned is the protection of the individual and family against the vortex which threatens to draw them into an all-embracing socialization, at the end of which looms the very real nightmare of 'Leviathan'. He said that the Church would conduct this fight to the utmost because the highest things were at stake: human dignity and the salvation of the soul.[15]

When Pius XII wrote this letter the spectre of communism loomed large. The 'Leviathan' to which he referred was an all-controlling communist state. However, individuals and families are under no less a threat today from the all-embracing dictates of unfettered corporate capitalism and the control being exercised over the lives of ordinary men and women by that soulless entity which modern economic parlance calls 'the free market'.

In the same address Pius was mindful of the considerable advancement which had been made in the conditions of the proletariat and workers generally during the sixty years since the promulgation of *Rerum Novarum*. The worker had attained a status and dignity which they had not had previously and had been endowed with clearly defined rights, and the Catholic world had honestly and effectively contributed to these advances.

Capitalism
Like Pius XI, he was critical of many aspects of the capitalist system. In an address to women on 21 October 1945, he spoke of some of the economic and social effects that issued from the capitalist system. He said that some of the results had been: excessive concentration of population in cities, the constant all-absorbing increase of big industries, the difficult and precarious state of others, notably those of artisans and agricultural workers, and the disturbing increase of unemployment.[16]

Taking up Pius's theme in a pastoral letter published on 8 September 1949, the French cardinals said that by condemning the actions of communist parties, the Church does not support capitalist regimes.

> It is most necessary that it be realised that in the very essence of capitalism – that is to say, in the absolute value that it gives to property without reference to the common good or to the dignity of labour – there is a materialism rejected by Christian teaching.[17]

These are strong words from the French cardinals, but they are a clear and concise statement of the Church's consistent teaching on the liberal capitalist system. In his encyclical *Optatissima Pax,* promulgated on 18 December 1947, in which the Pope dealt primarily with the policies associated with post-war reconstruction, he further illustrated his distrust of the capitalist system when he said that there was no lack of those who, sad to say, embittered and exploited the working man in his distress following a secret and astute plan and thereby obstructing the efforts of the forces of justice and order which were seeking to rebuild scattered fortunes.[18]

Wages
Pius XII makes his first reference to the issue of the workers' wages in his letter to Italian workers of 13 June 1943. His address reiterates *Rerum Novarum* and *Quadragesimo Anno* in its advocacy of a family wage. Recalling the teaching of his predecessors he said that he himself had not lost any opportunity of making all men understand by his repeated instructions the personal and family needs of the workers, proclaiming as fundamental prerequisites of social concord those claims which

the workers had so much at heart: a salary which would cover the living expenses of a family and would make it possible for the parents to fulfil their natural duty to rear healthy, nourished and clothed children; a dwelling worthy of a human person; the possibility of securing for children sufficient instruction and a becoming education; of foreseeing and forestalling times of stress, sickness and old age.[19]

Six years later on 20 September 1949, in an address to the International Union of Family Organizations, Pius XII said that the popes in their social messages had strongly favoured the family or social wage which gave the family the power to rear children in proportion to their increasing number. Naturally, he said, it was fitting to note that more attention was needed for large families: reduction of taxes, the granting of subsidies and allowances considered not as pure gifts but as a modest grant for the most valuable service rendered by the family, and especially the large family.[20]

In extending support to Pius XI in his advocacy of some form of family allowances which increase according to the number of children in the family, Pius XII does not suggest that these payments be part of the wages structure, although this is suggested by Pius XI in *Quadragesimo Anno*.[21] The linking of family allowances to wages does not appear in any subsequent social encyclicals. However, it is clear that there is papal endorsement from both Pius XI and Pius XII of the principle of family allowances.

Pius XII makes what is probably the last reference to wages of his pontificate, in a broadcast to thousands of Spanish workers, assembled in Madrid and other centres, on 11 March 1951. Speaking of the need for greater diffusion of property, he said that there were many factors which contributed to this, but the principal one would always be the payment of a just wage. A just wage, and the better distribution of natural wealth, constituted two of the most impelling demands of the Church's social programme.

Replying to those arguing that the Church does not know how to help men in their earthly life, Pius XII said that as far as solving the social question was concerned, nobody has offered a programme better than that contained in the teaching of the Church. It was safe, strong and practical, and has not been bettered.[22]

The worker and property

Like Pius XI and Leo XIII, Pius XII thought that private property should be made available to as many as possible and was a right existing in all persons as a natural foundation of life, and as a right to the use of the goods of the earth. Here again, the doctrine of the 'stewardship' of the world's goods as taught by the Church Fathers is evident. Pius XII further believed that the state has an important role to play in ensuring a just allocation of the world's goods:

> But if legislation is to play its part in the pacification of the community, it must prevent the worker, who is or will be the father of a family, from being condemned to an economic dependence and slavery which is irreconcilable with his rights as a person.[23]

National episcopal conferences

United States Catholic bishops

During the pontificates of Pius XI and Pius XII various episcopal conferences took up many of the issues expounded upon by the popes and reissued them as pastoral letters pertaining to their peculiar national situations. The American bishops were in the forefront of this development. On 25 April 1933 they published a pastoral letter entitled *Present Crisis* in which they took to task the behaviour of large corporations and their misuse of trusts. The American bishops argued for the application of the principle of subsidiarity and suggested that the rights of smaller units and bodies should be protected and smaller units of business and production encouraged. The law of the state should protect them and the court safeguard them. The bishops further argued that both capital and labour should be convinced that greed was a vice and that a just division of profits can and should be a virtue. Capital and labour, they said, should work for the common welfare and, for their mutual interest, workers should be encouraged to organize in trade unions.[24]

On 7 February 1940 the administrative board and assistant bishops of the National Catholic Welfare Conference of the United States issued a statement on behalf of the American bishops which dealt *inter alia* with workers and their wages. The bishops expressed their support for the suggestion of Pius XI in *Quadragesimo Anno* that a contract between employers and employees would serve both individual worker and social welfare more effectively if it were modified by some form of partnership which would permit the worker a graduated share in the ownership and profits of business and also some voice in its management. The bishops went on to say that the first claim of labour was one which took priority over any claim of the owners to profits, namely the right to a living wage.

The bishops defined the term 'living wage' as one sufficient not only for the worker but also the worker's family. They said that a wage so low that it must be supplemented by the wage of wife and mother or by the children of the family before it could provide adequate food, clothing, and shelter together with essential spiritual and cultural needs could not be regarded as a 'living wage'. They added that the term 'a living wage' meant sufficient income to meet not merely the present necessities of life but those of unemployment, sickness, death and old age as well. In other words, they said, a saving wage constituted an essential part of the definition of a 'living wage'. The bishops added that if a business was prevented by unfair competition from paying a living wage, and if such competition reduced prices to such a level that decent and just wages could not be paid, then those responsible were guilty of wrongdoing and sin grievously against moral principles as well as against the common good. The bishops said that it was a truth that the payment of the 'living wage' constituted a first charge on industry.[25] This reference to a 'living wage' being a first charge on industry marked a new and significant development in the concept of the living wage. In the current neo-liberal capitalist environment, it is a concept being honoured increasingly in its breach than in its observance.

Australian Catholic Bishops Social Justice Statement 1943

In 1943 the Australian Catholic bishops in their annual social justice statement entitled *Pattern for Peace* boldly set forth positive suggestions for the application of social encyclicals and the teachings of Pius XII to the world of industry and labour.

The bishops recommended that industrial policy should be directed to the most widespread distribution of the ownership of the means of production:

1. by means of co-partnership of workers in industrial enterprises
2. by marshalling the inventive resources of the nation to secure the greatest possible reduction in the size of industrial units consistent with efficiency in production.

They said that ownership, which in many instances was in the hands of a few monopolists, should be spread more widely throughout the community. Ownership was the best guarantee of political, economic and social freedom. The bishops said that special measures were called for in the public control of monopolies and the regulation of 'big business' to curb the power derived from immense financial resources.[26]

The Australian bishops developed the concept of solidarism as first mentioned by Pius XI in *Quadragesimo Anno*. They advocated the formation of industrial councils as the instrument for the control and regulation of industry. The industrial council was to be a body constituted by the state and endowed with sufficient legal powers to control all the operations of a particular industry. It was to be representative of workers, employers and other interests connected with the industry. The bishops believed that the industrial council would govern an industry at least as efficiently as the public utility corporation or a government department since it was composed of men with particular knowledge of the problems of the industry. The industrial council would avoid the extension of state bureaucracy and domination, so inimical to the principle of freedom.

Some of the functions envisaged by the bishops for the industrial council were:

1. the determination of wages and industrial conditions throughout the industry
2. to control the prices, wholesale and retail, of the products of industry
3. to control the maximum rates and dividends from year to year
4. to plan the amount and quality of production from year to year
5. to plan the marketing of the product
6. to control, with due regard for the demand and to the interests of all concerned, the number of enterprises operating in the industry
7. to determine conditions for the entry of workers into the industry and to ensure their efficient training
8. to arrange for pensions, insurance schemes and other social benefits within the industry
9. to exercise complete control (in general) over the policy and development of the industry, including, in the case of secondary industry, the supply of raw materials to other enterprises
10. to enable workers to suggest improvements and modifications which would improve productivity and lessen class hostility.

These recommendations, which no doubt were considered radical at the time, were a direct application of the principles laid down in *Quadragesimo Anno* for the recommended formation of 'vocational groups'.[27]

On the question of wage determination the Australian bishops were equally forthright. They advocated the application of a principle of graduated family wage. Under this system the basic wage for a single man or woman would be fixed. The same wage would be paid irrespective of the sex of the worker. As soon as the male worker married he would receive an increase in his wage to the full amount necessary to provide for his wife in addition to himself. On the birth of each child there would be a further increase to fulfil the same purpose.

So that there would not be an incentive for an employer not to employ married men with families, the bishops suggested that the employer himself directly pay the same basic wage to all his employees, married or single. They suggested, however, that employers at the same time contribute to a national equalization fund out of which the various endowments would be paid to married men. These endowments would consist of an increased payment to married men, increasing with the birth of each child. This is in accordance with the suggestion of Pius XI in *Quadragesimo Anno*.[28]

Australian Catholic Bishops Social Justice Statement 1947

The 1947 social justice statement of the Australian Catholic bishops was written by the redoubtable Catholic layman, intellectual and activist, B. A. (Bob) Santamaria and published under the imprimatur of all of the Australian Catholic bishops with the exception of the Archbishop of Brisbane, Dr James Duhig, who was out of Australia at the time the statement was published. Santamaria is credited with having written a number of the social justice statements from the late 1940s to early 1950s. The statement was entitled *Peace in Industry* and was published at a time in Australian history when the trade union movement was a battleground between the Communist Party and the Australian Labour Party industrial groups, logistically supported and assisted by the Catholic Social Studies Movement, of which B. A. Santamaria was the national president, for the control of the Australian trade union movement.

The statement was most significant in the direction which it gave to Australian trade unionists in connection with the use of the strike weapon. It said that under modern conditions, the right to organize in trade unions and the right to strike, under certain defined conditions, were inseparable. It said that it would be futile to urge the formation of trade unions if the Church did not realize that this involved recognition of the right to strike, as a last resort, and when other measures of achieving social justice had failed. The statement laid down four conditions for a just strike, which it said had been commonly accepted by theologians. These were:

1. The cause of a threatened strike must itself be just and rightful.
2. There must be sufficient hope of success. It was morally wrong to plunge workers into a strike in which they have no hope of success and from which they will emerge in a worse condition than before. Nevertheless, it did not always follow that because a strike was lost it was in vain.
3. The benefit to be gained must not be out of proportion to harm inflicted. In the case of strikes that seriously affect the entire community, the onus thus placed on those who decide to strike is therefore very great.
4. Before a strike is declared, every effort must first be made to settle the dispute peacefully through conciliation, arbitration, and other more peaceful methods.[29]

Australian Catholic Bishops Social Justice Statement 1948

In 1948 the social justice statement of Australian Catholic bishops, also written by B. A. Santamaria and published under the imprimatur of all the bishops, was entitled *Socialisation.* In the preamble to the statement, the bishops defined the term 'socialisation' in the heading of the statement to mean 'the state ownership of public utilities such as railways, electricity supply or the state ownership and control of basic industries and monopolies which could not be safely left in private hands'. In a reference to the origins of class warfare, the social justice statement says that it was precisely because the community had failed to establish a social order in which the ownership of productive property was so widespread as to set the tone of society, that the nation was riven by the great spasms of class warfare. The bishops said that the supreme pontiffs had never failed to point out that a community cannot be stable if in effect it was divided into two classes – the tiny few who controlled the vast bulk of the means of production, and the very many who owned nothing.

The bishops went on to state that the attitude of the Church to philosophies such as communism, which elevated class warfare to a principle of action, had been made abundantly clear. The Church, however, did not restrict its condemnation to the agents of revolution. At the same time she condemned in equal measure the social system of monopoly capitalism which had denied property to the masses and thus created the division of classes on which all class warfare was based.[30]

The bishops' statement dealt with a number of other matters pertaining to economic policy and monopolies but is perhaps best remembered for its support for the nationalization of certain key industries in certain circumstances. The Church recognized that, under present conditions, there were certain forms of enterprise and industry which were of quite extraordinary importance to the community, and which may legitimately come under public control in one form or another, although not necessarily by means of nationalization.

The bishops went on to say that some of these enterprises included banking; insurance; the manufacture of steel and heavy chemicals; rail, sea and air transport; public utility services (electricity, gas, tramways); and armaments. The bishops acknowledged that some of these concerns were no doubt efficiently conducted, but the question of efficiency was of secondary importance only. These, they said, were industries which, if they remained in the hands of uncontrolled private bodies, conferred upon those bodies the 'dominating power' referred to by Pius XI in *Quadragesimo Anno* as a power so great that it could not, without danger to the general welfare, be entrusted to private individuals.[31] The bishops said that it was beyond doubt that the companies which operated in these fields, few in number and extensive in power, were often in a position to dominate their customers, their suppliers, their employees, their potential competitors, and, at times, even the public authorities.

The bishops were careful to confine their recommendation to only certain circumstances. They said that where the meaning given to the word 'socialization' was simply that the state had the right to place under public control those industries which were too vital to the common good to be left safely in private hands, in that sense socialization was not opposed to Christian teaching. They added that the nationalization of any particular industry within this particular and restricted group was not opposed to Christian teaching, so long as it was not intended as one step on the road to total socialism. A key test for the citizens to apply in determining whether or not nationalization of a particular enterprise was justified, was for them to endeavour to discover whether the overall result of a government's policy had been to extend the ownership of productive property or to restrict it. In the former case, nationalization of a particular industry was far less suspect than in the latter. The nationalization of industries in which numerous small firms operated, or which was capable of being run by small units, was not legitimate.[32] These caveats and restrictions are in accordance with the principle of subsidiarity.

In language which is reminiscent of Belloc and Chesterton, the bishops said that the normal economic order – that order which is best adapted to the real meaning of mankind – is one in which the majority of men are working proprietors; that is to say, where they earn a living for themselves and their families by working their own property, whether that property is a farm, a shop, a workshop or a factory. They said that this was the best economic order precisely because the institution of the family is strongest where this system prevailed.[33]

Hierarchy of Quebec

In a pastoral letter in February 1950, the bishops of Quebec spoke of an obligation for workers to exercise their right to join unions. This was perhaps the first time the joining of trade unions was referred to as an obligation. The bishops said that present circumstances rendered more pressing and more imperative the obligation for workers to exercize this right to join unions. They said that every man had an obligation to seek to protect the security of his professional (economic) interests. He had the duty to seek to obtain for himself and his family all that was necessary in order to live a truly human life and to safeguard them against future hazards. He had the duty to contribute to the welfare of his fellows, especially those united to him in common interests. They said that he had the duty to collaborate in restoring a social order which would be more balanced in favouring respect for justice in all the activities of labour, industry and commerce. The isolated worker, they said, could not do this. The worker, by union with his fellow workers, could fulfil this important social duty. In the present state of things, accordingly, there existed a moral obligation to participate actively in one's economic organization.[34]

The Quebec bishops have here expressed one of the pivotal exhortations of Catholic action: for all Christians to be active and to participate in the trade union, professional calling, trade association, industrial or commercial organization or political party to which they belong.

Statement of bishops of Ohio

On 25 March 1958 the bishops of the State of Ohio issued a statement in which they said in effect that compulsory unionism was necessary and desirable in certain cases. They said that for reasons of social justice it may be desirable and often advantageous to the common good that a man's right be restricted by certain specified conditions. One of the imposed conditions may require that he belong to a labour union or at least be obliged to join a union subsequently, so as to share responsibility with his fellow workmen in support of the union. They said that a worker has a right and duty to work for his livelihood. This right cannot be circumscribed to the extent that a man loses his liberty of choice of a vocation, nor to the extent that he is deprived of an opportunity to support himself and his family. It does not follow, however, that a man has the unconditional right to work in any and every industry or business at will.[35]

The bishops were in effect saying that whereas the right to work was a general right and could not be denied to men in the aggregate, the right to work in a specific industrial plant or business could be subject to special conditions, such as the requirement that they be a member of a labour union. Compulsory unionism became the norm in western industrialized nations from the late 1950s onwards. However, beginning in the mid–1980s due to the pressure upon governments from corporate interests, compulsory unionism gradually faded as the strength of unions vis-à-vis corporate capitalism was weakened.

Notes

1 'Pius XII, Address to Austrian Catholics, September 14, 1952', in Cronin, *Social Principles and Economic Life*, p. 147.
2 *Quadragesimo Anno*, p. 36.
3 Pius XI, *Sertum Laetitiae*, Encyclical letter to the United States Bishops, 1 November 1939, in Rankin, *The Pope Speaks*, p. 260.
4 Pius XII Christmas Broadcast 1942, in Cronin, *Social Principles & Economic Life*, p. 46.
5 Pius XII Christmas Message 1942, in *A World to Reconstruct*, Gonella, Guido, p. 316.
6 Pius XII Christmas Message December 1942, in *Justice in the Marketplace*, ed. Byers, p. 103.
7 Letter to Italian Workers in Pollock, pp. 34, 35.
8 Pius XII Christmas Broadcast 1942, in Cronin, *Social Principles and Economic Life*, p.163.

9 Pius XII Christmas Message 1955 in ibid.
10 Pollock, p. 75.
11 Cronin, *Social Principles and Economic Life*, p. 127.
12 Calvez, *Social Thought of John XXIII*, p. 108.
13 Cronin, *Social Principles and Economic Life*, p. 124.
14 Ibid. p. 164.
15 Ibid. p. 8.
16 Ibid. p. 86.
17 Ibid. p. 87.
18 *Optatissima Pax*.
19 Cronin, *Social Principles and Economic Life*, p. 218.
20 Ibid. p. 197.
21 *Quadragesimo Anno*, p. 36.
22 Maurice Quinlan (ed.), *Guide for Living – selected addresses and letters of His Holiness Pope Pius XII,* Pan Books Ltd, London, 1959, p. 178.
23 Cronin, *Social Principles and Economic Life*, p. 249.
24 Byers, p. 414.
25 Ibid. p. 435.
26 Hogan, p. 44.
27 *Quadragesimo Anno*, pp. 42, 43, 44.
28 Ibid. p. 36.
29 Hogan, pp. 87, 88.
30 Ibid, p. 102.
31 *Quadragesimo Anno*, p. 55.
32 Ibid. p. 111.
33 Hogan, p. 101.
34 Cronin, p. 167.
35 Ibid. p. 168.

Chapter 10

MATER ET MAGISTRA

Background

Angelo Giuseppe Roncalli became pope on 28 October 1958 following the death of Pius XII earlier that month. He adopted the name John XXIII. He was consecrated bishop in March 1924 and appointed Apostolic Delegate to Bulgaria in April 1925 and later to Turkey and Greece. In 1944 he was appointed apostolic nuncio to France and was made a cardinal on 15 January 1952 by Pius XII. Soon after, he was appointed Patriarch of Venice, a position which he held until his election to the papacy.

As apostolic nuncio to France he had initially shown some sympathy for the worker-priest movement but later found that the form taken by this movement did not fit in with his own predilections, which lay in the direction of a regular and disciplined personal life, based on the practice of piety and following the liturgy of the Church and of a continual manifestation of the supernatural.[1]

Mater et Magistra

Mater et Magistra was promulgated on 15 May 1961 to commemorate the seventieth anniversary of *Rerum Novarum*. John XXIII had requested Mgr Pietro Pavan, who had served as professor of social economy at the Lateran University in Rome, to assist him in the drafting of the encyclical. Vivienne Boland says that Pietro Pavan is credited with a large share in the drafting of John's encyclical, but the Pope himself is said to have pondered long and earnestly over it. Its style and approach is, according to her, undoubtedly his own and the beliefs it expressed were also his.[2] The extraordinary changes which had occurred in the world since the end of the Second

World War provided the immediate social, economic and political context of *Mater et Magistra*. Krier Mich believes that the Pope was also influenced by the conclusions of the 47th Congress of the Semaines Sociales de France, which met in Grenoble in July 1960 to discuss the theme 'Socialization and the Human Person'. He believes that the encyclical was also influenced by the works of Pesch, Nell-breuning and Gundlach.[3]

The methodology of *Mater et Magistra* is in keeping with that of the previous social encyclicals *Rerum Novarum* and *Quadragesimo Anno* in that it is based on natural law. According to Curran, the natural law methodology allows one to address all human beings because the arguments proposed are not primarily based on uniquely Christian sources.[4]

John XXIII continued to use the same methodology in proclaiming a social message which was based on the requirements of human nature itself and conforming to the precepts of the Gospel and reason.[5]

Wage justice

In *Mater et Magistra* John XXIII substantially expanded on the social teaching in respect of wages and worker participation. In paragraph 74 of the encyclical he deals with the situation of productive enterprises which finance replacement and plant expansion from their own revenues, yet continue to pay their workers a minimum wage. In this case, he says, workers should be entitled to some share in the enterprise.[6]

In paragraph 77 he takes it further and says, 'It is very desirable that workers gradually acquire some share in the enterprise in which they work by such methods as seem most appropriate.'[7] He then reiterates what Pius XI said in *Quadragesimo Anno,* namely that every effort should be made that, at least in the future, only an equitable share of the fruits of production accumulate in the hands of the wealthy, and a sufficient and ample portion go to the working men.[8] John's reasoning here is based upon that of Pius XI in *Quadragesimo Anno* when he said that it was totally false to ascribe to a single factor of production what is in fact produced by joint activity; and it was completely unjust for one factor to arrogate to itself what is produced, ignoring what has been contributed by other factors.[9] Simple justice would indicate that, as the returns of certain enterprises are the result of joint efforts of capital and labour, workers should be rewarded by an appropriate share in the enterprise. For determining what was a just and moral wage, John XXIII laid down the four basic principal guidelines to be taken into account in the assessment of such a wage.

Firstly, there was the contribution of the individual worker to the economic effort; secondly, the economic state of the enterprises within which they worked; thirdly, the requirements of each community especially as regards to overall employment; and finally, the dictates of the common good of all the people and of the various states associated among themselves, but differing in character and extent. The Pope said that these standards of judgement were binding always and everywhere.[10]

John Cronin provides an interesting example of the circumstances which may arise to define the allocation of shares in an enterprise to its workers. He referred to the situation of West German industry in the decade 1949–1958 following the Second World War. He said that during that time German workers accepted relatively low wages so that capital funds would become available for rebuilding the war-shattered economy. As high as forty per cent of national income was diverted for investment during this period. Consequently, Germany developed one of the best industrial systems in the world. Its new prosperity was the envy of Europe. But the moral issue was bound to arise: what right do stockholders have to the tremendous increase in value of their shares caused by this rapid growth? They did not contribute the additional funds which financed these advances. It was mostly a contribution made by labour, which accepted low wages in order to make this capital available. He says that simple justice would dictate that workers be rewarded by an appropriate ownership share of this enormous new investment.[11]

In *Mater et Magistra* John XXIII directly alludes to the disproportionately high rate of directors' fees in certain corporations vis-à-vis the wages and salaries of ordinary employees.

> In economically developed countries, relatively unimportant services, and services of doubtful value, carry a disproportionately high rate of remuneration, while the diligent and profitable work of whole classes of honest, hard working men gets scant reward. Their rate of pay is quite inadequate. It in no way corresponds to the contribution they make to the good of the community, to the profits of the company for which they work, and to the general national economy.[12]

John XXIII was the first pope to make such a comparison.

In a statement which would be a cause of unease to the economic rationalists of the twenty-first century, the Pope said

Mater et Magistra

that the remuneration for work was not something that could be left to the laws of the market; nor should it be fixed arbitrarily. Wages should be determined in accordance with justice and equity, which meant that they should be paid a wage that allowed them to live a truly human life and to fulfil their family obligations in a worthy manner. John XXIII then refers to the four principles to be used in determining a just wage referred to earlier.[13]

One of these is that of the common good. John XXIII gives a detailed illustration of the meaning of the common good, which is one of the best given in any encyclical. In answering the question 'What are the demands of the common good?' he said that on the national level they included the employment of the greatest number of workers; care lest privileged classes arose, even among the workers; the maintenance of equilibrium between wages and prices; the need to make goods and services accessible to the greatest number; the elimination, or at least the restriction, of inequalities in the various branches of the economy, i.e. between agriculture, industry and services; the creation of a proper balance between economic expansion and the development of social services; the best possible adjustment of the means of production to the progress of science and technology; the need to make the prosperity of a more human way of life available not only to the present generation but to coming generations as well.[14]

John XXIII set yet another new direction in teaching on the social question when he drew attention to what he considered a very important social principle, namely that economic progress must be accompanied by a corresponding social progress, so that all classes of citizens could participate in the increased productivity. He said that the utmost vigilance and effort was needed to ensure that social inequalities, so far from increasing, were reduced to a minimum.[15]

The idea that economic progress must be accompanied by social progress occurs frequently in the encyclical. In Cronin's opinion it represents one of the key principles in John XXIII's social philosophy. Economic progress refers to the physical growth of an economy, its increasing ability to produce goods and services. On the other hand, social progress refers to the equitable and widespread sharing of the fruits of economic growth. In the later sections of the encyclical the term is used in the context of public services. From its frequent use in the encyclical, one can probably assume that it is meant to reinforce the workers' right to a living wage.[16]

Paragraph 73 of the encyclical can also be seen as tacit support for the concept of the provision of social security payments to workers on low incomes so that they are able to participate more fully in society's wealth.

Paragraph 112 of the encyclical has been said to show John XXIII's support for the concept of a productivity wage index. This idea is spoken about with some frequency today although its application is not widespread. In recent decades it had some support in the social democratic parties of the industrialized West, although since the 1980s the concept has been under attack from the advocates of economical rationalism and globalism. The Pope said that in recent years the productive efficiency of many national economies has been increasing rapidly. Justice and fairness therefore demand that, within the limits of the common good, wages too shall increase. This means that workers are able to save more and thus acquire a certain amount of property of their own. In view of this it is strange that the innate character of right which derives its force and validity from the fruitfulness of work should ever be called in question – a right which constitutes so efficacious a means of asserting one's personality and exercising responsibility in every field, and an element of solidity and security for family life and of greater peace and prosperity in the state.[17]

In *Pacem in Terris,* published on 11 April 1963, John XXIII specifically emphasizes that the worker has a right to a wage determined according to criteria of justice – and sufficient, therefore, in proportion to the available resources – to give the worker and his family a standard of living in keeping with the dignity of the human person.[18]

Worker participation

As we saw in the chapter dealing with *Quadragesimo Anno*, Pius XI had approached the subject of worker participation in 1931 and had made certain suggestions involving the sharing of profits with workers and decisions in ownership and management.[19]

In the years immediately following the Second World War there developed in Germany the idea that workers were automatically entitled to participate in the management of economic enterprises. A declaration to this effect, called in German *Katholikentag,* was made in Bochum in 1949. As discussed in the previous chapter, Pius XII felt moved to declare that no such right existed. John A. Coleman believed that Pius XII exhibited a decided coolness towards workers codetermination schemes in industry, but that John XXIII reversed Pius's decision in *Mater et Magistra*.[20] This issue, which mainly involved declarations by a section of the Church in Germany, was called 'the question of codetermination'.

In this writer's view, John XXIII did not directly contradict Pius XII on the question of worker participation in ownership and management, although some Catholic writers such as Calvez are of the opinion that John XXIII dispelled the suspicion that still lurked in some people's minds in connection with the text of Pius XI on what became known as the question of codetermination.[21] However, he made it clear in a number of recommendations that the partnership of capital and labour in economic enterprise was desirable.

In paragraphs 91 and 92 of the encyclical the Pope referred to the company as a true community of persons concerned about the needs, activities and standing of each of its members. He said this demanded that the relations between management and employees reflect understanding, appreciation and goodwill on both sides. It demanded too, that all parties cooperate actively and loyally in the common enterprise, not so much for what they could get out of it for themselves, but as discharging a duty and rendering a service to their fellow men. All this implied that the workers had their say in, and made their own contribution to, the efficient running and development of the enterprise. He said that any firm which was concerned for the human dignity of its workers must also maintain a necessary and efficient unity of direction. The enterprise must not treat those employees who spend their days in service with the firm as though they were mere cogs in the machinery, denying them any opportunity of expressing their wishes or bringing their experience to bear on the work in hand, and keeping them entirely passive in regard to decisions that regulate their activity.[22] The Pope went on to say that the present demand for workers to have a greater share in the conduct of the firm accorded not only with man's nature, but also with recent progress in the economic, social and political spheres.[23]

In a new insight, John XXIII recognized that, due to the driving impulse of scientific and technical advances, productive systems were rapidly becoming more modernized and efficient. In view of that, greater technical skills and more exacting professional qualifications were required of the workers. This meant that they must be given more assistance and more free time in which to complete their vocational training, as well as their cultural, moral and religious education. He believed that modern youth was enabled to devote a longer time to basic schooling in the arts and sciences. As a result, an environment was created in which he believed workers were encouraged to assume greater responsibility in their own sphere of employment. He said that in politics, too, it was of no small consequence that citizens were becoming daily more aware of their responsibility for furthering the common good in all spheres of life.[24]

It is significant that in paragraph 91 the Pope referred to the importance of ensuring that the company is indeed a true community of persons, concerned about the needs, the activities and the standing of each of its members. This is a development of the worker participation concept of *Quadragesimo Anno* referred to earlier and *Rerum Novarum's* idea of the partnership between labour and capital.[25] The reference by John XXIII to a community of persons was drawn from Pius XII's expression 'community of work' stated in an address to the International Conference on Human Relations in Industry in 1956. In this address he also gave the name of 'associates' to the various components of a company, again contributing to the idea of a community.[26]

In addition to worker participation in the management of industry, John XXIII expanded this idea to include worker participation in the economic institutions of the state and of public authorities which tackle the various economic problems on a national or international basis. John XXIII took the idea of worker participation to another level when he indicated his support for worker participation in the public authorities and institutions that dealt with economic problems on a national or international scale. He said that it was not the decisions made within the individual productive units which had the greatest bearing on the economy, but those made by public authorities and institutions which tackled the various economic problems on a national or international basis. He said that it was therefore high time that these public authorities and institutions brought into their discussions the workers and those who represented the rights, demands and aspirations of the working classes, and did not confine their deliberations to those who merely represented the interests of management.[27]

John XXIII's reference to a 'community of work' is reminiscent of Jacques Maritain writing in the 1950s, who said that the idea of a planned economy should be replaced by a new idea based on the progressive adjustment due to the activity and the reciprocal tension of autonomous agencies which, from the bottom up, would bring producers and consumers together, in which case it would be better to say an 'adjusted' rather than a 'planned' economy. Likewise, he said, the notion of collectivization should be replaced by that of associative ownership of the means of production, or of joint ownership of the enterprise substituting, as far as possible, joint ownership for the wage system.[28]

The International Labour Organization

John XXIII spoke in glowing terms of the work of the International Labour Organization (ILO). He said that for many years it had been making an effective and valued contribution to the establishment in the world of an economic and social order marked by justice and humanity, an order which recognized and safeguarded the lawful rights of the working classes.[29]

Cronin thought that the Pope's commendation of the ILO was significant not only as it directed approval for the work of this group, but also contained an implied rebuke to those who had tried to destroy it. Cronin referred to an incident in the late 1950s when there was pressure on the United States government to withdraw from the International Labour Organization because communist states participated in its deliberations. The Republican administration elected to remain affiliated to the International Labour Organization.[30]

Trade unions

John XXIII felt no need to deal at length with the role of trade unions. His support for the trade unions and collective bargaining is implicit in much of what *Mater et Magistra* said in connection with wage justice and worker participation. For instance, when he spoke of worker representation in the public authorities and institutions dealing with economic problems, he spoke of representation of the workers by those who represented them. Likewise, he referred to workers' associations and their general recognition in the judicial codes of states and nations, saying that they no longer recruit members in order to agitate, but to cooperate principally in the method of collective bargaining.[31]

Worker cooperatives

John XXIII was the first pope to give unequivocal support to the idea of cooperative enterprises. Pius XII had referred to the benefit of establishing what he called 'cooperative unions' in small and medium agricultural holdings, in the arts and trades, and in commerce and industry, but these were not worker cooperatives as we generally know them and were mainly for acquiring of purchasing and selling power.[32] In *Mater et Magistra* John referred to cooperatives in two contexts, firstly in relation to artisans and cooperative enterprises, and secondly pertaining to all farmers and rural workers.

> Hence the craftsman's business and that of the family farm, as well as the cooperative enterprise, which aims at the completion and perfection of both these concerns – all these are to be safeguarded and encouraged in the name of the common good and technical progress.[33]

Speaking of artisan and cooperative enterprises, he said:

> First of all it is necessary to emphasise that if these two kinds of undertaking are to thrive and prosper, they must be prepared constantly to adjust their productive equipment and their productive methods to meet new situations created by the advance of science and technology and the changing demands and preferences of the consumer. This adaptation must be effected principally by the workers themselves and the members of the cooperatives. Both these groups therefore, need a thorough going, technical and general education, and they must be organised professionally. In addition, the government must take the proper steps regarding their training, taxation, credit and social security.[34]

In praise of the spirit of cooperatives throughout the world, he said that by the force of their example they were helping to keep alive in their own community a true sense of responsibility, a spirit of cooperation, and the constant desire to create new and original work of outstanding merit. Both craftsmen and cooperatives were fully entitled to the protective surveillance of the state, as they were upholding true human values and contributing to the advance of civilization.[35]

John XXIII's support for the cooperative movement is significant. Worker cooperatives exist in various parts of the world in diverse industries. Perhaps the most well-known example of the worker cooperatives in operation are those operating in the Basque country of Spain in the district of Mondragon. This worker cooperative is engaged in the fields of manufacturing, education, health, transport, banking and other related activities. It has been a highly successful example of one of the alternatives to existing industry structure based on the capital-labour relationship. The operation and structure of the Mondragon cooperative is discussed more fully in a later chapter.

Baum makes the point in respect of worker cooperatives that the ethical foundation for them is pluralistic. He says that the values implicit in cooperativism are affirmed and defended by people coming from various ethical traditions. Cooperativism is counter-cultural. It is at odds with the individualism and utilitarianism characteristic of contemporary capitalist society. The people who do endorse cooperative social values appear to do so, according to Baum, on explicitly Christian grounds on the basis of a less-specific religious humanism, or on the basis of a secular humanism, classical or radical, that recognizes – beyond empiricism – the solidity and unity of the human family and the social responsibility of people for one another. Baum says that these values have actually been communicated more effectively when people act together rather than simply talk about them.[36]

State intervention
John XXIII believed that the present advances in scientific knowledge and productive technology made it more than ever possible for the public authority to reduce imbalances which existed between different branches of the economy, or between nations, or between different regions within the same political community. It also put into the hands of public authority a greater means for controlling fluctuations in the economy and effectively preventing the recurrence of mass unemployment. He said that since those in authority were responsible for the common good, there was a need for them to increase the degree and scope of their activity in the economic sphere and to devise ways and means of setting the necessary machinery in motion for the attainment of that end.[37] This injunction on government is, perhaps, derived from John XXIII's view in *Mater et Magistra* that the economic prosperity of the nation was not so much its total assets in terms of wealth and property, as the equitable division and distribution of this wealth. This, he believed, was what guaranteed the personal development of the members of society, which was the true goal of a nation's economy.[38]

In *Mater et Magistra* John XXIII said that the whole *raison d'être* for the state was the realization of the common good in the temporal order. Accordingly, it could not hold aloof from economic matters. He said it was the duty of the state to protect the rights of the whole citizen body, and particularly of its weaker members: the workers, women and children. It could never be right for the state to shirk its obligation of working actively for the betterment of the condition of the working classes.[39] It is clear that John XXIII was a firm advocate of state intervention in the economic affairs of the state in pursuance of the common good. In this he echoed the sentiments of Leo XIII in *Rerum Novarum* and of Pius XI in *Quadragesimo Anno*.

In *Pacem in Terris* John XXIII placed a duty on the state to ensure that workers who wish to work are able to find employment in keeping with their aptitudes, and that they receive a wage in keeping with the laws of justice and equity. On the question of codetermination he said that civil authorities should ensure that workers retain their proper responsibility in the work undertaken in industrial organization.[40]

Summary

Mater et Magistra was published a year before the opening of the Second Vatican Council and may well have been intended as a preface to it. DeBerri and Hug are of the opinion that the encyclical was written in response to severe imbalances between the rich and poor existing in the world, and that John XXIII internationalized Catholic social teaching by treating, for the first time, the situation of countries which were not fully industrialized. A subject not covered in this work is the important role of the laity, a matter discussed in the later part of the encyclical.[41]

Of considerable importance to working men and women is the encyclical's development of the concept of worker participation in the management of enterprises, and the concept of worker shareholding in the profits of industry as one of the contributors to building up of the fruits of production. Following the publication of *Mater et Magistra* the idea of a productivity wage index assumed greater prominence in the thinking of both Catholic and secular trade unionists.

Notes
1 Algisi, p. 206.
2 Dwyer, p. 579.
3 Krier Mich, p. 93.
4 Curran, p. 27.

5 *Mater et Magistra*, p. 7.
6 *Mater et Magistra*, p. 24.
7 Ibid. pp. 24, 25.
8 *Quadragesimo Anno*, p. 33.
9 Ibid. p. 28.
10 *Mater et Magistra*, paras 71, 72, p. 23.
11 Cronin, *Christianity and Social Progress*, p. 47.
12 *Mater et Magistra*, para. 70, p. 23.
13 Ibid., para. 71, p. 23.
14 Ibid., para. 79, p. 25.
15 Ibid., para. 73, pp. 23, 24.
16 Cronin, *Christianity & Social Progress,* pp. 45, 46.
17 Ibid., para. 112, p. 32.
18 *Pacem in Terris*, para. 20, p. 11.
19 *Quadragesimo Anno*, p. 34.
20 Boswell, McHugh and Verstraeten (eds.), *Catholic Social Thought, Twilight or Renaissance?* Article by John A. Coleman, p. 269.
21 Calvez, p. 40.
22 *Mater et Magistra*, paras 91 and 92, pp. 27, 28.
23 Ibid., para. 93, p. 28.
24 Ibid., paras 94, 95, 96, p. 28.
25 *Rerum Novarum*, p. 18.
26 Calvez, p.108.
27 *Mater et Magistra*, para. 99, p. 29.
28 Evans and Ward, p. 43.
29 Ibid., para. 103, p. 30.
30 Cronin, *Christianity & Social* Progress, p. 63.
31 *Mater et Magistra*, paras 97, 99, p. 29.
32 Cronin, p. 249.
33 Ibid., para. 85, p. 26.
34 Ibid., para. 87, pp. 26, 27.
35 Ibid., paras 89, 90, p. 27.
36 Baum, p. 242.
37 Ibid., para. 54, p. 19.
38 Ibid, para. 74, p. 24.
39 Ibid., para. 20, p. 11.
40 Ibid., para. 64, p. 21.
41 Deberri and Hug, p. 54.

Chapter 11

GAUDIUM ET SPES

Background

Gaudium et Spes, formally entitled the 'Pastoral Constitution on the Church in the Modern World', was promulgated on 7 December 1965, the last working day of the Second Vatican Council.

The Second Vatican Council had been called by Pope John XXIII and had deliberated during the years 1962–65. One of the thrusts of *Gaudium et Spes* was that Christian laity build up Christ's world in history: with faith that incarnates God in the temporal, hope that is not limited to the last things, and a charity that has no bounds. This would be God's kingdom in the world, not yet in its final and manifest stage. Riccardo Lombardi suggests that it was a call for a Church which was not static, isolated and possessed of mainly individualistic passive virtues to be one which continually roused everyone, including herself, and together with the sincere and good willed, tended towards bringing about an anticipation of the kingdom of eternity here on earth – knowing only too well that it will never be perfect in time.[1]

Paragraph 43 of the document signposts the thrust of *Gaudium et Spes*. It says:

> The Christian who shirks his temporal duties shirks his duties towards his neighbour, neglects God himself, and endangers his eternal salvation. Let Christians follow the example of Christ who worked as a craftsman; let them be proud of the opportunity to carry out their earthly activity in such a way as to integrate human, domestic, professional, scientific, and technical enterprises with religious values, under whose supreme direction all things are ordered to the glory of God . . . It is their task to cultivate a properly informed conscience and to impress the divine law on the affairs of the earthly city.[2]

The American Catholic bishops in their pastoral letter of 1987 in reference to *Gaudium et Spes* said that followers of Christ must avoid a tragic separation between faith and everyday life. They could neither shirk their earthly duties nor, as the Second Vatican Council declared, 'Immerse themselves in earthly activities as if these latter were utterly foreign to religion, and religion were nothing more than the fulfilment of acts of worship and the observance of a few moral obligations'.[3] The bishops' pastoral letter said that economic life raised important social and moral questions for each of us and for society as a whole. Like family life, economic life was one of the chief areas where we lived out our faith, loved our neighbour, confronted temptation, fulfilled God's creative design, and achieved our holiness. Our economic activity in factory, field, office, or shop feeds our families – or feeds our anxieties. It exercizes our talents – or wastes them. It raises our hopes – or crushes them. It brings us into cooperation with others – or sets us at odds. The bishops, referring to *Gaudium et Spes* paragraph 43, said that the Vatican Council instructed us 'to preach the message of Christ in such a way that the light of the gospel will shine on all activities of the faithful'.[4]

In *Gaudium et Spes* the Church offers herself as a servant of mankind. The distinctive note sounded in the document is that the Church is in the world to serve the world as did Jesus. Paragraph 3 of *Gaudium et Spes* states that the Church is not motivated by an earthly ambition but is interested in one thing only: to carry on the work of Christ under the guidance of the Holy Spirit, for He came into the world to bear witness to the truth, to save and not to judge, to serve and not to be served.[5]

In Townsend's view what the council committed the Church to appears especially in their declarations that human equality must receive increasing recognition in the social order, and that all forms of discrimination contrary to it must be eradicated. The council enunciated two principles which must govern the social order if it is to be truly human. The first is that whatever their difference of birth, talent and attainment, all men were basically equal by virtue of their natural dignity and supernatural destiny. The second was that whatever in social institutions and practices insults human dignity by treating men as tools rather than responsible persons, was as pernicious to society as poison was to the body. It destroyed life.[6]

Unjust economic structures

Of considerable importance to the rights of workers was the development in *Gaudium et Spes* of the idea that economic and social structures could, by their very nature, be unjust and flawed. Although maintaining the tradition of urging individual conversion, *Gaudium et Spes* recognized that economic life and economic justice were essentially dependent on the social and economic structures within which individuals lived and developed and that no important changes would take place unless these structures themselves were altered and reformed.[7]

Gaudium et Spes holds that certain social structures shape human personalities, so that men were often diverted from doing good and spurred toward evil by the social circumstances in which they lived and were immersed from their birth. Paragraph 25 goes on to say that because the structure of affairs was so often flawed by the consequences of sin, the social order required constant improvement. This implied that because all social structures were subordinate to man and not contrarywise, as Jesus had indicated when he said that the Sabbath was made for man and not man for the Sabbath, a radical structural change may be necessary if the social order was to achieve its purpose of respecting the dignity and rights of all human beings.[8]

This theme is developed later in *Gaudium et Spes* in those paragraphs dealing with the rights of workers to participate in the decision-making of the economic enterprises in which they are employed. This will be elaborated upon later.

The worker

Gaudium et Spes develops the theme of the dignity of work, the dignity of the human person, by relating it to the incarnation. The document says that by His incarnation, the Son of God has in a certain way united Himself with each man. He worked with human hands, He thought with a human mind, He acted with a human will, and with a human heart He loved. Born of the Virgin Mary, he has truly been made one of us, like us in all things except sin.[9]

Gaudium et Spes makes it clear that the social order exists to serve humanity, and not the other way around. It states that the social order and its development must constantly yield to the good of the person, since the order of things must be subordinate to the order of persons and not the other way around, as the Lord suggested when He said that the Sabbath was made for man and not man for the Sabbath.

Again, laying stress on the human person, the council said that everyone should look upon his neighbour (without any exception) as another self.[10] The council held that when men and women provided for themselves and their families through work in such a way as to be of service to the community as well, they could rightly look upon their work as a prolongation of the work of the Creator, a service to their fellow men, and their personal contribution to the fulfilment in history of the divine plan.[11] The council said that human activity proceeds from man: it is also ordered to him. When he works, not only does he transform matter and society, but he fulfils himself. He learns, he develops his faculties, and he emerges from and transcends himself. Rightly understood, this kind of growth is more precious than any kind of wealth that can be amassed.[12]

The council took a strong view that Christians were to give witness to their religious values in their calling as workers in whatever profession. It exhorted Christians to follow the example of Christ who worked as a craftsman, and to be proud of the opportunity to carry out their earthly activity in such a way as to integrate human, domestic, professional, scientific and technical enterprises with religious values, under whose supreme direction all things are ordered to the glory of God.[13]

The primacy of labour

Gaudium et Spes elevates the concept of the dignity of work and the worker to another level. The council said that in the sphere of economics and social life, the dignity and entire vocation of the human person as well as the welfare of society as a whole have to be respected and fostered – for man was the source, the focus and the end of all economic and social life.[14] Then, taking the idea of man as the source and focus of all economic and social life further, the council said that human labour was superior to the other elements of economic life. The latter had only the nature of tools. The council said that through work, the person became a partner in the work of bringing God's creation to perfection, and by offering that work to God, the labourer became associated with the redemptive work of Jesus Christ Himself. Thus, in view of the principle of the priority of labour thereby stated, the entire process of productive work must be adapted to the needs of the worker as a person and to the requirements of his life, particularly his domestic life. In stating that human work surpasses all other elements of economic life, as the latter were only means to an end, the council has firmly established the principle of the primacy of labour over capital.

Wages

Gaudium et Spes, unlike the social encyclicals of Leo XIII, Pius XI, John XXIII and the allocutions of Pius XII, makes no reference to a just wage. Various writers such as Daniel Finn have construed this as arising because of the dissonance between the idea of a just wage and the market system that characterizes the economies of most of the nations of the globe.[15] This writer puts no such construction on the omission. Implicit in *Gaudium et Spes,* particularly in those sections dealing with dignity and rights of the human person, is the right to receive remuneration for work sufficient to meet the needs of the person. Indeed, in a section headed 'The Common Good', the council says that there is a growing awareness of the sublime dignity of the human person, who stands above all things and whose rights and duties are universal and inviolable. He ought, therefore, to have ready access to all that is necessary for living a genuinely human life: for example, food, clothing, housing, the right freely to choose his state of life and set up a family, the right to education, work, to his good name, to respect, and to proper knowledge [*sic*].[16] It is submitted that this presupposes the receipt of a wage sufficient to enable the worker to attain these ends. Elsewhere, the council states that the ultimate and basic purpose of economic production does not consist merely in the increase of goods produced, nor in profit, nor prestige, but is rather directed to the service of man in his totality, taking into account his material needs and the requirements of his intellectual, moral, spiritual and religious life.[17] Here again the payment of a just living wage is presupposed.

In the section dealing with economic and social life the council, referring to *Rerum Novarum* No. 65, said that remuneration for work should guarantee man the opportunity to provide a dignified livelihood for himself and his family on the material, social, cultural and spiritual level corresponding to the role of the productivity of each, to develop economic factors in his employment, and for the common good.[18]

Again, using words reminiscent of John XXIII's reference to the 'community of the enterprise' in *Mater et Magistra,*[19] the council said that since economic activity was for the most part the fruit of the collaboration of many men, it was unjust and inhuman to organize and direct it in such a way that some of the workers were exploited. The council said that it frequently happened that workers were almost enslaved by the work they did. So-called laws of economics were no excuse for this kind of thing.[20]

In all of these passages from *Gaudium et Spes* there is an implied but clear call for wage justice.

Trade unions and strike action

Gaudium et Spes states that the rights of workers to form themselves into associations which truly represented them was among the fundamental rights of the individual. Governing this was the right of workers to play their part in the activities of their trade unions without risk of reprisal. The council went on to say that, thanks to such organized participation by workers in their trade unions together with progressive economic and social education, there will be a growing awareness among all people of their role and responsibility, and, according to the capacity and aptitude of each one, they will feel that they have an active part to play in the whole task of economic and social development and in the achievement of the common good as a whole.[21]

The council was unequivocal in stating that the right to strike was a necessary, although ultimate, means for the defence of workers' rights and the satisfaction of their lawful aspirations. The council said that in the event of economic–social disputes, attempts should be made to arrive at a peaceful settlement. Prior to any strike action sincere discussions should take place between all sides. If a strike did occur, all avenues should be explored as soon as possible to resume negotiations to effect reconciliation.[22]

Working conditions and structures

As mentioned earlier, *Gaudium et Spes* laid stress on respect for the human person, saying that everyone should look upon his neighbour without exception as another self.[23] The council then listed a variety of crimes against the human person, including such things as murder, genocide, abortion, subhuman living conditions, slavery, prostitution and – importantly for this discussion – degrading working conditions where men were treated as mere tools for profit rather than free and responsible persons.[24]

The council, in referring to economic activity, says that it is unjust and inhuman to organize and direct it in such a way that some of the workers are exploited. But, they observed, even today workers are almost enslaved by the work they do.[25] The council was forthright in its condemnation of such practice and said that there were no excuses for it to occur.[26] Is this not a condemnation of unjust economic structures? The council then went on to say that workers should have the opportunity to develop their talents and their personalities in the very exercise of their work. Is the council not saying that where enterprises, by their structure, deny workers the opportunity of so developing their talents and personalities, they are perpetuating unjust work structures? It is this writer's view that this inference can be drawn from the document.

Worker participation and codetermination

Gaudium et Spes established two basic norms as being at the centre of economic activity. The first was the principle that labour is superior to capital, referred to earlier. The second concerned the question of codetermination or worker participation in the decision-making processes of economic enterprises. In *Gaudium et Spes*, the council established beyond doubt that participation by workers was a 'must', not just a recommendation.

The council said that workers should have the opportunity to develop their talents and their personalities in the very exercise of their work.[27] It said, drawing from *Mater et Magistra* Nos. 91–98, that in business enterprises it was persons who associated together – that is, men who were free and autonomous, created in the image of God. Therefore, while taking into account the role of every person concerned – owners, employers, management and employees – and without weakening the necessary executive unity, the active participation of everybody in administration was to be encouraged.[28] The council did not end there. Echoing *Mater et Magistra*, it took the principle of worker participation beyond companies and enterprises into the public institutions who made the decisions governing economic and social conditions and said that workers ought to have a say in the decision-making of these institutions either in person or through their representatives.[29] In many industrialized nations, labour relations are determined by industrial tribunals of various sorts. *Gaudium et Spes* recommends the participation of workers or their representatives as members of these tribunals.

Broadly speaking, *Gaudium et Spes* established the principle of worker participation in three associated but different directions. Firstly, as we have seen, they should participate in the management and administration of the enterprises in which

Gaudium et Spes

they are employed. Secondly, the workers have the right to associate with others in the formation of trade unions and the right to participate in the activities of their unions without risk of reprisal. Through their trade unions, the council believed, they would be able to play an active part in the processes of economic and social development and participate in the achievement of the common good.[30] Thirdly, there is an implied recommendation for the participation of workers through their trade unions in international institutions dealing with matters with which they are concerned. The council said:

> Economic development must remain under man's direction; it is not to be left to the judgement of a few individuals or groups possessing too much economic power, nor of the political community alone, nor of a few strong nations. It is only right that, in matters of general interest, as many people as possible, and, international relations, all nations, should participate actively in decision making.[31]

As we shall see in a later chapter, the norms established by *Gaudium et Spes* in respect of the worker were to be a significant influence on the social encyclicals of John Paul II: *Laborem Exercens* and *Centessimus Annus*.

Manuel Velasquez draws two implications from the principle of the priority of labour over capital: firstly, that a just economic system must ensure that every citizen finds 'opportunities for adequate employment' with 'payment' sufficient for the worker to lead 'life worthily ... (with) his dependants';[32] and secondly, that 'any way of organising and directing' labour that makes the worker a 'slave' or that does not allow workers to 'develop their own abilities and personalities through the work they perform' is likewise wrong and cannot be justified 'by so-called economic laws'.[33]

Summary

Lukas Vischer said that *Gaudium et Spes* provided an almost dithyrambic description of the capabilities and accomplishments of mankind. He said that human progress was no longer grudgingly regarded instead, it was given a spiritual dimension. The work of men and women not only furthers creation; indeed, it perfected it.[34]

Hehir commented that *Gaudium et Spes* has been the fundamental reference point for the universal Church in keeping the balance of an engaged public ministry without compromising the Church's religious origin, nature and destiny. In his opinion, the decisive contribution of Vatican II to the social ministry of the Church was to locate a defence of the person and the protection and promotion of human rights at the centre of the Church's life and work.[35] Certainly from the perspective of the worker, *Gaudium et Spes* substantially expanded the scope of the idea of codetermination, setting it in concrete. It also firmly established the idea that human work is an extension of the work of the Creator, the contribution to the fulfilment in history of the divine plan.[36] The concept of the dignity of work is fortified by the council, which said that through the homage of work offered to God, man is associated with the redemptive work of Jesus Christ, whose labour with his hands at Nazareth greatly enobled the dignity of work. This, they said, was the source of every man's duty to work loyally, as well as his right to work.[37]

In establishing the principle of the priority of labour over capital and suggesting that economic work structures *per se* could be unjust, *Gaudium et Spes* broke new ground for further development in later encyclicals.

Notes
1 Lombardi, p. 91.
2 Flannery, para. 43, pp. 943, 944.
3 Lutz, p. 17.
4 Ibid.
5 *Gaudium et Spes*, para. 3.
6 Townsend, p. 91.
7 Dwyer, p. 188.
8 *Gaudium et Spes*, para. 26.
9 Ibid., para. 22.
10 Ibid., paras 26, 27.
11 Ibid., para. 34.
12 Ibid., para. 35.
13 Ibid., para. 43.
14 Ibid., para. 63.
15 Dwyer, p. 146.
16 *Gaudium et Spes*, para. 26.
17 Ibid., para. 64.
18 Ibid., para. 67.
19 *Mater et Magistra*, para. 91.
20 *Gaudium et Spes*, para. 67.
21 Ibid., para. 68.
22 Ibid.
23 Ibid., para. 27.
24 Ibid.
25 Ibid., para. 67.

26 Ibid.
27 Ibid.
28 Ibid., para. 68.
29 Ibid.
30 Ibid.
31 Ibid, para. 65.
32 Ibid., para. 67.
33 Dwyer, pp. 192, 193; *Gaudium et Spes,* para. 67, quoted in essay by Manuel Velasquez.
34 Lukas Vischer, *The Work of Human Beings as Creatures of God.* Lecture sponsored by The Ecumenical Leadership Foundation, The Second Visser T'hooft Memorial Consultation, June 1995.
35 Hessel, p. 183; essay by J. Bryan Hehir.
36 *Gaudium et Spes*, para. 34.
37 Ibid., para. 67.

Chapter 12

THE SOCIAL ENCYCLICALS OF PAUL VI

Background

John Baptist Montini was ordained to the priesthood on 29 May 1920. He soon joined the Vatican Diplomatic Service and acted as Assistant Secretary of State under Pius XII. On 5 January 1954 he was consecrated Cardinal Archbishop of Milan. John XXIII died on 3 June 1963 during one of the sessions of the Ecumenical Council. In the ensuing conclave, John Baptist Montini was elected pope on 1 July 1963 adopting the name Paul VI.

Populorum Progressio

Populorum Progressio was promulgated on Easter Sunday, 26 March 1967. This encyclical touches upon the subject of workers and work but incidentally, its main thrust being that of social justice generally in the community and internationally. In many ways the encyclical was a response by Paul VI to the appeal with which *Gaudium et Spes* began, with its reference to the joy, hope, the grief and anguish of the men of our time, especially the poor and afflicted, and the expression of the belief that their joy, hope, grief and anguish were also experienced by the followers of Christ.[1]

Work

Paul VI discusses the idea of labour as a participation with the Creator and creation itself. He said that everyone who worked was a creator. As he worked with material which resisted his efforts, man by his work gave an imprint to it, acquiring as he did so perseverance, skill, and a spirit of invention. Further, when work was done in common – and hope, hardship, ambition and joy were shared – it brought together and firmly united the wills, minds and hearts of men with the result that in work's accomplishment, men found themselves to be brothers.[2]

Worker participation

Paul VI then deals with the various contrary effects of work. He speaks of how in some it invites selfishness, in others revolt, in others money, pleasure and power, and in others it contributes to professional awareness and a sense of duty and charity to one's neighbour. Importantly, he writes that when work becomes more scientific and organized, it risks becoming dehumanizing for those who perform it by making them its servants. Work was human only if it remained intelligent and free.[3] Paul reiterates John XXIII's call in *Mater et Magistra* for enterprises to be true communities of persons where workers play an active part in the business of the company for which they work.[4]

Trade unions

In *Populorum Progressio* Paul VI says that the pluralism of professional organizations and trade unions was admissible if liberty was protected and emulation stimulated, provided that the religious orientation of life to its final end and human freedom and dignity were safeguarded. He gave a resounding endorsement to those people active in professional organizations and trade unions, by saying that he paid homage to all those who laboured in them and who gave unselfish service to their brothers.[5]

Octogesima Adveniens

Promulgated to celebrate the eightieth anniversary of *Rerum Novarum*, *Octogesima Adveniens* was promulgated on 14 May 1971. Like *Populorum Progressio* before it, the main thrust of *Octogesima Adveniens* was the application of principles of social justice to political and economic systems both national and international. Direct reference to workers is relatively minor.

Urban proletariat

Paul VI was the first pope to address the new problem created by urbanization, namely the growth of a new class of what may be termed the 'urban proletariat'. The Pope said that urbanization, undoubtedly an irreversible stage in the development of human societies, confronted humankind with difficult problems. He said that humanity is experiencing a new loneliness. This loneliness is not in the face of a hostile nature which it has taken centuries to subdue, but in an anonymous crowd which surrounds and in which mankind feels a stranger. In this disordered growth, new proletariats are born.[6]

Wages
Drawing upon *Gaudium et Spes* Paul VI reiterates that the beginning, the subject and the goal of all social institutions must be the human person. Following from this is the right of every person to work to develop their qualities and personality in the exercise of their calling, and their right to what he termed an 'equitable remuneration'.[7] An equitable remuneration must be sufficient to enable the worker and family to lead a worthy life on the material, social, cultural and spiritual levels.[8]

Trade unions – political strikes
Paul fully acknowledged and appreciated the role of trade union organizations in the economic advancement of society and the realization of the common good. He was, however, the first pope to make direct reference to what came to be known as 'political strikes', and indicated that such strikes were not a valid use of the strike weapon.[9] Political strikes are those in which the aim sought by strike action did not directly pertain to wages or conditions of labour, but to other matters of a purely political nature usually determined by the legislative authorities.

Worker participation
Paul VI reiterates John XXIII's principles of worker participation in the economic life of enterprises in *Mater et Magistra,* but widens the scope of participation to include participation in the social and political spheres.[10] He said that in order to counterbalance increased technocracy, modern forms of democracy must be devised not only making it possible for everyone to become informed and to express themselves, but also by involving them in a shared responsibility. Reiterating John XXIII's comments in *Mater et Magistra*[11] and his own teaching in *Populorum Progressio,*[12] he asserts that participation by all in the management of enterprises and in social and political spheres facilitates the ability of various groups to live together as communities.

Synod of the bishops 1971

Early in *Octogesima Adveniens* Paul VI foreshadowed the forthcoming synod of bishops to be held in Rome later in 1971.[13] The aim of the synod was to examine as Paul VI said, in greater detail the Church's mission in the face of grave issues raised today by the question of justice in the world. One of the documents prepared by the synod was entitled 'Justice in the World'. The synod said that the basic principles whereby the influence of the Gospel has made itself felt in contemporary social life were to be found in the body of teaching set out in a gradual and timely way from the encyclical *Rerum Novarum* to the letter *Octogesima Adveniens*. The synod said that, as never before, the Church had through the Second Vatican Council's constitution, *Gaudium et Spes*, better understood the situation in the modern world in which the Christian works out his salvation by deeds of justice. They said that *Pacem in terris* gave us an authentic charter of human rights. In *Mater et Magistra* international justice begins to take first place; it found more elaborate expression in *Populorum Progressio*, in the form of a true and suitable treatise on the right to development; and in *Octogesima Adveniens* is found a summary of guidelines for political action.[14] This document primarily dealt with the subjects of economic, political and social justice in the national community, and could be described as a summary of the synod's efforts to find practical ways for the implementation, by national hierarchies, of the social teaching of the Church from *Rerum Novarum* to *Octogesima Adveniens*.

Summary

Populorum Progressio and *Octogesima Adveniens* expanded the concept of worker participation as laid down in *Quadragesimo Anno* and *Mater et Magistra* to include the desirability of participation by all in the economic and political decision-making of society. *Octogesima Adveniens* expands *Mater et Magistra's* concept of community in economic enterprises brought about by worker participation, to include expanded communities created by participation by all in the social and political spheres in which they were engaged.[15] For the first time a clear reference is made to the illicit nature of strike action for purely political purposes,[16] and reference is made to the problems of modern urbanization with the development of a new underclass of urban proletariat residing both on the fringes of the cities and in the city centres.[17]

Notes
1 *Gaudium et Spes*, para. 1.
2 *Populorum Progressio*, para. 27, p. 18.
3 Ibid., para. 28.
4 *Mater et Magistra*, para. 91.
  Populorum Progressio, para. 28.
5 Ibid., para. 39.
6 *Octogesima Adveniens*, para. 10, p. 15.
7 Ibid., para. 14.
8 *Gaudium et Spes*, para. 67.
9 *Octogesima Adveniens*, para. 14.
10 Ibid., para. 47.
11 *Mater et Magistra*, para. 91.
12 *Populorum Progressio*, para. 28.
13 *Octogesima Adveniens*, para. 6.
14 Justice in the World, p. 12.
15 *Octogesima Adveniens*, para. 47.
16 Ibid., para. 14.
17 Ibid., para. 10.

Chapter 13

JOHN PAUL II

Background

If Leo XIII has been given the title 'The Workers' Pope', John Paul II may aptly be called 'The Worker Pope'. Baptized Karol Wojtyla, John Paul II was ordained priest on 1 November 1946. Before entering the seminary Karol Wojtyla had worked as a labourer in a limestone quarry for four years and for several years in a chemical factory. His worker background endeared him to Pope Paul VI, with whom he had a long and special relationship.[1] In 1956 he was appointed chairman of ethics at Lublin University, and in July 1958 was appointed Auxiliary Archbishop of Krakow. He was later appointed Archbishop of Krakow by Pope Paul VI during the third session of the Vatican Council. In the late 1950s he spent several years in France, and during this time came into contact with the worker-priest movement. Although the worker-priest movement had been banned by John XXIII in the late 1950s, Wojtyla had warm words for it and possessed a certain admiration for their work in the deChristianized milieux of the French working class. Szulc said that Wojtyla's contact with the worker-priest movement was a major turning point in his life.[2]

In the immediate preconciliar years Wojtyla was invited to contribute to the council agenda by the Papal Ante-Preparatory Commission. During the council he served on the central subcommission of the council, which dealt with the drawing of the *Gaudium et Spes* document.

Paul VI died on 6 August 1978, and on 16 October 1978 in the ensuing conclave Karol Wojtyla was elected pope, adopting the name John Paul II.[3]

John Paul II's interest in the 'worker question' was in evidence as far back as 1947 when he was on holidays from his doctoral studies, and during that time, went to Belgium where he fulfilled the role of a pastor to the miners. About the same time he went to Marseilles, Paris and Brussels, and met clergy involved with the worker-priest experiment.[4] His concern for the worker is evidenced in much of his poetry and drama. Examples of this are the play *Our God's Brother* and the poem 'The Quarry'.[5] In his preconciliar works *Love and Responsibility*, *Sign of Contradiction,* and *The Acting Person*, Wojtyla exhibits thoughts and ideas which would later appear in more detailed form in the encyclical *Laborem Exercens.* For example, in *Love and Responsibility* Wojtyla asks whether it is proper that a person may be used as a means to an end. His answer is that a person must not be merely the means to an end for another person. This, he says, is precluded by the very nature of personhood, for a person is a thinking subject and capable of making decisions. This insistence upon the impermissibility of stifling man's use of his unique faculties as a person and subject within the context of employer–worker relations reappears, as we shall see, in *Laborem Exercens.*

In *Sign of Contradiction* Wojtyla underlines the efforts of philosophical and everyday materialism to turn matter into an absolute. This, he says, is a major contemporary problem. He then links materialistic attitudes with disdain for the spiritual. He says that these attitudes lie at the root of all the ruthless exploitation of men by other men, including exploitation in industrial production and the division of society into warring classes.[6]

In *Laborem Exercens* John Paul II discusses these problems under the heading 'Materialistic Economism'. In his work *The Acting Person*, Wojtyla says that it is not only man's nature that forces him to exist and act together with others, but his existing and acting together with other men enables him to achieve his own development – that is, the intrinsic development of the person. This is why every human being must have the right to act, which means 'freedom in the action', so that the person can fulfil himself in performing the action.[7] He then describes 'participation' as that property of a person which enables him to exist and act 'together with others' and thus to reach his own fulfilment. Wojtyla then says that participation as a property of the person is a constitutive factor of any human community.[8] These concepts, as we shall see later, are contained and developed in paragraphs 12 to 15 of *Laborem Exercens*.

It is of interest that John Paul II's great encyclical *Work and the Worker*, more commonly known as *Laborem Exercens,* was promulgated in 1981, the year following the formation of the Solidarity labour movement in Poland. Edward Mechmann comments that it should not be a surprise that Pope John Paul II, former Archbishop of Krakow and a major supporter of Solidarity, had been an indefatigable defender and promoter of the interests of workers, and his encyclical *Laborem Exercens* was just such an example.[9] John Paul II died on 2 April 2005 and was succeeded in the ensuing conclave on 19 April 2005 by Josef Cardinal Ratzinger, the Prefect of the Sacred Congregation for the Doctrine of the Faith, who assumed the name of Benedict XVI.

Laborem Exercens

Laborem Exercens was promulgated on the 15 September 1981. It was originally intended to have been promulgated on the 15 May to mark the ninetieth anniversary of *Rerum Novarum*. This, however, was delayed by the assassination attempt of the 13 May. Perhaps coincidentally, its promulgation coincided with the rise of the Solidarity labour movement in Poland, the first national congress of which was held in Gdansk from 5 September to 7 October and, significantly, was the first free trade union assembly in the Soviet Bloc. The encyclical is broad and far-reaching. It contains a comprehensive theology of work, a comprehensive statement of the rights of labour and an analysis of the antinomy between labour and capital. The sections dealing with the theology of work are touched upon but briefly as they are beyond the ambit of this book. It is dealt with first as the relevant sections of the encyclical are discussed in generally the same sequence in which they appeared in the encyclical itself.

Theology of work

John Paul II explained that in the very first pages of the book of Genesis was found the source of the Church's conviction that work was a fundamental dimension of human existence on earth. He said that even though the words of Genesis 'be fruitful and multiply and fill the earth and subdue it',[10] did not refer directly and explicitly to work, beyond any doubt they indirectly indicated it as an activity for man to carry out in the world. Man was shown as the image of God, partly through the mandate received from his Creator to subdue and dominate the earth. In carrying out this mandate, man – every human being – reflected the very action of the Creator of the universe.[11]

John Paul II linked the words 'subdue the earth' with today's technology and machinery. He said that if the biblical words 'subdue the earth' addressed to man from the very beginning were understood in the context of the whole modern age, industrial and post-industrial, then they undoubtedly included also a relationship with technology, with the world of machinery which is the fruit of the work of the human intellect and a historical confirmation of man's dominion over nature. Accordingly, according to Himes, in Catholic social thought the focus remains on the human experience of work, even as the kind and manner of work changed. This permits the tradition to use human dignity as the baseline for examining the world of work even as that world undergoes many developments.[12]

Coexisting with this application of the words 'subdue the earth' in the objective sense is the application of these words in the subjective sense of man as the subject of work. John Paul said that, understood as a process whereby man and the human race subdued the earth, work corresponded to this basic biblical concept only when throughout the process man manifests himself and confirms himself as the one who 'dominates'. In fact, there was no doubt that human work had an ethical value of its own which clearly and directly remained linked to the fact that the one who carried it out was a person, a conscious and free subject – that is to say, a subject that decided about himself. The Pope said that this truth constituted the fundamental and perennial heart of Christian teaching on human work and had, and continued to have, primary significance for the formulation of the important social problems characterizing whole ages.[13]

He referred to the Second Vatican Council, which said:

> Throughout the course of the centuries, men have laboured to better the circumstances of their lives through a monumental amount of individual and collective effort. To believers, this point is settled: considered in itself, such human activity accords with God's will. For man, created to God's image, received a mandate to subject to himself the earth and all that it contains, and to govern the world with justice and holiness: a mandate to relate himself and the totality of things to him who was to be acknowledged as the Lord and Creator of all.[14]

Adding to this, he said that the word of God's revelation was profoundly marked by the fundamental truth that man, created in the image of God, shared by his work in the activity of the Creator and that, within the limits of his own human capabilities, man in a sense continued to develop that activity, and perfected it as he advanced further and further in the discovery of the resources and values contained in the whole of creation.[15]

He referred to the salvific value of work. Sweat and toil, which work necessarily involved in the present condition of the human race, presented the Christian, and everyone who was called to follow Christ, with the possibility of sharing lovingly in the work that Christ came to do. This work of salvation came about through suffering and death on a cross. By enduring the toil of work in union with Christ crucified for us, man in a way collaborated with the Son of God for the redemption of humanity. He showed himself a true disciple of Christ by carrying the cross in his turn every day in the activity that he was called upon to perform.[16]

John Paul II said that in work, thanks to the light that penetrated us from the resurrection of Christ, we always find a glimmer of new life, of the new good, as if it were an announcement of 'the new heavens and the new earth'[17] in which man and the world participate precisely through the toil that goes with work.[18]

Solidarity and the worker question
John Paul II recognized the existence of various types of works. He said that while one could say that, by reason of its subject, work was one single thing, when one takes into consideration its objective directions one is forced to admit that there exist many different types of work. The development of human civilization brought continual enrichment in this field. However, one of the consequences of this development was that not only did a new form of work appear, but others disappeared. Even if this was accepted as a normal phenomenon, it had to be seen whether certain ethically and socially dangerous irregularities crept in and to what extent. He said that it was precisely one such wide-ranging anomaly that gave rise in the nineteenth century to what has been called 'The Worker Question', sometimes described as 'The Proletariat Question'.[19]

'The rise of the worker question' and the problems connected with it, gave rise to a just social reaction and resulted in the emergence of a great burst of solidarity between workers, first and foremost industrial workers. He said that the call to solidarity and common action addressed to the workers – especially those engaged in narrowly specialized, monotonous and depersonalized work in industrial plants, where the machine tended to dominate man – was important and eloquent from the point of view of social ethics. It was, he said, the reaction against the degradation of man as the subject of work and against the unheard-of accompanying exploitation in the field of wages, working conditions and social security for the worker. He said that this reaction united the working world in a community marked by great solidarity and it was justified from the point of view of social morality.[20]

John Paul II said that although worker solidarity, together with a clearer and more committed realization by others of workers' rights, had in many cases brought about profound changes, at the same time various ideological or power systems and a new relationship which had arisen at various levels of society, have allowed flagrant injustices to persist or have created new ones. This was true both in countries which had attained a certain process of industrial revolution and in countries where the main working milieu continued to be agriculture or similar occupations.[21]

Planned structural unemployment, unregulated competition and deregulationist policies, with their disastrous consequences for small, independent economic units, and all of which are fruit of neoliberal capitalist ideology, are some examples of these new injustices.

Labour and capital in conflict – the priority of labour

John Paul II describes the conflict between labour and capital as the great conflict of the age of industrial development: one between the small but highly influential group of entrepreneurs, owners or holders of the means of production, and the broader multitude of people who lacked these means and who shared in the process of production solely by their labour. It arose from the fact that the workers put their powers at the disposal of the entrepreneurs and these, following the principle of maximum profit, tried to establish the lowest possible wages for the work done by the employees. In addition, there were other elements of exploitation, connected with the lack of safety at work and of safeguards regarding the health and living conditions of the workers and their families.[22]

John Paul II said that this conflict came to be interpreted by some as a socio-economic class conflict and found expression in the ideological conflict between liberalism, understood as the ideology of capitalism, and Marxism, understood as the ideology of scientific socialism and communism, which professed to act as the spokesman for the working class and the worldwide proletariat. As a result, he said, the real conflict between labour and capital was transformed into a systematic class struggle, conducted not only by ideological means but also and chiefly by political means.[23]

In an age of conflicts, most of which are caused by man, John Paul II stated that in this situation man must first recall a principle that had always been taught by the Church: the principle of the priority of labour over capital. This principle directly concerned the process of production. In this process, labour is always a primary efficient cause, while capital, the whole collection of means of production, remains a mere instrument or instrumental cause. He said that this principle was an evident truth that emerged from the whole of man's historical experience.

John Paul II explains the principle of the priority of labour by reminding us that the final analysis of all of man's work depended upon the leading role of the gift made by 'Nature' – that is to say, by the Creator. Further consideration of this confirms our conviction of the priority of labour over what in the course of time has come to be called capital. This is because the concept of capital includes not only the natural resources placed at man's disposal, but also the whole collection of means by which man appropriates natural resources and transforms them in accordance with his needs. He said that it must be noted that all these means are the result of the historical heritage of human labour. All the means of production from the most primitive to the most modern have been gradually developed by man's experience and intellect. Thus everything that is at the service of work, everything that in the present state of technology constitutes its ever more highly perfected 'instrument', is the result of work.[24]

From the foregoing it can be seen, as John Paul II said, that all the gigantic and powerful instruments – the whole collection of the means of production, in a sense, that have been considered as synonymous with 'capital' – are the result of work and bear the signs of human labour.[25] Put another way, the totality of the means of production does not exist without the intervention of human labour. Thus, John Paul II said, it remains clear that every human being sharing in the production process, even if he or she was only doing the kind of work for which no special training or qualifications were required, was the real efficient subject in this production process, while the whole collection of instruments, no matter how perfect they may be in themselves, were only a mere instrument subordinate to human labour. He said that this truth was part of the abiding heritage of the Church's teaching, and must always be emphasized with reference to the question of the labour system and with regard to the whole socioeconomic system. The Pope said that emphasis and prominence must be given to the primacy of man in the production process: the primacy of man over things. This truth, he said, had important and decisive consequences.[26]

In Gregg's view of *Laborem Exercens*, the real priority of labour involves ensuring that each individual's status – regardless of the precise character of their work – as a free and creative subject whose work-acts permit him to realize himself as a person, is the basic principle around which work-processes are organized.[27]

Worker participation

John Paul II substantially advanced the Church's teaching on worker participation in both expanding upon the application of worker participation, and in the philosophical argument in support of the principle. His philosophical argument has developed from the patristic view of the universal destination of goods and the right to common use of them. He says that the right to private property is subordinated to the right to common use – to the fact that goods were meant for everyone. Furthermore, he said that in the Church's teaching, ownership had never been understood in a way that could constitute grounds for social conflict in labour. In stating that a property was acquired first of all through work in order that it may serve work, this concerned in a special way ownership of the means of production. He said that isolating these means as a separate property in order to set it up in the form of 'capital' in opposition to 'labour' – and even to practise exploitation of labour – was contrary to the very nature of these means and their possession. The means of production cannot be possessed against labour. They cannot even be possessed for possession's sake, because the only legitimate title to their possession – in the form of private ownership or in the form of public or collective ownership – is that they should serve labour, and thus, by serving labour, that they should make possible the achievement of the first principle of this order, namely the universal destination of goods and the right to common use of them.[28]

The Pope said that from this point of view, and in consideration of human labour and of common access to the goods meant for man, one could not exclude the socialization, in suitable conditions, of certain means of production. In this context, socialization means the involvement, the association, and the participation of many in the processes.

It was right to confirm all the effort with which the Church's teaching had striven, and continued to strive, to ensure the priority of work and thereby man's character as a subject in social life and, especially, in the dynamic structure of the whole economic process. From this point of view, he said, the position of 'rigid' capitalism continues to remain unacceptable, namely the position that defended the exclusive right to private ownership of the means of production as an untouchable 'dogma' of economic life. He said that the principle of respectful work demanded that the exclusive right to private ownership of the means of production could undergo a constructive revision both in theory and in practice. The use of the word 'demands' by John Paul II is significant in that it is the strongest ever statement by any pontiff on the question of worker participation. The Pope said that if it were true that capital, as the whole of the means of production, was at the same time the product of the work of generations, it was equally true that capital was being unceasingly created through the work done with the help of all these means of production, and these means can be seen as a great workbench at which the present generation of workers is working day after day. The work referred to included different kinds of work, not only manual labour, but also the many forms of intellectual work, including white-collar work and management.[29]

Referring to some of the practical applications of a constructive revision of the exclusive right to private ownership of the means of production, John Paul II said that many proposals had been put forward by experts in Catholic social teaching and by the highest magisterium of the Church, which took on special significance. Referring to *Quadragesimo Anno* and *Gaudium et Spes*, he said that proposals for joint ownership of the means of work, sharing by the workers in the management and all profits of business, so-called shareholding by labour were examples. Whether these various proposals could or could not be applied concretely, it was clear that recognition of the proper position of labour and the worker in the production process demands various adaptations in the sphere of the right to ownership of the means of production. Again, the use of the word 'demands' is significant: worker participation is not simply a good idea, but something which is 'demanded'.

John Paul II said that the *a priori* elimination of private ownership of the means of production could not achieve the desired reforms. Any group in authority may carry out its task of administering the means of production satisfactorily, but it may also carry it out badly by claiming for itself a monopoly of the administration and disposal of the means of production and not refraining from offending basic human rights. Further, in converting the means of production into state property, the collective system is by no means equivalent to 'socializing' that property. We could speak of socializing only when the subject character of society was ensured – that is to say, when, on the basis of his work, each person was fully entitled to consider himself a part-owner of the great workbench at which he was working with everyone else. A way towards that goal could be found by associating labour with the ownership of capital, as far as possible, and by producing a wide range of intermediate bodies with economic, social, and cultural purposes.[30]

The 'intermediate bodies' to which John Paul II referred would be bodies enjoying real autonomy with regard to the public powers, pursuing their specific aims in honest collaboration with each other, and in subordination to the demands of the common good. He said they would be living communities both in form and in substance, in the sense that the members of each body would be looked upon and treated as persons and encouraged to take an active part in the life of the body.[31] John Paul II is here drawing upon John XXIII's *Mater et Magistra*.[32] It would also seem that the 'intermediate bodies' to which he refers are in accordance with the principle of solidarism and are a synonym for the 'vocational groups' advocated by Pius XI in *Quadragesimo Anno*.[33]

Another approach of John Paul II to the question of worker participation is what has become known as the 'personalist' argument. The Pope appears to derive it from the principle of the priority of labour over capital. He says that this principle has key importance both in the system built on the principle of private ownership of the means of production, and also in the system in which private ownership of these means has been limited even in a radical way. Labour is in a sense inseparable from capital; in no way does it accept the antinomy – that is to say, the separation and opposition with regard to the means of production that has weighed upon human life in recent centuries as a result of merely economic premises.[34] The Pope is in effect saying that the principle of the priority of labour has application in both capitalist and socialist economies.

There is also contained here a veiled criticism of that which brought about the antinomy between capital and labour. John Paul II said that when man worked, using all the means of production, he also wished the fruit of this work to be used by himself and others, and he wished to be able to take part in the very work process as a sharer in responsibility in creativity at the workbench to which he applied himself.[35] It must be emphasized in general terms that the person who worked desired not only due remuneration for his work, but also wished that, within the production process, provision be made for him to be able to know that in his work, even on something that is owned in common, he is working 'for himself'. The Pope said this awareness was extinguished within the worker in a system of excessive bureaucratic centralization which made the worker feel that he was just a cog in a huge machine moved from above, and that he was, for more reasons than one, a mere production instrument rather than a true subject of work with an initiative of his own.[36] The key words here are 'know' and 'for himself'. The work process must be such that the worker is fully cognisant that he is working for himself. He must have a full personal appreciation, belief, and experience of that fact.

John Paul II said that the Church's teaching had always expressed the strong and deep conviction that man's work concerned not only the economy, but also, and especially, personal values. These personal values were the principal reason expressed by Thomas Aquinas in the *Summa* in favour of the private ownership of the means of production. He said that whilst he accepted that for certain well-founded reasons, exceptions could be made to the principle of private ownership, he accepted that in his own time the system of 'socialized ownership' had been introduced. Nevertheless, the personalist argument held good both on the level of principles and on the practical level. If it were to be rational and fruitful, any socialization of the means of production must take the personalist argument into account and that every effort must be made to ensure that in this kind of system also, the human person could preserve his awareness of working 'for himself'.[37]

It is interesting that John Paul II uses the term 'workbench' three times in his dissertation on worker participation. It has inclusive connotations for the work processes. Rodger Charles comments that, properly considered, the employer and the employed are both workers on the same workbench, with different functions, but united by their common purpose of efficient production to meet the needs of their fellow citizens. He says that the tensions induced by the defects of the liberal capitalist tradition make it difficult for this ideal to be put into effect. He believed, however, that there were enough good employers and workers ready to respond to them to demonstrate that the Church's instinct here was sound.[38]

Samuel Gregg comments that because the person is a conscious human subject, he knows whether or not he is sharing in goods such as creativity and responsibility when working with others. It is not enough just to pay a wage to each participant in a work process. Enterprises must be organized so that people may work 'for themselves' in the sense that they are able to use the initiative which is theirs by virtue of being the subject of work, and thereby realize the personal values which people may attain through work in the subjective sense.[39]

Baum comments that John Paul II argues that workers were meant to be the owners of the giant workbench at which they laboured. He said that only then would they be able to work for themselves and not for another; only then would they overcome the alienation of labour. And yet in doing so, he said, they would at the same time serve the wellbeing of their co-workers and of society as a whole. Baum says that John Paul II assigns workers' ownership the highest place among the various ways in which industries could be owned. Yet, he said, even this ownership remains conditional, subject to the ethical test of whether the goods produced were made to serve the entire community.[40] In similar vein to *Gaudium et Spes* and *Mater et Magistra* John Paul II says that one way of ensuring the subjectivity of all involved in the work process is to build community-like relationships within enterprise structures.[41]

Materialistic economism

In the introduction to the second edition of *Ethics and the National Economy* by Heinrich Pesch, Rupert Ederer says that John Paul II uses the term 'economism' in precisely the same sense as used by Pesch.[42] Pesch had said that capitalism was an economic ambience which was marked essentially by the prevalence of money, capital and the interests of those who controlled it, and which was based on the principles of free enterprises and individualistic economism. Capitalism meant the control over economic life in the name of the unrestricted and unlimited acquisitive interests of those who own capital.[43] Materialistic economism drives a system in which the concept of profitability – the mercantile, capitalistic spirit that is oriented to the ways and means of making money – becomes the governing principle in all aspects of economic life: production, exchange and income distribution. The commercial end-purpose of enterprise prevails and enjoys virtually unrestricted freedom in the national economy. Everything serves the interest of those who own capital, and this gradually comes to mean financial capital.[44]

Materialistic economism is discussed here because, as a mindset, it played a major part in the development of antinomy between labour and capital. John Paul II first uses the term in *Laborem Exercens* when he speaks of the danger of treating work as a special kind of 'merchandise', or as an impersonal 'force' needed for production, and *Laborem Exercens* is the only social encyclical in which the term appears. The danger of treating work in this way always existed, especially when the whole way of looking at the question of economics was marked by the premises of materialistic economism.[45] The Pope said that the consequences of the development of a one-sided materialistic civilization, which gave high importance to the objective dimension of work, while the subjective dimension – everything in direct or indirect relationship with the subject of the work – remained on a secondary level, was a certain confusion or even a reversal of the order laid down from the beginning by words in the book of Genesis in that man was treated as an instrument of production, whereas he ought to be treated as the effective subject of work and its true maker and creator.[46]

Baum, speaking of what he called 'monetarism', which, in this writer's view, is a term synonymous with economism, said that 'monetarism' had been applied with more or less consistency in Britain and the United States and then in most of the nations of the West. What we had witnessed since then was increasing deregulation, new free trade agreements and a previously unheard-of globalization of the economy. The power of the corporate actors in this global economy had become so great that national governments must curry their favour, and, as a result, had become unable to protect the economic wellbeing of their own people. Baum believed that capitalism had entered a new phase and that the harsh critics of present-day economic globalization were not only economists with socialist sympathies, but also defenders of welfare capitalism, especially those who had vindicated it on ethical grounds. They had provided us with a literature that documented the tragic consequences of monetarist economics. He was of the opinion that modern Catholic social teaching had become more critical of the Western economic system.[47]

Baum's comments are supported by the frequent observations of eminent Australian intellectual, social activist, and writer, the late B. A. Santamaria, who expressed concern that modern governments had become so beholden to global capital that national sovereignty was being increasingly compromised.[48]

Robert A. Destro believes that the moral error of 'economism' is one in which businesses, representatives of labour, and governments are susceptible. Common labourers can be as materialistic as the captains of their industries: the corruptions of the commissars of the planned economies of central and eastern Europe are now on display for all to see. He says that just as economics is not mere bookkeeping, so 'economism' is a moral error with practical consequences. Destro's view was that those consequences could prompt a pragmatic and moral reflection that could lead a trade union, a business, or even a government in a better direction.[49]

Indirect employer

One of the new terms introduced by John Paul II in *Laborem Exercens* is the concept of the 'indirect employer'. The term applies to the various ministries or public departments and various social institutions whose task is to act in the interests of protecting the rights of workers. On an international level he lists such agencies as the International Labour Organization and the United Nations organization itself as such bodies. He says that all of these organizations have a role to play in achieving full respect for workers' rights, since the rights of the human person are the key element in the whole of the social moral order. The concept of the indirect employer is determined in a sense by all the elements that are decisive for economic life in a given society and state, and also by much wider links and forms of dependence. The attainment of workers' rights cannot be deemed to be merely the result of economic systems, which on a larger or smaller scale are guided chiefly by the criterion of maximum profit. On the contrary, he says, it is respect for the objective rights of the worker – every kind of worker: manual or intellectual, industrial or agricultural,[50] that must constitute the adequate and fundamental criterion for shaping the whole economy, both on the level of the individual society and state, and within the whole of the world economic policy and the systems of international relationships that derive from it.

John Paul II said that when we consider the rights of workers in relation to the indirect employer – that is to say, all the agents at the national and international level that are responsible for the whole orientation of labour policy – we must first direct our attention to a fundamental issue, namely that of finding suitable employment for all who were capable of it. The role of the agents included under the title of 'indirect employer' was to act against unemployment, which in all cases was an evil, and which, when it had reached a certain level, could become a real social disaster. One of the functions of the indirect employer was to make provision for overall planning with regard to the different kinds of work by which not only the economic life but also the cultural life of a given society was shaped. They should give attention to organizing that work in a correct and rational way. This organization was to take place, not in a one-sided centralized way by public authorities, but by way of a just and rational co-ordination in the framework of which the initiative of individuals, free groups and local work centres and complexes must be safeguarded, keeping in mind the subject character of human labour.

He said that the indirect employer potentially determines one or other facet of the labour relationship, thus conditioning the conduct of the direct employer when the latter determines in concrete terms the actual work contract and labour relations. The concept of indirect employer was applicable to every society and in the first place to the state. This is because it was the state that must conduct a just labour policy. However, in the present system of economic relations in the world there are numerous links between individual states, links that find expression in the import and export processes – that is to say, in the mutual exchange of economic goods whether raw materials, semi-manufactured goods or finished industrial products. These links, he said, also created mutual dependence. It would seem, in this writer's view, that those government departments and those organizations which determine trade policies, to the extent in which those trade policies influenced employment within national boundaries, are deemed indirect employers.[51] It is appropriate therefore, in my view, that their policies be subject to the scrutiny of trade unions and all bodies concerned with the rights and welfare of workers generally.

Wages

John Paul II approaches the question of wages as a deontological question. It is a problem of social ethics which requires the payment of just remuneration for work done. He said that in the present context there is no more important way for securing a just relationship between the worker and the employer than that constituted by remuneration for work.[52] In his analysis, John Paul II refers to the first principle of the whole ethical and social order, namely the principle of the common use of goods. In every system, regardless of the fundamental relationships within it between capital and labour, wages – that is to say, remuneration for work, are still a practical means whereby the vast majority of people can have access to those goods which are intended for common use: both the goods of nature and manufactured goods.[53] He says that the payment of a just wage is an important means of checking that the socio-economic system is functioning justly. It is a concrete means of verifying the justice of the whole socioeconomic system.[54]

In keeping with the teaching of the magisterium on the primacy of the family, John Paul II speaks of the payment of a family wage, which is described as a single salary given to the head of the family for his work, sufficient for the needs of the family without the other spouse having to take up gainful employment outside the home. Alternatively, other social measures such as family allowances or grants to mothers devoting themselves exclusively to their families should be made to supplement a wage. John Paul II's support for a family wage capable of supporting a single income family, for the concept of the wife acting as a full-time carer for any children of the marriage, is a direct statement of what is implied in prior social encyclicals, although in *Rerum Novarum* Leo XIII makes clear his preference for women to work in the home, which he considers more appropriate for the welfare of the children and the family.[55]

John Paul II takes the argument further when he says that experience confirms that there must be a social re-evaluation of the mother's role, of the toil connected with it, and of the need that children have for care, love and affection in order that they may develop into responsible, morally and religiously mature and psychologically stable persons. He says that it would redound to the credit of society to make it possible for a mother – without inhibiting her freedom, without psychological or practical discrimination, and without penalizing her as compared with other women – to devote herself to taking care of her children and educating them in accordance with their needs, which vary with age. Having to abandon these tasks in order to take up paid work outside the home is wrong from the point of view of the good of society and of the family when it contradicts or hinders these primary goals of the mission of a mother. Here John Paul II is drawing upon *Gaudium et Spes* and the central role which the Vatican Council ascribed to the work of the mother in the home.[56]

John Paul II says that the true advancement of women requires that labour should be structured in such a way that women do not have to pay for their advancement by abandoning what is specific to them and at the expense of the family, in which women as mothers have an irreplaceable role.[57] It is unfortunate that one of the consequences of neoliberal capitalism has been the economic conscription of mothers with young children into the workforce, accompanied by a belittling of the importance of the role of full-time mothers and a devaluing of the work they perform within the context of the home.

John Paul II makes reference to certain benefits besides wages which should accrue to the worker. These include the right to proper health care, especially in the case of work-related accidents, and the ready availability of medical assistance to workers. It also refers to the right to a pension and appropriate insurance for old age and work-related accidents. The provision of a safe system of work and a safe working environment are also deemed by him to be rights to which the worker is entitled.[58]

Trade unions

Continuing with his theme of workers' rights, John Paul II says that the need for workers to secure the various rights to which they are entitled gives rise to another right: the right of association – that is, to form associations for the purpose of defending the vital interests of those employed in the various professions. He introduces a new element into social teaching in respect of trade unions when he says that the task of unions is to defend the existential interests of workers in all sectors in which their rights are concerned. The key words here are 'all sectors', which is an all-embracing term including matters of a political and social nature affecting them in their capacity as workers. He advances the magisterium's endorsement of trade unions when he describes them as an indispensable element of social life.[59]

Perhaps in keeping with his sympathy for the Solidarity trade union movement in Poland, John Paul II ascribes to trade unions a role not ascribed to them in previous encyclicals. He said that they are indeed a mouthpiece in the struggle for social justice. But it was not, he said, a struggle against others.[60] There was a danger of union demands turning into a kind of group or class 'egoism'. Union demands can and should aim at correcting – with a view to the common good of the whole of society – everything defective in the system of ownership of the means of production or in any way these were managed.[61] This too represents a further development of the magisterium in respect of its teaching on trade unions, in recognizing that trade union activity may enter the field of politics in its prudent concern for the common good. John Paul II says that the role of unions is not to 'play politics' in the sense that the expression is commonly understood today. Unions do not have the character of political parties and should not be subjected to the decision of political parties or have links with them which were too close. Close contact of that type could, he said, result in their losing contact with their specific role, which was to secure the just rights of workers within the framework of the common good of the whole of society. They would then become an instrument used for other purposes.[62]

John Paul II indicates a new role for trade unions in the education and training of their members. He traces the work of what he termed 'peoples' universities' and 'worker schools' which fostered the self-education of workers. This is an extension of the understanding of John XXIII in *Mater et Magistra* of the greater technical skill training required by workers in an age of scientific and technical advance.[63] He said that, thanks to the work of their unions, workers would not only have more, but above all, be more. They would realize their humanity more fully in every respect.[64]

His position in respect of strike action is similar to that of the Second Vatican Council. However, the Pope refers to workers being entitled to the right to strike without being subjected to personal penal sanctions for taking part in a strike. As Gregg says, this represents a variation on *Gaudium et Spes*, teaching that workers should be able to participate in unions without fear of reprisals. He says that the word 'penal' implies that the state is a primary retaliatory body. The detail into which *Laborem Exercens* teaching about unions enters reflects in part Wojtylan influences.[65] John Paul II repudiates the idea of the struggle of trade unions being a class struggle in the Marxist sense, and says that it is not a struggle 'against' others. The workers' unions remain a constructive factor of social order and solidarity, even if it is because of their work needs that people unite to secure their rights.[66]

Centesimus Annus

Alienation

In *Centesimus Annus,* promulgated on 1 May 1991, John Paul II adopts and develops what is normally thought of as the Marxist notion of alienation. He is, however, critical of the Marxist understanding of the word. He says that whereas Marxism criticized capitalist bourgeois societies, blaming them for the commercialization and alienation of human existence, this rebuke was based on a mistaken and inadequate idea of alienation, derived solely from the sphere of relationships of production and ownership – that is, they were given a materialistic foundation – and the legitimate positive value of market relationships, even in their own sphere, was denied. He said that Marxism ended up by affirming that only in a collective society could alienation be eliminated. However, historical experience in socialist countries had sadly demonstrated that collectivism did not do away with alienation but rather increased it, adding to it a lack of basic necessities and economic inefficiency.[67]

The Pope said that alienation was also a reality in western societies. This was due to consumerism, when people were ensnared in a web of false and superficial gratifications, rather than being helped to experience their personhood in an authentic and concrete way. Alienation was found in work when it was organized so as to ensure maximum returns and profits with no concern whether the worker, through his own labour, grew or diminished as a person, either through increased sharing in a genuinely supportive community, or through increased isolation in a maze of relationships marked by destructive competitiveness and estrangement, in which he is considered only a means and not an end. The Pope said that the concept of alienation fell back upon the Christian vision of reality by recognizing in alienation a reversal of means and ends. When man does not recognize in himself and in others the value and grandeur of the human person, he effectively deprives himself of the possibility of benefiting from his humanity and of entering into that relationship of solidarity and communion with others for which God created him.[68]

In this the Pope is drawing upon his earlier writing in *The Acting Person* where he said that alienation, when it occurred in life, involved estrangement from that which properly belonged to the human person – his personhood.[69] In *The Acting Person* Wojtyla agreed that the system of things described in Marxist theory could contribute to human alienation. But like *Laborem Exercens*, Wojtyla does not consider it as the primary cause. Gregg says that the claim then, that alienation is ultimately caused by 'systems of things' is to deny man's ascendancy over the material world. If man is indeed master, then he – and not things or structures – is the ultimate cause of alienation.[70]

In *The Acting Person* Wojtyla explains that alienation from other men stemmed from a disregard for, or a neglect of, that real depth of participation which was indicated by the term 'neighbour'.[71] As Gregg points out, although *Centisimus Annus* does not use the word 'neighbour', its point is the same. Alienation ultimately stems not from relationships of production, but from man's failure to recognize and treat others as persons.[72] This is, of course, clearly contrary to Marxist analysis.

John Paul II makes the interesting point that whilst exploitation in the forms analysed and described by Marx had been overcome in western society, alienation had not. Alienation existed in various forms of exploitation when people used one another and when they sought an ever-more refined satisfaction of their individual and secondary needs, while ignoring the principal and authentic needs which ought to regulate the matter of satisfying the other ones too. A person who was concerned solely or primarily with possessing and enjoying, who was no longer able to control his instincts and passions, or to subordinate them by obedience to the truth, could not be free. Obedience to the truth about God and man was the first condition of freedom, making it possible for a person to order his needs and desires and to choose the means of satisfying them according to a correct scale of values, so that the ownership of things may become an occasion of growth for him.[73]

Thus it would seem, in this writer's view, that failure to live one's life in a right relationship with God could in itself result in a form of alienation.

Rodger Charles makes the interesting point that some Marxist insights – the alienation of the worker in particular – contain a strong element of truth. He says that liberal capitalism has been curbed through legislation, social and political pressures and countervailing forces, but its philosophy still dominates the wishes and will of modern capitalism. This is shown whenever it is given the freedom to do as it wishes without hindrance.[74]

Worker participation

Centisimus Annus adds little to *Laborem Exercens* in respect of worker participation. However, John Paul II, speaking of the role of trade unions and other worker organizations as defenders of workers' rights and protectors of their interests as persons so as to enable workers to participate more fully and honourably in the life of their nation, speaks of their struggle as one in which they proposed '*a society of free work, of enterprise, and of participation*'.[75] Such a society, he says, is not directed against the market, but demands that the '*market be appropriately controlled*'[76] by the forces of society and by the state, so as to guarantee that the basic needs of the whole of society are satisfied.[77]

Capitalism – yes or no?

Centisimus Annus contains what some Catholic writers construe as papal endorsement of the capitalist system. In answer to a rhetorical question as to whether capitalism should be the goal of the countries now making efforts to rebuild their economy and society, and whether the capitalist model ought to be proposed to the countries of the Third World, the Pope made the following answer. If capitalism meant an economic system which recognized the fundamental and positive role of business, the market, private property and the resulting responsibility for the means of production, as well as free human creativity in the economic sector, then the answer was certainly in the affirmative. He qualified this, however, by saying that it would perhaps be more appropriate to speak of a 'business economy', 'market economy', or simply 'free economy'.

In this writer's view, these qualifications strongly indicate a reluctance by the Pope to give his approval to the capitalist system per se. The Pope went on to say, however, that if 'capitalism' meant a system in which freedom in the economic sector was not circumscribed within a strong judicial framework which placed it at the service of human freedom in its totality, and which saw it as a particular aspect of that freedom, the core of which was ethical and religious, then the reply was certainly negative.[78]

The question then arises as to which of these two potential definitions of capitalism prevails at this point of time. It is the opinion of this writer, that the characteristics of the Pope's second definition of capitalism prevail in the global liberal capitalism of our time. The Pope himself alludes to this possibility when he says that although the Marxist solution has failed, the realities of marginalization and exploitation remained in the world, especially in Third World countries, as did the reality of human alienation in countries which are more advanced. He added that although the collapse of the communist system removed one of the obstacles to facing these problems, there was a risk that a radical capitalist ideology could spread which refused even to consider these problems, in the *a priori* belief that any attempt to solve them was doomed to failure, and which blindly entrusted their solution to the free development of market forces.[79]

Following the collapse of communism in Eastern Europe and in Russia in particular, neocapitalist ideologies were imposed willy-nilly upon societies which had no experience of a free market. The results have been, in a majority of cases, the development of economic systems the feature of which has been exploitation, alienation, poverty, and the concentration of wealth in the hands of a few to the detriment of the many. Whilst it may be tempting for some Catholic writers to attribute to John Paul II an endorsement of the capitalist system, it would, in this writer's view, be drawing rather a long bow. It would be disregarding the totality of *Centisimus Annus* and all prior social encyclicals, particularly *Quadragesimo Anno*.

The way is clearly open for the consideration of structures which are neither socialist nor capitalist, and which give free and full rein to the personalist approach to work. These alternatives are canvassed in chapter 15.

Summary

Protestant theologian Lukas Vischer said that the praise of human work by John Paul II reached almost incredible heights.[80] Lukas believed that it may have been his experiences in his native Poland which motivated John Paul II, as it was precisely among Poland's workers that a growing resistance to the communist system was seen. He described the encyclical *Laborem Exercens* as an effort to show that the Church disposed over a coherent and ongoing understanding of human work.[81] In both its content and detail, *Laborem Exercens* goes far beyond *Rerum Novarum* and even beyond *Gaudium et Spes*. The Pope's ideas on materialism and economism are a major factor in analysis of work structures and how unjust work structures can contribute to the exploitation of the worker. His expansion of the teaching in respect of the rights of workers as detailed earlier, particularly in relation to worker participation, the personalist approach to work and the role of trade unions, are but some examples of the way in which John Paul II exhibited his love and concern for the working men and women of the world. John Paul II will be remembered for many reasons. His solicitude for workers and their rights will certainly be one of them.

Notes
 1 Szulc, p. 232.
 2 Ibid. p. 149.
 3 Walsh, p. 6.
 4 Gregg, p. 122.
 5 Ibid. p. 123.
 6 Ibid. pp. 112, 113.
 7 Wojtyla, p. 332.
 8 Ibid. p. 333.
 9 Mechmann, p. 50.
10 Gen. 1:28
11 *Laborem Exercens*, para. 4, p. 20.
12 Hines, p. 79.
13 Ibid., para. 6, p. 27.
14 *Gaudium et Spes*, para. 34.
15 *Laborem Exercens*, para. 25, pp. 94, 95.
16 Ibid., para 27, pp. 104, 105.
17 2 Peter 3:13; Rev. 21:1.
18 *Laborem Exercens*, para. 27, p. 106.
19 Ibid., para. 8, p. 33.
20 Ibid., para. 8, pp. 33, 34.
21 Ibid., para. 8, p. 35.
22 *Laborem Exercens*, para. 11, pp. 46, 47.
23 Ibid., para.11, p. 47.
24 Ibid., para. 12, pp. 51, 52.
25 Ibid., para. 12, p. 52.
26 Ibid., para. 12, pp. 52, 53.
27 Gregg, p. 130.
28 *Laborem Exercens*, para. 14, pp. 59, 60.
29 Ibid., para. 14, p. 61.
30 Ibid., para. 14, p. 63.
31 Ibid.
32 *Mater et Magistra*, para. 61, pp. 21, 22.
33 *Quadragesimo Anno*, ch. 5, pp. 41, 42, 43.
34 Ibid., para. 15, p. 64.
35 The italics are the writer's.
36 Ibid., para. 15, pp. 64, 65.
37 Ibid., para 15, p. 65.
38 Charles, p. 64.

39 Gregg, p. 131.
40 Baum, p. 241.
41 *Laborem Exercens*, para. 14, p. 63; *Mater et Magistra*, para. 91, p. 27; *Gaudium et Spes*, para. 68.
42 Pesch, p. 32.
43 Ibid. p. 159.
44 Ibid. p. 161.
45 *Laborem Exercens*, para. 7, pp. 30, 31.
46 Ibid., para. 7, p. 31.
47 Baum, p. 214.
48 The writer has personal knowledge of these statements from various lectures given by the late B. A. Santamaria.
49 Weigel and Royal, p. 149.
50 *Laborem Exercens*, para. 17, pp. 70, 71, 72.
51 Ibid., para. 18, pp. 73, 74.
52 Ibid., para. 19, p. 77.
53 Ibid., para. 19, p. 78.
54 Ibid.
55 *Rerum Novarum*, para. 60, p. 37.
56 *Gaudium et Spes*, para. 52.
57 *Laborem Exercens*, para. 19, p. 80.
58 Ibid., para. 19, pp. 80, 81.
59 Ibid., para. 20, p. 82
60 Ibid, para. 20, p. 83.
61 Ibid., para. 20, p. 84.
62 Ibid.
63 *Mater et Magistra*, para. 94, p. 28.
64 Ibid., para. 20, p. 85.
65 Gregg, p. 119.
66 *Laborem Exercens*, para. 20, p. 83.
67 *Centisimus Annus*, para. 41, pp. 73, 74.
68 Ibid., para. 41, pp. 74, 75.
69 Samuel Gregg, p. 139.
70 Ibid. p. 140.
71 Ibid. p. 140.
72 Ibid. p. 140.
73 *Centisimus Annus*, para. 41, pp. 75, 76.
74 Charles, p. 80.
75 The italics are the writer's.
76 The italics are the writer's.
77 *Centisimus Annus*, para. 35, p. 64.
78 Ibid., para. 42, pp. 76, 77.
79 Ibid., para. 42, p. 77.
80 Vischer, p. 2.
81 Ibid.

Chapter 14

RECENT STATEMENTS OF NATIONAL EPISCOPAL CONFERENCES, *DEUS CARITAS EST* AND OTHER CHURCH DOCUMENTS

Following *Laborem Exercens* various episcopal conferences have commented upon, and in some instances been highly critical of certain aspects of neoliberal capitalism, which they generally referred to as the monetarist economy. Baum quotes the American and Canadian bishops as having said that the monetarist economy produces structural unemployment, creates spreading pockets of poverty, leads to growing insecurity of employment, increases economic inequality and produces dramatic housing shortages, to name but a few.[1]

United States Catholic bishops

In 1984 working papers were prepared for the bishops' pastoral statement entitled *Economic Justice for All,* published on 18 November 1986. One of the working papers, written by Rudi Oswald, expressed concern that workers and their unions in the United States were facing extraordinary challenges and attacks from employers, who used intimidation and coercion to prevent workers from making a free choice of association and to forestall any effective participation by workers in fixing the conditions under which they worked.[2]

In what can only be regarded as an example of the threats posed to the basic rights of workers by neoliberal capitalism, Oswald said that in 1980 there were 18,000 workers fired from their jobs for asserting their right to associate themselves in a labour union. He said that many more thousands whose names will never be known were too frightened, too intimidated, to assert this right.³ Governmental restrictions upon the rights of trade unions and trade unionists is not confined to the United States. In 2004 a bill was introduced into the Australian federal parliament entitled 'the Workplace Relations Amendment (Right of Entry) Bill 2004', which sought to amend the Workplace Relations Act to place restrictions on the right of trade union officers and employees to enter workplaces in pursuit of their varying responsibilities in representing employees. It is significant that during the debate on this bill in April 2005 the then Opposition spokesman for industrial relations, Mr Kevin Rudd, an Anglican, referred to the encyclicals *Rerum Novarum*, *Laborem Exercens* and *Centisimus Annus*, indicating that legislation of this type was in direct contradiction to the social teachings of the Catholic Church.⁴ One would hope that legislators throughout the world would not be backward in challenging such legislation whenever and wherever it arises.

The introduction to the bishops' pastoral letter lists a number of basic moral principles on which the social teachings of the Church are based. Some of these principles are:

> Every economic decision and institution must be judged in light of whether it protects or undermines the dignity of the human person.
>
> Human dignity can be realised and protected only in community.
>
> All people have a right to participate in the economic life of society.[5]

Worker participation

The bishops restated the recommendation made by them in their 1919 programme of social reconstruction, referred to in an earlier chapter, for the majority of workers in some way to become owners, at least in part, of the instruments of production. They said that that judgement remained valid to the present day.⁶ The bishops said that workers in firms and on farms were especially in need of stronger institutional protection, because their jobs and livelihood were particularly vulnerable to the decisions of others in today's highly competitive labour market. They expressed support for arrangements which they saw as gaining increasing support in the United States: profit sharing by the workers in a firm; enabling employees to become company stockholders; granting employees greater participation in determining the conditions of work; co-operative ownership of the firm for all who work within it;

and programmes for enabling a much larger number of Americans, regardless of their employment status, to become shareholders in successful corporations.[7] One would hope that such initiatives become the norm. However, given the apparent dominance of neo-liberal capitalist philosophy, it is difficult to envisage widespread acceptance of such efficacious and socially just arrangements. We must however, continue to place before society the social teachings of the Church wherein lies the promise of a just social order.

Trade unions

Drawing on *Gaudium et Spes* and *Laborem Exercens*, the bishops strongly supported the role of organized labour securing the rights of its members. The bishops expressed concern regarding the decrease in the percentage of US workers who were in trade unions. They said that the greatest challenge facing United States workers and unions today was that of developing a new vision of their role in the United States economy of the future. American workers were facing pressures that threatened their jobs. The restrictions on the right to organize in many countries abroad made labour costs lower there, threatened American workers and their jobs, and led to the exploitation of workers in these countries. In these difficult circumstances, guaranteeing the rights of US workers called for imaginative vision and creative new steps, not reactive or simply defensive strategies. They suggested that organized labour could play a very important role in helping to provide the education and training needed to help keep workers employable.[8] This is reminiscent of John Paul II in *Laborem Exercens*.[9]

The bishops expressed their opposition to the organized efforts currently seen in the US to break existing unions and prevent workers from organizing. They said that migrant and agricultural workers were particularly in need of protection, including the right to organize and bargain collectively. They called for reform of the US labour law to meet these problems and to provide more timely and effective remedies for unfair labour practices.[10] The bishops said that along with the rights of workers and unions came important responsibilities. Individual workers had obligations to their employers, and trade unions also had duties to society as a whole. Union management in particular carried a strong responsibility for the good name of the entire union movement. Drawing upon *Laborem Exercens* they said that workers must use their collective power to contribute to the wellbeing of the whole community and should avoid pressing demands the fulfilment of which would damage the common good and the rights of more vulnerable members of society.[11]

Referring to the changing nature of the United States economy in what he said could be termed a post-industrial economy 'information society' or a 'service economy', Himes said that while the nature of the economy in nations like the United States was undergoing dramatic alterations, these changes were viewed in Catholic social thought as neither cause for despair nor uncritical optimism. Human dignity, human rights and the common good remained touchstones for Catholic social thought to scrutinize the emerging economies of the post-industrial societies.[12]

Wages

The American bishops expressed the view that the way power was distributed in a free-market economy frequently gave employers greater bargaining power than employees in the negotiation of labour contracts. They said that such unequal power may press workers into a choice between an inadequate wage and no wage at all. But, they said, justice not charity demanded certain minimum guarantees. The provision of wages and other benefits sufficient to support a family in dignity was a basic necessity to prevent the exploitation of workers. Drawing upon *Laborem Exercens*, the bishops said that the dignity of workers also required adequate health care, security for old age or disability, unemployment compensation, healthy working conditions, weekly rest, periodic holidays, recreation and leisure, and reasonable security against arbitrary dismissal. These provisions were all essential if workers were to be treated as persons rather than simply as 'factors of production'.[13]

Speaking on the necessity for wage demands, and taking into account the common good of the whole community and the rights of more vulnerable members of society, the bishops noted, however, that the wages paid to workers were but one of the factors affecting the competitiveness of industries. Thus it was unfair to expect unions to make concessions if managers and shareholders did not make at least equal sacrifices. This is one ethical standard being honoured increasingly in its breach.

Employment

The bishops emphasized the role of government in bringing about the conditions for full employment. The general or macroeconomic policies of the federal government were essential tools for encouraging the steady economic growth that produced more and better jobs in the economy. They recommended that the fiscal and monetary policies of the nation – such as federal spending, tax, and interest rate policies – should be coordinated so as to achieve the goal of full employment. The bishops made further recommendations. They recommended the expansion of job training and apprenticeship programmes in the private sector, administered and supported jointly by business, labour unions, and government. They also recommended increased support for direct job creation programmes targeted at the long-term unemployed and those with special needs. They said that the first line of attack against poverty must be to build and sustain a healthy economy that provided employment opportunities at just wages for all adults who were able to work.[14] In this regard, Catholic social teaching finds itself in direct conflict with neoliberal capitalist concepts of structured unemployment and so-called 'labour market flexibility'.

In November 1995, the United States bishops, commemorated the tenth anniversary of *Economic Justice for All* in a pastoral letter entitled *A Decade after Economic Justice for All*. The principles stated in the earlier pastoral letter were reiterated.

Sacred Congregation for the Doctrine of the Faith

– *The Instruction on Christian Freedom and Liberation*

It is interesting that the strongest endorsement for worker participation of any church document is contained in the document entitled *The Instruction on Christian Freedom and Liberation,* promulgated by the Sacred Congregation for the Doctrine of the Faith on 22 March 1986 and signed by the present Pope, the then Josef Cardinal Ratzinger, the Prefect of the Congregation, and Alberto Bovone, the Titular Archbishop of Caesarea in Namibia, the secretary of the congregation. The congregation maintained that wages, which could not be considered as a mere commodity, must enable the worker and his family to have access to a truly human standard of living in the material, social, cultural and spiritual orders. They said that it was the dignity of the person which was the main criterion for judging work, not the other way round. Echoing the personalist approach of John Paul II in *Laborem Exercens,* the congregation said that whatever the type of work, the worker must be able to perform it as an expression of his personality. There followed from this the necessity of a participation[15] which, over and above a sharing in the fruits of work, should involve a purely communitarian dimension at the level of projects, undertakings and responsibilities.[16]

The congregation stated that the priority of work over capital placed an obligation in justice upon employers to consider the welfare of the workers before the increase of profits.[17] The congregation said that the fact that the value of any human work did not depend on the kind of work done but was rather based on the fact that the one who performed the work was a person, was an ethical criterion with implications that could not be overlooked. Every person had a right to work, and this right must be recognized in a practical way by an effective commitment to resolving the tragic problem of unemployment. The fact that unemployment kept large sectors of the population and notably the young in a situation of marginalization was intolerable. For this reason the creation of jobs was a primary social task facing individuals and private enterprise, as well as the state.[18] Here again we see the conflict between Catholic social teaching and the tenets of neoliberal capitalism.

The Canadian Catholic bishops

The Canadian bishops have been amongst the most outspoken of all of the national episcopal conferences on issues affecting the sanctity of work and the rights of workers. They have been particularly critical of the deleterious effects of governmental trade and industry policies which they perceive as contributing to a worsening of the conditions of workers and the eroding of the concept of the dignity of work.

In a submission to the Commission of Enquiry on Unemployment Insurance made on 13 February 1986, the bishops said that work was one of the characteristics that distinguished human beings from the rest of creation, so work in a sense was of the very nature of humanity. Through the activity of work, people are able to exercise their creative spirit, realize their human dignity, and participate in the development of society. Work corresponds to human dignity, expresses this dignity and increases it. They said that from this vision of the human person followed a key principle of Catholic social teaching: the priority of labour over capital. This principle concerned the production process, where working people were the subjects of production. All capital and technology are mere instruments or objects as they are historically the fruit of human labour and always subordinate to labour. They said that the basis for determining the meaning and value of work lay in the subjective dimension of work. Work had value because the worker was a person. People working are not commodities or objects whose work is determined by the market.[19]

The Canadian bishops said that full employment should always be a primary objective of government planning. It was not realistic, nor was it admissible, to expect to provide suitable employment for all who were capable of it relying on a private sector strategy wherein unemployment was seen as a possible secondary effect, somewhere down the road. Work, they said, was a human right for all, not a privilege for a few.[20] We see here a thinly veiled criticism of the tenets of neoliberal capitalism in respect of structured unemployment and labour market flexibility. Commenting upon the Canadian government's proposed changes to Canada's unemployment insurance programme, the bishops said that the present review of the programme came at a time when social expenditures in general were being seriously cut back and social programmes restructured. They added that the government had designated the 'private sector' as the engine for growth. Deficit reduction appeared to be the main preoccupation – yet in the last few months alone, billions of dollars had been handed over to banks, oil companies, wealthy individuals and money markets. The bishops said that the core of this agenda was a renewed vision of 'market society' where human beings and safe relations were defined in terms of demand and supply for and of the market. The dominant tendency was to subordinate human dignity and human needs to the abstract rhetoric of the market. They believed that these disturbing trends were symptomatic of a moral disorder in the country. In effect, the protection of capital took priority over labour, over people, over communities.[21] These observations of the bishops are pertinent not only to Canada but, unfortunately, to other western industrialized economies.

The bishops showed an awareness of John Paul II's concept of the indirect employer.[22] In a document entitled *Free Trade: At What Cost?* published in 1987 the Canadian bishops expressed strong reservations in respect of the free-trade negotiations then taking place between the Canadian and United States governments. Under John Paul II's idea of the indirect employer, governments, governmental departments and agencies, various national and international agents, commerce and trade fall under the category of indirect employer. The Canadian bishops' concern was that the trade policies being pursued would have a deleterious effect upon workers in labour-intensive industries such as textiles, clothing, electrical products, leather products, toys and games who feared for their jobs. They said that service workers, mostly women, were increasingly concerned about the potential threat to their jobs posed by trade and services – for example, financial services, clerical work, data processing – with the United States. Farmers feared the loss of their farms and income due to the gradual elimination of marketing boards and subsidy programmes which are alleged to be 'unfair trade practices'.

This last comment is interesting as the decline of rural industries and small farms is evident in the United States, Canada, and Australasia due mainly to the deregulation of industries and national competition policies which render rural price support systems invalid. Significantly, in the European Union, where the social benefits of the maintenance of strong rural communities is recognized, government policy is directed towards maintaining and supporting the family farm. The bishops also expressed concern for workers in the branch plants of United States companies in Canada who faced the prospects of layoffs and plant shutdowns as Canadian subsidiaries were able to shift more production back to their parent corporations under a free-trade accord.[23] The bishops were particularly critical of the report of the McDonald Royal Commission, which stated *inter alia* that unemployment was natural, 'normal', 'voluntary' and even 'healthy' from an economic point of view.

From the point of view of Catholic social teaching, comments such as this fly directly in the face of Catholic social thought and are an example of some of the worst features of neoliberal capitalism.

Australian Catholic bishops' conferences

The Australian Catholic bishops have had a long history of concern for the worker which has been reflected in many of the social justice statements from 1943 onwards. Some of these statements have been referred to earlier. In 1992 the

Australian bishops issued a statement entitled *Common Wealth for the Common Good*. In the introduction to the statement, the Archbishop of Sydney, Cardinal Clancy, referred directly to the unjust effects of economic rationalism in language that could leave no doubt as to the bishops' concerns about the negative effects of neoliberal capitalism on the social order. Cardinal Clancy said that behind the adoption of some economic policies and the advocacy of others, one could discern the influence of that set of ideas which has been labelled 'economic rationalism'. It is characterized by a strong belief in the free market, in the need to reduce government spending and intervention, and in the principles of privatization and user pays. He said its advocates stressed the importance of competition, the desirability of reducing both welfare payments and income tax (replacing lost revenue, if possible, with a consumption tax), and minimizing the influence of the trade-union movement.[24]

In language which can only be described as scathing, he said that, taken to extremes, this trend could be equated with the promotion of individualism, the 'survival of the fittest' philosophy (sometimes labelled 'social Darwinism') and the 'greed is good' mentality.[25]

Cardinal Clancy said that it may be an exaggeration to suggest that an extreme form of economic rationalism has totally dominated the Australian scene in recent years. Nevertheless, its spirit undoubtedly exists in a notable way among those who have exercised power. There is evidence that it was a significant influence on the thinking of both the Commonwealth government and the opposition over a number of years, as it has been in countries like Britain, the USA, Canada and New Zealand during much of the 1980s and beyond.[26]

The Australian bishops recognized that economic rationalist philosophy had contributed to a decline in the real wages of workers and a disproportionate increase in income at the top end. They said, quoting from a study by Professor Stilwell:

> The share of the national income going to workers in the form of wages and salaries has fallen substantially while the share going to the owners of capital in the form of profits, rents and interest payments had risen correspondingly. Effectively, 10 per cent of the national income was taken away from workers and given to the owners of capital in the period between 1983 and 1989. This was a massive redistribution between social classes. The reason for the switch is not difficult to see – wage restraint kept down the wage share in national income, but there has been no restraint on incomes

from profits, rents and interest. Falling unit wage costs bolstered the profitability. High interest rates redistributed incomes to those with surplus funds to lend. The high rents associated with the housing crisis further added to incomes from property ownership.[27]

The bishops strongly supported the concept of worker participation and took the teaching of the Church a step further in this regard by openly pressing their support for what is frequently known as 'worker cooperatives':

> We recommend that Church members urge political parties to adopt coherent socio-economic policies which address the roots of the nation's problems; combine social objectives with economic goals; aim at securing worker participation in the ownership and management of companies (as is done in Germany); and aim at securing the co-operation of those sectors of society which are concerned to create a more co-operative social system.[28]

The reference to worker participation policies in Germany is interesting as it recognizes the influence Catholic social teaching has had in the formulation of social policies in many of the countries of western Europe. The Catholic bishops made reference to the Mondragon industrial cooperative in Spain where 21,000 workers effectively owned the ninety manufacturing cooperatives. They said that increased worker participation in business and industrial enterprises was a trend which reflected papal social teaching and deserved full encouragement.[29] The bishops' reference to the worker cooperatives of Mondragon is significant as there is a growing body of Catholic social thought which sees in the worker cooperative movement, as implemented in places such as Mondragon, an alternative to existing capitalist structure.

On industrial relations, the bishops recommended that workplace disputes be settled as far as possible by a process of conciliation – a principle which could be consistent with the policy of enterprise bargaining, provided that the unions themselves retained an appropriate role in the process. This is a clear recognition by the bishops of the important role of trade unions in the conciliation and arbitration process. Confronting some of the tenets of economic rationalism head-on, the bishops recommended *inter alia*:

1. that governments take long-term measures to address the problem of structural unemployment, paying attention to regional differences and to the effects of unemployment on

different groups, especially the young
2. that governments legislate against policies or practices which lead to the exploitation of workers, and monitor compliance with such legislation
3. that governments show awareness of the immediate effects on employment of the lowering of tariffs, even if it can be argued that the long-term effect will be favourable; and that any government advocating large scale tariff reduction be obliged to spell out the consequences of such a policy for employment
4. that in practice, governments and all employers take more heed of the legislation which covers equal pay and career opportunities for women in the workforce.[30]

The bishops' concern for the effects of lowering tariffs echoes the concerns expressed by the Canadian Catholic bishops and for much the same reasons. Like the Canadian bishops, the Australian bishops acknowledged the role of the indirect employer[31] in determining the levels of employment and unemployment.

Vatican Intervention at the World Summit on Social Development, Copenhagen 1995

In an intervention at the World Summit on Social Development in Copenhagen on 12 March 1995 the Vatican Secretary of State, Cardinal Angelo Sodano, told the conference that the principle reaffirmed several times in the Summit's documents, that the person was at the centre of sustainable government, should also be applied to the laws in the sphere of economics. Referring to *Centesimus Annus*, he said that Pope John Paul II had affirmed that, even prior to the system of the exchange of goods and free market, there existed something due to the person given their very nature, by reason of the lofty dignity of the person.[32]

Pastoral Letter of United States bishops 1991

In a letter of the United States bishops described as a pastoral letter of the Bishops of the United States on the one-hundredth anniversary of *Rerum Novarum*, the bishops said:

> In Catholic teaching, economy exists to serve people, not the other way around.[33]

The bishops repeated this statement just five years later in a document entitled 'A Catholic Framework for Economic Life' approved by them on 12 November 1996 during their fall meeting in Washington DC, when they said that the economy existed for the person, not the person for the economy.[34]

It is a teaching that is well recommended to the world's legislators.

In the 'Catholic Framework for Economic Life', the bishops detailed ten ethical principles as a framework for reflection on economic life and as criteria for judgement and directions for action. These principles were drawn directly from Catholic teaching on economic life and included the following:

> All economic life should be shaped by moral principles. Economic choices and institutions must be judged by how they protect or undermine the life and dignity of the human person, support the family and serve the common good.
>
> A fundamental moral measure of any economy is how the poor and vulnerable are fairing.
>
> All people have the right to economic initiative, to productive work, to just wages and benefits, to decent working conditions as well as to organise and join unions or other associations.[35]

Importantly, referring to John Paul II in *Centesimus Annus* paragraph 35, the bishops said that the State has a proper role in the marketplace in ensuring that the market works in a proper and just manner. Governments, they said, have essential responsibilities and limitations in respect of the operation of free markets.[36] This is analogous to *Centesimus Annus* where John Paul II said that what is required is a society of free work, of enterprise and of participation in which the market was appropriately controlled by the forces of society and by the state so as to guarantee that the basic needs of the whole of society were satisfied.[37]

Catholic bishop's conference of England and Wales 1996

In a document entitled 'The Common Good and the Catholic Church's Social Teaching', published in 1996, the bishops commented, *inter alia*, on developments which they considered to be at odds with the principle of the common good.

They said that Catholic social teaching recognized the fundamental and positive value of business, the market, private property and free human creativity in the economic sector. But, they said, sometimes market forces cannot deliver what the common good demands, and other remedies have to be sought. In its social teaching, the Catholic Church explicitly rejected belief in the automatic beneficence of market forces and said that the end result of market forces must be scrutinized and if necessary corrected in the name of natural law, social justice, human rights, and the common good. Adam Smith himself did not envisage markets operating in a value-free society, but assumed that individual consumer choices would be governed by moral considerations, not least the demands of justice.

The bishops reiterated what the American bishops had said in their pastoral letter a few years earlier; that the economy exists for the human person, not the other way round.[38]

Deus Caritas Est

In his first encyclical, *Deus Caritas Est*, promulgated on Christmas Day 2005,
Benedict XVI revealed his empathy with the worker when he said:

> The rise of modern industry caused the old social structures to collapse, while the growth of a class of salaried workers provoked radical changes in the fabric of society. The relationship between capital and labour now became the decisive issue – an issue which in that form was previously unknown. Capital and the means of production were now the new source of power which, concentrated in the hands of a few, led to the suppression of the rights of the working classes, against which they had to rebel.[39]

In March 2006, in an address to members of Italy's Union of Christian Entrepreneurs and Business Executives, Benedict XVI said that business owners must avoid every form of worker exploitation and must recognize the importance of family life for their workers. He said that upholding the importance of people in the workforce and in the world of business and respecting their needs and talents, were values that often faced the risk of not being pursued by business owners who lacked solid moral inspiration.[40]

Summary

The various episcopal conferences, whilst applying the social teaching of the magisterium as laid down in the various social encyclicals, managed to impart their own distinctive slant in applying the social teachings of the Church to the difficulties and injustices arising in their respective nations. In doing so, they have developed the application of the Church's social teaching in various degrees and sometimes significantly. They also provide an example of the application of Catholic social teaching in diverse social conditions.

Notes

1 Baum, p. 214.
2 Houck and Williams, p. 86.
3 Ibid.
4 Hansard I, 15 March 2005.
5 Lutz, pp. 19-20.
6 *Economic Justice for All: Pastoral letter on Catholic social teaching and the US economy*, National Conference of Catholic Bishops, Washington DC, 1986, p. 149.
7 Ibid., p.148.
8 Ibid., pp. 54, 55.
9 *Laborem Exercens*, para. 20, p. 85.
10 *Economic Justice for All: Pastoral letter on Catholic social teaching and the U.S. economy*, pp. 53, 54.
11 Ibid., p. 54.
12 *Responses to 101 Questions on Catholic Social Teaching*, Kenneth R. Himes, Paulist Press, New York, 2001, p. 79.
13 *Economic Justice for All*, p. 53.
14 Ibid., pp. 78, 79, 80, 97.
15 The italics are the writer's.
16 *Instruction on Christian freedom and liberation*, para. 86, pp. 83, 84.
17 Ibid., para 87, p. 84.
18 Ibid., para 85, pp. 82, 83.
19 Sheridan, p. 307.
20 Ibid. p. 308.
21 Ibid. pp. 306, 307.
22 The italics are the writer's. *Laborem Exercens*, para. 18, p. 73.
23 Ibid. p. 352.
24 *Common Wealth for the Common Good*, p. viii.
25 Ibid. p. ix.
26 Ibid.
27 Article in *Australia Can Work: an alternative to recession*, ed. Terry Flew, quoted in *Common Wealth for the Common Good*, p. 58.
28 Ibid. p. 92.

29 Ibid. p. 97.
30 Ibid. p. 98, 99.
31 *Laborem Exercens*, para. 18, p. 73.
32 Declaration at the World Summit on Social Development in Copenhagen.
33 National Conference of American Catholic Bishops 1991.
34 *A Catholic Framework for Economic Life*.
35 Ibid.
36 Ibid.
37 *Centisimus Annus*, para. 35, p. 64.
38 'The Common Good and the Catholic Church's Social Teaching', Catholic Bishops Conference of England and Wales, 1996, published by Office For Social Justice, St Paul, Minnesota, pp. 11, 12, 16. Viewed on their web site.
39 *Deus Caritas Est*, para. 26, p. 10.
40 *The Catholic Leader*, 12 March 2006.

Chapter 15

CATHOLIC SOCIAL TEACHING AND THE WORKER IN THE NEOLIBERAL CAPITALIST ERA

This work has sought to illustrate the manner in which the social teachings of Scripture and the Church's magisterium have ameliorated and changed the conditions of workers in different ways in different times through the ages. The need for the application of Christian social principles to the present-day relationship between capital and labour is as pressing as it ever was.

The worker in the twenty-first century is living in an era in which the ideology of 'globalism' is eroding the social justice and social welfare gains of working men and women, made from the late nineteenth century through to the twentieth century. This is happening to the extent that there is a re-emergence of the laissez-faire capitalist mindset with many of its attendant evils.

Globalization and globalism

It is useful to distinguish the term 'globalism' from the term 'globalization'. Globalization, like most words ending with the letters 'ion', indicates a process. For instance, we have the processes of electrification, mechanization, and automation. Globalization is then a result of normal human creativity leading to technological development, better organization and economic development. Globalism is entirely different. It is an ideology, a blind faith in free-market economics and minimal government intervention, in the belief that capitalism can work best without economic regulation. Globalism could perhaps be described as the international manifestation of neoliberal capitalism. International bodies like the World Trade Organization and the International Monetary Fund have engineered the deregulation of national economies so that multinational corporations can freely shift their capital, technology and products around the world to maximize profits. The argument is that this will see a rising tide of economic growth lift all people's standard of living. The opponents of globalism argue that the reverse has occurred.

Injurious policies of the indirect employer

As governments and their agencies are one of the many facets of the 'indirect employer' of *Laborem Exercens* referred in the previous chapter, they must share the responsibility for the increasingly disadvantageous position of the worker and the increasingly unjust conditions under which they labour. Some policy areas in which the ideology of globalism has manifested itself are:

- Corporatization and privatization
  Since the 1930s some areas of what we may call the 'public sector' such as railways and public works were used to absorb the otherwise unskilled, unemployed workers. That last 'employment safety net' has now been denied to these people as these public utilities are downsized, corporatized and privatized.
- Labour market deregulation
  This is merely a euphemism for emasculating the unions and decreasing their power, replacing collective bargaining with workplace contracts in order to keep down wages. Accompanying this is the growing casualisation of the workforce.
- Trade policies
  Some trade policies include the slashing of import tariffs to a level resulting in a marked decline in certain industries causing ever-increasing unemployment.

Laissez-faire and neoliberal capitalism compared

George Soros, in describing some of the features of laissez-faire capitalism, which he believes is more appropriately termed 'market fundamentalism', says that it is market fundamentalism that has rendered the global capitalist system unsound and unsustainable. This, he says, is a relatively recent state of affairs. At the end of the Second World War, international movement of capital was restricted, and the Bretton Woods institutions were set up to facilitate trade in the absence of capital movements. Soros says that restrictions were removed only gradually, and it was only when Margaret Thatcher and Ronald Reagan came to power around 1980 that market fundamentalism became the dominant ideology. Soros says that it is market fundamentalism that has put financial capital into the driver's seat. He adds that, according to market fundamentalism, all social activities and human interactions should be looked at as transactional, contract-based relationships and valued in terms of a single common denominator: money. Activities should be regulated, as far as possible, by nothing more intrusive than the invisible hand of profit – maximizing competition. He says that the incursions of market ideology into fields far outside business and economics are having destructive and demoralizing social effects. Of particular concern is his observation that market fundamentalism has become so powerful that any political forces that thereto resist it are branded as sentimental, illogical and naive.[1]

Comparing the global capitalist system of the late nineteenth century with the contemporary version, Soros makes the interesting observation that the Judaeo–Christian ethical tradition which influenced the values which then existed in the system does not exist at the present time. He says that monetary values and transactional markets did not provide an adequate basis for social cohesion.[2] Although a supporter of the globalization process, Soros considered that the present arrangements in which capital was free to move around, but in which social concerns received short shrift, was a distorted form of a global open society.[3]

Robert Simons refers to another aspect of global neoliberal capitalism: the need for society not to become overwhelmed by the steadily increasing power of multinational or transnational corporations. He says that the increased power becomes visible especially in two trends. One is the formation of oligopolies, where whole industrial sectors are dominated worldwide by a handful of firms. A second is the formation of conglomerates where a single TNC (transnational corporation) has interests in a wide variety of unrelated activities. These two trends have enormously enhanced TNC power in relation to national governments, consumers and, importantly to this study, the labour force.[4]

Moreena Hertz, associate director of The Centre of International Business & Management at the Judge Institute of the University of Cambridge, describes the situation in which we find ourselves at the dawn of the new millennium. She describes it as the world of the silent takeover where government's hands are tied and we are increasingly dependent on corporations. It is a world where business is in the driving seat, corporations determine the rules of the game, and governments have become referees, merely enforcing rules laid down by others.[5] Others, such as Michael Novak, see the large corporation as a counterbalance to what is perceived as the growing ambitions of the administrative state. Novak asserts that were the state to acquire control over large corporations, the political system would thoroughly dominate the economic system.[6] With respect to Novak, as we have seen, it is the vacation by governments of their responsibilities to the common good, and the exponents of neoliberal capitalism assuming a greatly enlarged role in the determination of financial policy that poses a threat, not just of the domination of the financial system but to the existence of the open, free and democratic society. Moreover, democratic governments are, in theory at least, answerable to the people. Corporations broadly speaking are answerable to no one other than their shareholders.

The injustices and inequalities resulting from neoliberal capitalism are compounded today by the fact that major political parties in developed countries increasingly rely on corporate funding for electioneering. Further governments depend on corporations and capital markets for foreign investment. All major political parties these days share an ideological orthodoxy that favours corporations and the rentier class. All of this may well explain the benign attitude of governments towards oligopolies.

Ramesh Mishra sums up the situation when he says that today we are faced with a situation where national economies have become far more open and internationalized, but the site for democratic regulation of economic activity remains the nation state. As a result, he said, there is an inevitable conflict between the demands of a globalizing process seeking to establish universal laissez-faire with scant regard for its social and human (including environmental) consequences, and the democratic nation state with its mandate of collective responsibility for the wellbeing of the national community – a mandate Mishra says that, given the systems of social protection, face the prospect of erosion through what he describes as the neoliberal thrust of globalization which would make the market sovereign.[7] Mishra says that systems of social protection represented the outcome of more than a century of struggle in which democratic political rights have played a major part. He says that it was not surprising then that the attempt on the part of capital to undo these gains of democratic struggle by denationalizing the economy, and thus moving economic policy beyond the pale of democratic decision-making, appears as a major, covert and indirect assault on democracy. He concluded with the observation that what he termed globalization, which this writer would describe as global neoliberal capitalism, was not only threatening to roll back the welfare state but was, given its unregulated and undemocratic character, also threatening to roll back democracy.[8] This writer concurs.

Employment and wages

The reality of the declining living standards of the poor and middle class in the United States is highlighted by an article in the *Wall Street Journal* of 1 October 1999 under the heading 'The pain behind the gain'. The article deals with the annual US Census Bureau report on wages and household incomes. Referring to the report, the *Wall Street Journal* says:

> [It] offers stark proof that life is still a struggle for millions of Americans. All the fanfare about this record-breaking expansion . . . masks statistics showing that, overall, wages have barely budged for the decade as a whole. Last year's poverty rate was still 1.6 percentage points higher than it was in 1973 . . .[9]

The *Wall Street Journal* said that whilst the US boom had generated more wealth for more Americans, it also showed that the fruits of the booming years economy had been heavily skewed towards the rich. Income inequality rose sharply through the 1980s and early 1990s. From 1994 onwards, the disparity had been locked in at an historically high level. The *Wall Street Journal* said that although wages for low-paid workers had been rising slightly, they were still not high enough to lift significant numbers out of poverty.[10]

The *New York Times* took a similar view in an article published shortly before the US Census Bureau report on wages and household incomes:

> The gap between rich and poor has grown into an economic chasm so wide this year that the richest 2.7 million Americans, the top 1%, will have as many after-tax dollars to spend as the bottom 100 million ... Among the most prosperous one-fifth of American households, or about 54 million people, whose share of the nation-

al income grew, that fatter slice of the pie was not sliced evenly. More than 90% of the increase is going to the richest 1% of households ...

The *New York Times* called attention to another revelation. The census report found that the rise in average income during the late 1990s was due in part to Americans working longer hours. In 1998 Americans spent an average of sixty hours a week at work.[11]

Referring to the increasing rate of job losses in the United States, Danni Rodrik says that the causes of these job losses are consistent with a picture of labour markets in which greater openness to trade, interacting with the short-term fluctuations in the labour demand, have resulted in greater inequalities across and within skill groups and greater instability in wages and employment. He believes it plausible that the deep sense of insecurity felt by participants in today's labour market was related to the fact that globalization had made their services much more easily substitutable than before.[12] A feature of neoliberal capitalist economies is one in which secure and well-paid jobs are eliminated and replaced by a plethora of part-time and insecure jobs.[13]

Many corporations hold the threat over their workforce that if wages are not held at a level acceptable to a corporation, the enterprise will be moved elsewhere. It is increasingly the case that the justice of the workers' wage demands and the necessity for the payment of a living wage to workers is disregarded in favour of the attaining of desired profit levels. This is but one of the many ways in which the practical application of neoliberal capitalist ideology comes into direct conflict with the social teachings of the Catholic Church.

Mishra makes the point that what international agencies such as the International Monetary Fund and the World Bank are advocating is a simple market model which regards labour power as a mere commodity.[14] This notion is in direct conflict with the Church's teaching on the dignity of work, the necessity for a just and living wage, the partnership of labour and capital, the personalist approach to labour as enunciated by John Paul II, and the Church's teaching on labour as being a sharing in the work of creation.

Mishra adds that there is evidence from the US that employers can no longer be relied upon to provide workers with good wages and benefits such as health insurance and pensions. Increasingly workers and their families are being left to fend for themselves, which they are less able to do in a situation of job insecurity and declining wages.[15] Explaining the rationale for the neoliberal capitalist assault upon what we would regard as social security and the tenets of the welfare state, Mishra says that measures such as full employment, employment protection, unemployment benefits, minimum wage laws, health and safety legislation and trade union rights brought about the institutionalization of basic social standards and to that extent limited the scope of the market. These regulations appeared as so many impediments which prevented the deployment of labour freely as a commodity. The neoliberal capitalist argument is that these safeguards for workers 'distort' the price of labour. In a globally competitive but unregulated environment, competitive advantage appears to lie with 'flexible' labour markets – hence the emphasis of neoliberal capitalism in removing the 'rigidity' in the name of becoming more competitive.[16]

A working paper presented to a meeting of Australian participants in the Asia – Pacific network of National Institutes for Labour Studies in August 1995 listed certain of the components and features of what is termed the neoliberal state. These included:

- low wages – reduced union influence
- weakening of employment legislation and trade unions
- decentralization of the local wage system to tailor wages to local/regional market conditions, i.e. from the national to the state and from the state to the region
- deregulation – aimed to free all local markets of bureaucratic impediments
- reduction in public infrastructure – education, health, and so on.[17]

The working papers state that both at the regional level as well as at the national level in Australia, as in many other countries, one has witnessed the breakdown of the Keynesian welfare state and the emergence of what is termed a neoliberal state.[18]

Richard Sennett details some of the staggering wage inequalities that have arisen in the United States in recent years. Quoting investigations made by the economist Simon Head, Sennett said that for the bottom 80 per cent of the American working population, average weekly wages (adjusted for inflation) fell by 18 per cent from 1973 to 1995, while the pay of the corporate elite rose 19 per cent before taxes, and 66 per cent after the tax accountants had worked their magic. Sennett said that another economist, Paul Krugman, postulated that the top 1 per cent of American wage earners more than doubled their real incomes in the decade 1979-89 in comparison with a much lower rate of wealth accumulated in the decade before. Quoting from *The Economist*, Sennett said that in Britain the top 20 per cent of the working population earned seven times as much as the bottom 20 per cent, while twenty years ago the spread was only four times. An American Secretary of Labour has stated that the United States was on the way to becoming a two-tiered society composed of a few winners and a larger group left behind, a view seconded by the Chairman of the Federal Reserve Bank who declared that unequal income could become a major threat to (American) society.[19]

In Australia, Dr Ernest Healy of Monash University's Centre for Population & Urban Research described the shift to longer working hours as a social and political crisis in the making. After examining the Australian Bureau of Statistics Quarterly ABS Labour Force survey, Dr Healy wrote in *People & Place* that:

> During the period 1986-87 to 1998-99 the proportion of the labour force working long hours (45+) increased far more than the proportion working fewer than 35 hours. This trend was particularly marked for older men and to a lesser degree for older married women.
>
> In 1998-99 more than 47% of men in the labour force aged 35-54 worked for longer than the standard working week, compared to just under 36% in 1986-87.[20]

He said that the cause of this major change was a direct consequence of labour market deregulation. He added that while it was now more frequently recognized that part-time workers often desire more work, it is still not sufficiently recognized that the trend to long hours may be, for many workers, involuntary – even coercive.[21]

Another recent Australian study by Professor Gregory of the Research School of Social Sciences Australian National University, revealed some alarming social trends in respect of families and work. Surveys showed that between 1979 and 1998 the percentage of children growing up in families where no parent had a job rose from 11 per cent to 18 per cent. The survey showed that since 1975, the number of men in full-time employment as a percentage of the population had fallen by 26 per cent, and this had not been adequately compensated for by female full-time employment, which rose only 1 per cent over the same period. Over this time, unemployment rose from 4.6 per cent in 1975 to 7.3 per cent in 1999, with the average duration of unemployment increasing from 12.7 weeks to a staggering 55.7 weeks. Professor Gregory's research showed that the major cause of the growth in the number of jobless families was the destruction of full-time jobs amongst men. In 1998, 12 per cent of these men in couple families were without work, double the figure of 1979. He said that Australia was experiencing a 'hollowing out' of its middle class. Families have been moving towards either two jobs (the 'work rich') or no jobs (the 'work poor'). Although there has been a considerable growth in part-time employment, this was not sufficient to offset full-time job losses over the period.[22]

Professor Gregory's findings have been supported by a recent study commissioned by *The Australian* newspaper, by Anne Harding from the National Centre for Social and Economic Modelling, which looked at changes in personal and family incomes from 1982 to 1996–97. The study confirmed that there had been a hollowing out of the middle class. Middle income earners shrank from 45 per cent to 35 per cent of all wage earners. About half moved up into high-income brackets and half moved down into lower-income brackets. Figures published by Bob Birrell and Virginia Ropson of the Centre for Population and Urban Research at Monash University in October 1998 showed that almost one-third of 25–44-year-old men were not in full-time work, with dramatic effects on their marriage rates, divorce rates and accompanying rise in female single-parent families.[23]

The Bulletin of Labour Relations No.45 of 2002 verifies the findings of Professor Gregory referred to earlier. It generally refers to what it calls the 'massive growth of non-standard or precarious employment' and especially in the number of workers employed on a casual basis. The report says that on a conservative estimate, by the late 1990s, at least 45 per cent of the Australian labour force was employed on a non-standard basis. Of this group more than half were casual, making casual employment in Australia higher than in any other OECD (Organization for Economic Co-operation and Development) country. It said that the level of casual employment had more than doubled since the mid-1980s. Furthermore, there had been a dramatic increase in the number of workers employed as full-time casuals. Between 1984 and 1997 the number of full-time casuals increased to 10.6 per cent of all full-time workers in Australia. These workers do not enjoy formal employment protection. In particular he noted that with the movement of regulation from awards to single-employer enterprise agreements in the early 1990s there was an extensive liberalization of casual clauses, including the gradual erosion of casual loadings, in agreements.[24]

In May 2007, the chairman of the Australian Social Justice Council, Bishop Christopher Saunders said families struggling to meet costs of living and higher levels of household debt, had not been well served by a labour market that has produced more jobs that are low paying, insecure, and involve irregular hours. He added that a recent joint study by the Human Rights and Equal Opportunity Commission and Relationships Australia had confirmed that more than twenty years of labour market deregulation with its consequences of longer and more irregular working hours, had upset the work and family balance.[25]

Guy Standing details several emerging trends in the UK which evidence an employment insecurity which has induced instability in the labour market and income assessment. He says three emerging trends are evident:

- in industrialized countries, at least, employment separation has been increasingly likely to lead to joblessness
- for those who become jobless, employment separation has been associated with increasing duration of joblessness
- for those who find a job, employment separation is increasingly likely to be followed by a job with a lower income.

He says that one reason for this may be that entry level wages have fallen relative to average wages, as was the case in the United Kingdom.[26] Standing's findings in respect of the increased duration of joblessness following employment separation are interesting, as they mirror the results of Professor Gregory's research in Australia referred to earlier.

Do we not see in all of this an example of the social dislocation and injustices which flow from the disordered ideology and financial structures being increasingly imposed on an unsuspecting, perhaps overtrusting society, by the ideologues of neo-liberal capitalism?

Trade unions

The International Labour Organization's World Labour Report 1997-98 provides interesting empirical evidence on trade union density for sixty-five countries in 1985 and 1995. The results are summarized as follows:

- 51 per cent (33) of the countries saw a decline of union membership by more than 20 per cent
- 25 per cent (16) of the countries saw a decline of more than 5 and less than 20 per cent
- 11 per cent (7) of the countries had a more or less stable union density (5 per cent)
- 3 per cent (2) of the countries experienced a growth of more than 5 and less than 20 per cent
- 11 per cent (7) of the countries experienced a growth of more than 20 per cent membership.[27]

These figures show the general decline of trade union membership on a worldwide basis. Peter Leisink says that one of the reasons for the decline is the attitude of global bodies such as the OECD. He says that one of the measures for improving business competitiveness which the OECD advises, is the lowering of production costs and prices by removing market imperfections in the supply of production factors, including labour (OECD 1996, p. 56).

This represents the line of thought which, in his analysis of orthodox economic theory, Campbell, of the International Labour Office criticizes as an approach that assumes that labour market interventions largely interfere with and impede efficient adjustments, and that all rules work to the detriment of economic growth and job creation. Leisink says that Campbell argues these assumptions are unsubstantiated, and raises empirical studies which show that high labour standards do not go hand in hand with poor economic performance. According to Leisink, Campbell concludes that labour standards and good economic performance are complements rather than substitutes.[28]

Danni Rodrik is of the view that one of the factors leading to the weakening of unions has been the greater substitutability of labour, which alters the nature of bargaining between workers and employers. He says that to the extent that wages are determined in bargaining between workers and employers, an increase in the substitutability of workers results in a lower share of the enterprise surplus ending up with workers. A related consequence of this is that the unions become weaker.[29]

Rodrik says that the political salience of labour's voice in the United States, and to a lesser extent in Europe, is currently diminished by at least three forces. First, he says that the same pressures that reduce the bargaining power of labour in the workplace also reduce its power in the political marketplace. As governments increasingly compete for enterprises and capital, the interests of workers – who, after all, have nowhere else to go – are relegated to second place. 'Competitiveness' becomes another word for a labour cost, something that can be enhanced by slashing benefits and wages. Second, he says, the excessive attachment of labour to a single political party as is the case in the United States, United Kingdom and Australia, diminishes its political power. Political parties are naturally more responsive to the interests of those who are ready to shift their allegiances to competing parties rather than to the interests of captive groups. Third, according to Rodrik, the receptivity of the general public to the ideas of labour advocates is greatly reduced by the perceived protectionist tenor that often characterizes these ideas.[30]

It is perhaps unfortunate that trade unions have been largely unable to educate the general populace as to the differences between free trade and fair trade. William Tabb says that a preferred solution for assisting workers by trade policy is not protectionism but protection for vulnerable people in socially equitable ways. For most people, if not for many economists, fairness needs to be taken seriously and made integral to the evaluation of international trade policies. Market economies, however, are not inclined to pursue justice issues as part of economic analysis or trade policy.[31] This failure of the market system, from the viewpoint of Catholic social thought, is one of the many errors of the neoliberal financial system. As Rodrik says, nations hold the right – and should be allowed – to restrict trade where it conflicts with widely held norms at home or undermines domestic social arrangements that enjoy broad support.[32] It is the duty of the 'indirect employer' as defined by John Paul II in *Laborem Exercens*,[33] in accordance with the common good, to bear in mind the same considerations as ought to be borne in mind by the direct employer towards the worker in upholding wage justice, the dignity of labour, just working conditions and the right to work. It is the view of this writer that governments, in their role as 'indirect employers' are, in the developed economies, shedding this responsibility in favour of the tenets of neoliberal capitalism.

Kenneth Davidson, writing in *The Age* of 19 November 2000, said that globalization and associated neoliberal policies over the past few decades had eroded workers' bargaining power. The US labour market was effectively de-unionized during the 1980s. Between 1979 and 1997, real wages fell in the United States. He said that the fruits of rising labour productivity were channelled not even partly into wages but into profits and a rising share market.[34]

In the developed economies there has been a systematic and concerted attempt to weaken the role of trade unions and to roll back protective employment regulations. Guy Standing says that in western Europe there have been numerous legislative enactments directed to that aim. The result was increased employment insecurity. These measures included:

- regulations barring certain groups from employment protection, or allowing employers to hire them without giving them such protection
- regulations limiting compensation for those laid off
- regulations lengthening the period of employment required before protection is provided and regulations reducing the number of weeks of notice required for retrenchment
- regulations increasing the conditions required of workers to enable them to have employment protection
- tripartite or bipartite national agreements to reduce employment protection and compensation for dismissal in return for something else.

Such 'concession bargaining' was a feature of collective agreements in the USA in the 1980s and spread in Europe, a prominent case being the agreement between the employers and unions in Spain in April 1997.

Tabb says that in the United States low union density, effectively the lowest among the advanced economies, might be considered a matter of worker choice except that it is so hard for workers to speak freely and organize without retribution. The threat and the experience of activists being fired are pervasive. He says that 80 per cent of workers believe it 'very' or somewhat 'likely' that non-union workers will get fired if they try to organize a union. There is ample evidence that most non-unionized workers fear victimization and that their fears are warranted. The labour regime in the United States is one of

Catholic social teaching and the worker

the most regressive of any of the advanced economies. Human Rights Watch research into the exercise of labour rights in different industries, occupations and regions of the United States found that freedom of association was a right under severe, often buckling, pressure wherever workers tried to exercize it.[35] Any employer intent on resisting workers self-organization can drag out legal proceedings for years, fearing little more than an order to place a written notice in the workplace promising not to repeat unlawful conduct. Tabb said that when employers are ordered to pay back pay with interest, any income received by the employee from other employment in the interim is deducted from the amount they need to return to the wronged worker. In any event, he said, back pay is a small price for getting rid of union militants and organizers and is considered a routine cost of doing business. The Human Rights Watch report says that, as a result, a culture of near impunity has taken shape in much of US labour law and practice.[36]

Tabb relates the case of Wal-Mart as an example of a US corporation that will go to extreme lengths to stay union-free. He says that in 2000, when just eleven linked department workers in a Jacksonville, Texas' super centre voted to join a union, the retailer approached a friendly judge in Bentonville who slapped the union with a highly unusual 'national temporary restraining order'. The order prohibited the union – the United Food and Commercial Workers, which had launched a recruiting drive – from soliciting workers inside its stores on the grounds that 'union members were entering private store areas and potentially endangering public health'. Tabb says that the Wal-Mart experience is not an extreme case, only one of the best known. The erosion of labour laws, that in the 1930s were passed in the United States under intense pressure from a mobilized trade union movement to protect workers, has transformed into emasculation in recent decades. Tabb makes the pertinent point that it will be necessary to build a global workers' movement so that core labour can be made viable not only in Third World police states, but in the United States as well.[37]

Another example of the erosion of the position of labour within the jurisdiction of the United States was the example of Levi-Strauss, whose business partners on the Pacific Island of Saipan, a USA protectorate, put the 'Made in the USA' label on sweatshop-produced products from a factory in which the contractor was underpaying workers and keeping them in padlocked barracks. According to Tabb, this particular situation has now been reviewed following sustained adverse publicity.[38] Tabb describes one common method used by employers to force labour to toe the line. This is the threat and practice of what he calls 'runaway shops' – that is, moving production offshore.[39] The employers simply threaten the labour force that the enterprise will be moved offshore if they do not accept the working conditions and wages laid down by the management. Employer strategies such as this are yet a further example of the necessity for the building of an effective and strong global workers' movement. In this writer's view there is a definite role for the Church in the building of such a movement by means of the practical application and promulgation of the wealth of Catholic social teaching directly applicable to rights and duties of capital and labour.

Apart from widespread employer and governmental opposition to trade unions, Standing lists a number of other factors which have contributed to the global decline of unionism. He says that labour-market insecurity has eroded membership, with fewer workers being employed, making it easier for employers to resist or derecognize unions and making it harder for workers to organize or have the confidence to do so. External flexibility has made an increasing proportion of jobs less able to be unionized. There is extensive evidence that temporary, part-time and other non-regular workers are less likely to be in unions. The changing composition of the labour force and increased labour force flexibility tended to lower unionization, since intermittent and marginal labour force participants are less inclined to join or stay in unions. He also refers to what he terms the establishing of 'pet unions' by our firms and governments. These unions are set up as the company-based alternatives to independent unions and are easily influenced by management. In this writer's view such unions are contrary to the idea of independent trade unions formed through recognition of the right of workers to associate, enshrined in nearly every social encyclical since *Rerum Novarum*.[40]

However, it should be said that the attitude of many workers themselves has not been helpful to the cause of unionization. This is particularly the case with white-collar employees whose level of remuneration and general work conditions may be such that they do not readily identify with unions which some may perceive as having greater application to blue-collar workers. There is also the prevalence amongst higher paid workers of what is termed in labour relations as the 'I'm all right Jack syndrome'. It is submitted that there is an educational role here for those entrusted with the promulgation of Catholic social teaching, particularly in reference to the principles of solidarity, the primacy of labour and worker participation.

Will Hutton makes the point that the American labour market is characterized by impermanence, from which not even the professional and managerial classes are immune. He says that in 1993, for the first time ever, more white-collar workers than blue-collar workers were unemployed. As the labour market tightened in the second half of the 1990s, impermanence worked to the advantage of those workers with skills, who were able to bid up their wages in the talent war. However, he said, this cyclical effect did not disguise the underlying trends. Over time the story is one of rising turnover rates, more contingent work, an explosion of the use of agencies supplying temporary workers, and longer hours. The average American now has nine jobs in a lifetime, and almost three in ten Americans work in jobs on non-standard terms – part-time, temping, on-call, or day labour. Average wages fell steadily in real terms for more than twenty years up until 1995 for all but the top 20 per cent of the workforce. To compensate, those four-fifths of Americans who faced a fall in real wages worked longer hours over the same period and continued to do so into the second half of the 1990s, even as wage rates in real terms began to harden. On average, Americans now work around fifty hours a week, up from about forty in 1973 – more than any other industrialized country except Portugal. American workers also have the least paid holidays.[41]

Worker participation – a move towards more just work structures

While the tenets of neoliberal capitalism hold sway in the greater part of the industrial world, a number of alternative enterprise structures have arisen which, it is submitted, are in accordance with the social teachings of the Church as enunciated in this work. In his essay on managers as distributors of justice, James Murphy suggests that when people work, they leave – in the form of their products, but in virtue of who they are as images of the Creator – an irrepeatable imprint on the world which is, in its turn, an image of the creative activity of God. Murphy believed that no price, no usable good, nothing exchangeable for goods, could stand as adequate recompense for this. Accordingly wage remuneration in itself can never truly compensate – never exhaust – the human act of labour.[42]

Murphy sees gainsharing as one way of building equity into a firm's wage system. Gainsharing is based on the improved productivity of the individual worker or work team. Since profits and productivity are not always increased in tandem, gainsharing establishes a direct connection between workers' productivity and their pay. He says that gainsharing is based upon a formula which connects increased individual or team productivity to increases in compensation, irrespective of the company's overall performance. In short, gainsharing rewards those who make improvements at any organizational level, thereby increasing equity within the organization.[43] Gainsharing in many industrialized countries with central wage fixing systems is often referred to as a productivity wage, and the basis of its calculation is termed the 'productivity wage index'. Along with the company gainsharing programmes are employee stock ownership plans. This, according to Murphy, contributes to the growth of an 'ownership culture'. Employees are encouraged to regard the company as 'their' company and authority is derived not so much from seniority, neither is it exercised in an arbitrary manner, but rather is derived from demonstrated competence, knowledge and skill. Referring to the firm of Herman Miller, who had in place a gainsharing programme and an employee stock ownership plan, Murphy says that the company also observed an equity pay ratio which stipulates that the highest paid employee, usually the chief executive, cannot be paid more than twenty times the pre-tax income of the firm's manufacturing employees.[44]

Gainsharing needs to be differentiated from the more familiar profit-sharing. Profit-sharing is based on the level of performance of the firm. It rewards or penalizes all members of the organization according to the profitability of the whole. It takes no account of the fact that factors other than the employees' productivity and outside the employees' control can be determining factors. Legislative enactments would be required to protect and ensure the efficiency of economic democracy of this kind, and regulations would be required to overcome potential external influences from the years of operation of the systems. For instance, to prevent profit-sharing or stakeholder firms from reverting to conventional firms dominated by external blockholder principals (banks, pension funds, and so on), there would have to be mechanisms in place ensuring that all the stakeholders were involved in the regulation of the allocation of economic surplus and the timing of its realization.

Standing further says that the surplus sharing system must embrace the intermittently employed flexi-workers and the community around the firm. Among the benefits would be that income inequalities between those inside and outside employment would be reduced, and social pressures would be placed on those not in employment to play the role of socially responsible citizens.[45]

He says that a system of communal profit-sharing would strengthen the sense of community and citizenship. The challenge was to give voice to groups that would check 'winner takes all' mechanisms. High taxes do not work well in an open global economic system. Yet unless the inequalities are addressed, distributive justice is impossible. Sharing through the democratic control over the identification, monitoring and allocation of economic surplus could ensure a balance between competing claims. He added, however, that stakeholder democracy must incorporate what he termed the 'Difference Principle' so that checks would be implemented to prevent powerful combinations. If control were concentrated in the hands of any particular type of shareholder, that interest might opt for short-term, high-return investment and distribute dividends as quickly as possible to a few shareholding institutions. This, he said, would have adverse consequences for others, including actual and potential workers in the firm and in the community. The challenge was to ensure that all stakeholder groups have a meaningful voice in the control process, and that sustainable investment coexisted with sustainable redistribution to the vulnerable, the insecure and the surrounding community.[46]

Helen Alford and Michael Naughton quote Jeff Gates as having said that the more connected capital was to labour and to the communities that supplied labour – that is, through ownership – the more it could serve the common good. They said that Gates, Norman Kurland, Robert Ashford and others proposed not only employee stock ownership plans but also customer stock ownership plans and related enterprise share ownership plans, and other stock ownership plans to reconnect capital to the communities that generated it. Gates aimed for a 'close capitalism' in which those who stood to be affected by the uses of corporate property considered those uses from the perspective of owners and spoke for or against them with the voices of owners.[47]

Jacques Maritain, writing on what he termed the co-proprietorship of the means of work, said that means of work should serve as the material basis of a form of personal possession, the possession no longer of a thing in space, but of a form of activity in time, the possession of a 'trust' or 'workers title' which assured a man that his employment was rightly his, was judicially linked with his person, and that his operative activity will therefore have room to progress; it should serve to give a title and a social guarantee to bring into action what was functionally and inalienably the property of the worker: his personal powers, his intelligence, the skill of his hands. This was the profound human truth understood by the medieval guilds.[48]

Reform of the institution of the corporation

In the related matter of corporate responsibility, advocates such as Ralph Nader suggested the adoption of a 'Corporate Bill of Obligations' providing for a measure of control over management by shareholders, consumers and employees, and removing the veil of corporate secrecy over such details as earnings by subsidiaries, the identity of the real owners, safety-testing procedures and product-control standards. In addition, this suggested bill of obligations would contain antitrust restrictions, for example, by limiting to 12 per cent the share that any one corporation may own in any oligopolistic industry. Other positions would protect consumers against shoddy and dangerous products. It is important that statutory provisions relating to such obligations possess adequate enforcement powers as there was always the danger, as Nader pointed out, that a federal chartering agency would become as unresponsive and inefficient as were some of the present regulatory and enforcement agencies.[49]

Antonides points out that, generally speaking, proposals for corporate reform have centred on ways to impose restraints from the outside or on ways to democratize the corporation from within. A number of specific proposals were put forward by various participants in the Conference on Corporate Accountability. For example, John J. Flynn advocated that employees of the large corporations be nominated as the 'constituency' and given a voice in management, which would provide a meaningful check and balance upon corporate power. He said that this would change the position of the worker from 'seller of his labour' to 'owner of the enterprise' and would drastically change the function of labour unions. Another proposal by Robert Townsend, former chairman of Avis Rent-a-Car and author of *Up the Organization,* presented a modest proposal in the form of advocating the appointment of a 'public director' to all manufacturing companies with over $1billion in assets. Townsend recommended that each public director have a budget of $1million a year of the company's money with which he would be able to hire all the staff needed to examine the performance of the corporation. Directors would be appointed from a pool that was created especially for that purpose and assigned to corporations by lot. They would be rotated every four years.

There is a growing argument that the institution of the corporation itself requires examination and reform. If government intervention in the free market of Adam Smith's time created the corporate capitalism of today, and if this system is prone to injustice and instability, then governments individually and as an international community have not only the right but the moral obligation to regulate their own creation. Firstly, if citizens granted the privilege of limited liability and incorporation to corporations, then citizens have a right to share in the enormous wealth corporations create. This dispels the claim that the fiduciary duty of a corporate manager is only to his shareholders as an economic heresy – that is, it is only part of his duty, not the whole moral duty. Chief executives have a responsibility to the citizens who granted their corporations these privileges in the first place. Those free market advocates who today argue for *laissez nous faire* are in fact arguing for the granting of even more privileges to the corporate sector.

Secondly, if corporate capitalism's financial system is prone to instability and massive market failures, then governments and the international community have a moral responsibility to regulate the system to prevent or lessen the impact of market failures. It should not be forgotten that it was the gross nineteenth-century injustices and massive market failure that was the Great Depression, that made corporate capitalism the midwife of both communism and Nazism. Certainly, there is a powerful moral argument for corporate capitalism. It can produce wealth like no other system in history. There is, however, an equally powerful argument for it to be regulated. Unregulated, it does not know how to justly distribute this wealth or stabilize its financial system. Equally it can be said that citizens and families have the right to have their government intervene in the economy to ensure that there is a breadwinner's just wage, legal protection for working conditions and hours, taxation concessions for families, allowances for a wife and children, and a savings system so that people can provide for their own needs.

Worker cooperatives

Worker cooperatives exist in both developed and undeveloped countries. The best examples of worker cooperatives are those of the Mondragon region in the Basque country of northern Spain. The first cooperative was established in 1959 on the initiative of Father Don José Maria, commonly known in the Mondragon region as Arizmendi, Luis Usatorre, Jesús Larrañaga, Alfonso Gorroñogoitia, José Maria Ormaechea and Javier Ortubay.[50] Many of their founding principles were based on those of Robert Owen and the Rochdale Pioneers who founded the first cooperative in Great Britain in 1844. The cooperative, known as ULGOR (an anacronym of the initial letters of the names of the founders), was to be directly owned by the workers and met at least once a year in a general assembly which elected the board of directors who held office for a period of four years. Half of the board retires every two years. The general assembly operates on the principle of one worker, one vote. The board of directors appoints the general manager who is the chief executive appointed for four years. The general manager has no vote on the board of directors and acts as an adviser only. The board consists of a broad cross-section of the workers, and no fees are paid to directors.

A social council elected from the various departments of the cooperative deals with the board of directors on matters concerning personnel, discipline, working conditions, wages and welfare.

On joining the workers' cooperative each member has to make a capital contribution. This remains his own property and can only be withdrawn by him if he retires from the cooperative.

The workers receive a monthly salary. The greater the job responsibility, the higher the salary. It is provided, however, that the highest paid worker cannot receive more than three times the salary of the lowest paid worker. If the co-operative makes a profit, 10 per cent is paid back into the community for such things as schools and cultural activities, 20 per cent is paid to the cooperative's reserves or reinvestment funds and 70 per cent is available for division amongst the members of the cooperative. Each member's share is proportional to his or her salary. This payment, which cannot be withdrawn by the worker, is added to his or her capital holding and receives an interest payment of 6 per cent. Like their initial capital contribution, these moneys can only be withdrawn on the worker's retirement from the cooperative. By insisting that members must take their capital holdings on leaving, the cooperatives are protected from external control. On retiring from the cooperative the worker receives in addition their capital holdings and their normal pension entitlements.

In Mondragon a cooperative bank has been established to assist with the formation of other cooperatives and to monitor their progress. Once a cooperative exceeds 500 members, the excess is split off and a new cooperative formed.[51] The cooperatives are involved in manufacturing, education, both general and tertiary, banking, housing and health. They are perhaps the best example of worker participation and ownership in practice.

Conclusion

One of the developments of most concern in this neoliberal age is the deep disdain with which the opinions of those opposed to the injustices which are inherent in the neoliberal capitalist system are treated. When referring to the World Trade Organization's meeting in Seattle in 1999, John McMurtry said that what those opposed to the World Trade Organization's agenda were trying to emphasize has never been publicly understood. The systematic overriding of elected government policies, laws and historically won social goods, that the protesters have stood against has not yet even been acknowledged. He said that a no-alternative agenda operates on the ontological as well as the ideological level. The existing financial regime exudes the idea that what the regime overrides does not exist, or is evil.[52]

This situation is exacerbated by the fact that the bulk of the mass media is under the control of multinational corporations, the overriding philosophy of which is that of the open market and neoliberal capitalism. McMurtry says that the general problem confronting those concerned with the effects of what he terms 'the global war of occupation' is that the ruling economic paradigm is structured to increase the money-demand of transnational investors rather than the lives of peoples and their life conditions. Societies and environments are understood as means of corporate stockholders' profit maximization, rather than stock markets as means of promoting the shared life good. The world of value is in this way turned upside down.[53]

McMurtry's observations are ones with which this writer concurs. It is this writer's view that neoliberal capitalism is largely a mimic of nineteenth-century laissez-faire capitalism, having embraced most of its worst features.

It is important that society be aware of the threat posed to the existence of a free, socially responsible society by the excesses of global neoliberal capitalism. If we are not vigilant in this regard, the servile state of which Belloc warned may well descend upon us. In his preface to the work *The Catholic Church and the Destitute*, Belloc said that this slavery would not be the slavery of an alien or inferior race, but the slavery of the mass of citizens compelled by social organization to work for the benefit of the few.[54]

In an address to the Pontifical Academy of Social Sciences on 6 March 1999, John Paul II referred to new and disturbing aspects of the conflict between capital and labour. He said that in our present day this conflict showed aspects that were new and more disquieting than previously. Scientific and technological progress and the globalization of markets, of themselves a source of development and progress, exposed workers to the risk of being exploited by the mechanisms of the economy and by the unrestrained quest for productivity.[55] In God's order of things, all of creation, and all that exists in this world, including the financial system, is at the service of humanity. Humanity is not the servant of the financial system. Yet this is the regime imposed upon humanity by neoliberal capitalism. It is an error which compels a breach of the Gospel, 'You cannot serve both God and money'.[56]

Under the sway of the neoliberal ideology, the worker is being once again reduced to the status of a cog in the mechanism of production. Once again, he or she is becoming an object in the processes of production rather than its subject. It is the view of this writer that global neoliberal capitalism poses a greater threat to the free society and the common good than that posed in relatively recent times by fascism and communism. Accordingly, it is necessary that governments and society address the injustices and inequities spawned by this ideology. Nations and governments would do well to heed the warning of Nobel prize-winning Russian historian, novelist, and Soviet dissident, Alexander Solzhenitsyn, who said:

> Although the earthly ideal of socialism–communism has collapsed, the problems it purported to solve remain: the brazen use of social power and the inordinate power of money, which often direct the very course of events. And if the global lesson of the twentieth century does not serve as healing inocculation, then the vast red whirlwind may repeat itself in its entirety.[57]

It is arguable that capitalism, in the form most commonly and historically known to us, has proved incapable of providing equitable and just structures conducive to the building of the common good on a permanent basis. Perhaps, in the form known to us, it has run its course? It may be that new, more equitable structures for the cooperative partnership of labour and capital need to be tested.

Rerum Novarum was a watershed in the conflict between liberal capitalism and the social teaching of the Church. Given the global nature of neo liberal capitalism in our time, this conflict is likely to be even more marked. In this writer's view, it cannot be otherwise.

Notes
1 Soros, *The Crisis of Global Capitalism*, Introduction, pp. xx, xxvi, xxvii.
2 Ibid. p. xxi.
3 Soros, *George Soros on Globalisation*, p. 7.
4 Simons, p. 199.
5 Hertz, p. 7.
6 Novak, *The Spirit of Democratic Capitalism*, p. 178.
7 Mishra, p. 106.
8 Ibid. p. 108.
9 *Wall Street Journal*, 1 October 1999.
10 Ibid.
11 *New York Times*, 5 September 1999.
12 Rodrik, p. 22.
13 Ibid. p. 23.
14 Mishra, p. 22.
15 Ibid. p. 28.
16 Ibid. p. 107.
17 Gollan, p. 46.
18 Ibid. p. 45.
19 Sennett, p. 54.
20 Article by Dr Ernest Healy in *People & Place*, January 2000.
21 Ibid.
22 Gregory, R. G., 'Labour market trends and family policies: implications for children' in *News Weekly*, 31 July 1999.
23 *News Weekly*, 15 July 2000.
24 *Bulletin of Labour Relations* No.45, 2002, pp. 48, 49.
25 *The Catholic Leader*, 6 May 2007.
26 Standing, pp. 182, 183.
27 Leisink, p. 19.
28 Ibid. pp. 1, 2.
29 Rodrik, pp. 23, 24.

30 Ibid. pp. 75, 76.
31 Tabb, p. 54.
32 Ibid. p. 80.
33 *Laborem Exercens*, para. 18, pp. 73, 74.
34 Kenneth Davidson, *The Age*, 19 November 2000.
35 Tabb, p. 125.
36 Ibid. pp. 125, 126.
37 Ibid. p. 136.
38 Ibid.
39 Ibid. p. 126.
40 Tabb, pp. 199, 202.
41 Hutton, pp. 204, 205, 206.
42 Cortright, p. 89.
43 Ibid. p.106.
44 Ibid. p.108.
45 Standing, p. 375.
46 Ibid. p. 374.
47 Alford and Naughton, p. 163.
48 Maritain, p. 182.
49 Antonides, p. 83.
50 Whyte, William Foote and Whyte, Kathleen King, pp. 27, 33.
51 BBC Horizon, written and produced by Dominic Flessati, BBC, 1980.
52 McMurtry, p. 57.
53 Ibid. p. 7.
54 O'Grady, p. 6.
55 John Paul II, Address to the Pontifical Academy of Social Sciences, *L'Osservatore Romano*, English edition, 17 March 1999, p. 3.
56 Matt. 6:24.
57 *New York Times*, 28 November 1993.

Chapter 16

EPILOGUE

The binding threads

Running like threads through the fabric of the Church's social teaching are certain basic principles, briefly summarized here, which provide both the foundations and cohesion of Catholic social teaching – past, present and future.

Justice

Both the Old and New Testaments contain numerous references to justice or justice issues. Some twelve of the Psalms for instance contain references to justice. These references are generally to the poor and the weak or the orphan and the needy and are detailed in Chapter 2 of this work. Likewise, in the Gospels we have the 'Golden Rule': 'So always treat others as you would like them to treat you; that is the meaning of the law and the prophets' (Matt. 7:12). This rule contains a strong call for justice as it is one of the things for which humanity 'hungers and thirsts' (Matt. 5:6).

Service

The call to service of others features prominently in the Gospels. For example, in Luke 22:25–7 Jesus says: 'Among Pagans it is the "kings" who lord it over them, and those who have authority over them are given the title "benefactor". This must not happen with you. No; the greatest among you must behave as if he were the youngest, the leader as if he were the one who serves.' Again, at the Last Supper, Jesus said: 'If I then, the lord and master, have washed your feet, you should wash each other's feet. I have given you an example that you may copy what I have done to you' (John 13:13–15). And again, in Mark 10:43–5 Jesus said: 'The Son of Man himself did not come to be served but to serve, and to give his life as the ransom for many.'

St Paul, in Philippians 2:6-8, speaks of Jesus becoming a servant to all: 'His state was divine, yet he did not cling to his equality with God but emptied himself to assume the condition of a slave . . .'. In Philippians 2:3-4 Paul says: 'Always consider the other person to be better than yourself, so that nobody thinks of his own interests first, but everybody thinks of other people's interests instead.' The instruction of service to others in the Scriptures is clear.

The equality of all before God

Presenting another thread is the biblical concept of the equality of all before God. This is closely associated with the fatherhood of God over all humanity. In Ephesians 4:1-6, Paul says that there is one Lord, one faith, one baptism, one God and Father of us all, who is above all and through all and in all. Indeed, the Lord's Prayer opens with the words, 'Our Father'. In Galatians 3:26-9, Paul preaches of the equality of all believers in Christ regardless of their social status. He says that there are no more distinctions between Jew and Greek, slave and free, male and female, but that all are one in Christ Jesus. Another illustration of this concept is contained in Paul's letter to Philemon where he says that Onesimus should return to Philemon not as a slave but as something much better than a slave, as a dear brother and brother in the Lord.

Stewardship

Stewardship necessarily involves ourselves and others. The fruits of our labour, for example, provide for our own needs and the needs of others.

The Patristic Fathers developed and expounded upon the concept of stewardship. St John Chrysostom, in his treatise on wealth and poverty, said that the rich, by accumulating their wealth, had stolen from the poor. He adds, quoting from Ecclesiasticus 4:1 that the failure of the rich to realize that they hold their goods for the poor is to deprive the poor of their living.

Gregory of Nazianzus, Bishop of Constantinople, said that God spreads out the earth for all the animals, with its fountains, rivers and forests. God gave air to winged animals, water to aquatic creatures, and to all the basic elements of life. These elements of life were not dominated by any power, not restricted by any law, not separated by any boundaries, but were placed by God at the disposal of all and abundantly so that no one would lack anything.[1]

In chapter 16, Book 5 of the *Divine Institutes* the North African, Lactantius, spoke of the equality of all before God and stated what was in effect the essence of stewardship. He said:

> Some will say, are there not among you some poor, and others rich; some servants and others masters? Is there not some difference between individuals? There is none; nor is there any other cause why we mutually bestow upon each other the name of brethren, except that we believe ourselves to be equal. Riches do not render men industrious, except that they are able to make them more conspicuous by good works. For men are rich, not because they possess riches, but because they employ them on works of justice; and they who seem to be poor on this account are rich because they are not in want, and desire nothing.[2]

The common good

Proximate to stewardship is the concept of 'the common good'. Basil the Great, a noted liturgical reformer and social activist, discusses the social nature of mankind in what has become known as 'The Long Rules'. He said that nothing was so compatible with human nature as living in society in dependence upon one another and loving our own kind.[3]

For Ambrose of Milan the idea of the common good was based upon nature itself. In Book 1 of the *Hexameron*, Ambrose said that God had ordered all things to be produced so that there should be food in common to all, and that the air should be a common possession of all.[4] In Book 3 of the same work, Ambrose said:

> It is clear, then, that we should consider and admit that what benefits the individual is the common good, and we should judge nothing as useful unless it benefits all. For how can one be benefited alone? What is useless to all is harmful. I certainly cannot concede that what is useless to all can be of use to anyone at all. For if there is much one law of nature for all, there is also but one state of usefulness for all. And we are bound by the law of nature to act for the good of all. It is not, therefore, right for the person who wishes the interests of another to be considered according to nature, to injure him against the law of nature.[5]

The dignity of the human person

We are all sons and daughters of God and brothers and sisters of Christ. The fatherhood of God confers the status of dignity upon the human person.

St Paul, writing as a prisoner in Rome, said that there was one Lord, one faith, one baptism and one God and Father of us all.[6]

Christianity thus taught, that whilst not ceasing to be God's creature, humanity had now become His children. This dignity of the human person, is, as stated in the Catechism: 'rooted in his creation in the image and likeness of God, and is fulfilled in his vocation to divine beatitude'.[7]

The magisterium

These threads are at the core of Catholic social teaching in general, but particularly teaching on the 'worker question' in particular from *Rerum Novarum* to the present.

Binding these threads together, and imbuing its social teaching with authority and cohesion is the magisterium of the Church. Because of this, the social teaching of the Church is a veritable beacon of light in the social order, to all people in every age.

Notes
1 Phan, p. 125.
2 McDonald, p. 326.
3 Ragner, p. 239.
4 *Hexameron*, Book 1, ch. 28, paras 130, 132 in *Early Church Fathers and other works*, W. M. B. Eerdmans Publishing Co., Edinburgh, 1867.
5 *Hexameron*, Ambrose of Milan, Book 3, para. 25 in Phan, p. 179.
6 Ephesians 4:1–6.
7 Catechism of the Catholic Church, St Pauls Edition, 1998, p. 424.

BIBLIOGRAPHY

Encyclicals
Caritate Christi Compulsi, Pius XI, 3 May 1932, Human Life International CD Library.
Casti Conubii, Pius XI, 31 December 1930, Human Life International CD Library, Front Royal, 2000.
Centesimus Annus, John Paul II, 1 May 1991, Editiones Paulines, author: place, date?
Cum Summi, Clement XIV, 12 December 1969, Human Life International CD Library, Front Royal, 2000.
Gaudium et Spes, Vatican Council II, published in *The Conciliar and Post-Conciliar Documents,* General Editor Austin Flannery, Dominican Publications, Dublin, 1992.
Laborem Exercens, John Paul II, St Paul's Publications, Homebush, 1981.
Mater et Magistra, John XXIII, Catholic Truth Society, London.
Mater et Magistra, John XXIII, St Paul Editions, Boston.
Nostis et Nobiscum, Pius IX, 8 December 1849, Human Life International CD Library, Front Royal, 2000.
Nova Impendet, Pius XI, 2 October 1931, Human Life International CD Library, Front Royal, 2000.
Octogesima Adveniens, Paul VI, A. C. T. S. Publications, Melbourne.
Optatissima Pax, Pius XII, 18 December 1947, Human Life International CD Library, Front Royal, 2000.
Pacem in Terris, John XXIII, St Paul Books & Media, Boston.
Populorum Progressio, Paul VI, Pauline Books & Media, Boston.
Quadragesimo Anno, Pius XI, St Paul Editions, Boston.
Quanta Cura, Pius IX, 8 December 1864, Human Life International CD Library, Front Royal, 2000.
Quanto Conficiamur Moerore, Pius IX, 10 August 1863, Human Life International CD Library, Front Royal, 2000.
Qui Pluribus, Pius IX, 9 November 1846, Human Life

International CD Library, Front Royal, 2000.
Quod Apostolici Muneris, Pius IX, 28 December 1878, Human Life International CD Library, Front Royal, 2000.
Rerum Novarum, Leo XIII, St Paul Books and Media, Boston, 1942.
Sertium Laetitiae, Pius XI, Encyclical letter to the United States Bishops, 1 November 1939, in *The Pope Speaks*, ed. Charles Rankin, Faber & Faber Ltd, London, 1940.
Solicitudo Rei Socialis, John Paul II, Pauline Books and Media, Boston.
Ubi Arcano Dei Consilio, Pius XI, 23 December 1922, Human Life International CD Library, Front Royal, 2000.

Episcopal and church references
A Catholic Framework for Economic Life, United States Catholic Bishops, 12 November 1996, Human Life International CD Library, Front Royal, 2000.
Common Wealth for the Common Good, A Statement on the Distribution of Wealth in Australia, Australian Catholic Bishops Conference, Collins Dove Publishers, Melbourne, 1992.
Declaration at the World Summit on Social Development in Copenhagen, 12 March 1995, Human Life International CD Library, Front Royal, 2000.
Economic Justice for All: Pastoral Letter on Catholic Social Teaching and the US Economy, National Conference of Catholic Bishops, Washington DC, 1986.
Hierarchy of Quebec, Pastoral Letter, February 1950, in Cronin, *Social Principles and Economic Life*.
Instruction on Christian Freedom and Liberation, Sacred Congregation for the Doctrine of the Faith, St Paul Publications, Homebush, 1986.
John Paul II, Address to the Pontifical Academy of Social Sciences, *L'Osservatore Romano*, English Edition, 17 March 1999.
Justice in the World, Document presented for study at the Second General Assembly of the Synod of Bishops, 1971, International Commission for Justice and Peace, Brickfield Hill, New South Wales.
Pastoral Letter of the Hierarchy of the United States, 26 September 1919. Human Life International CD Library, Front Royal, 2000.
Pastoral Letter of French Cardinals, 8 September 1949, in Cronin, *Social Principles and Economic Life*.

Pius XII, Christmas Broadcast 1942, in Cronin, ibid.
Pius XII, Christmas Message 1942, in Gonella, *A World to Reconstruct*.
Pius XII, Christmas Message December 1942, in Byers, *Justice in the Marketplace*.
Pius XII, Address to Italian Workers, 13 June 1943, in Cronin, *Social Principles and Economic Life*.
Pius XII, Radio Address, 1 September 1944, ibid.
Pius XII on Women's Duties, 21 October 1945, ibid.
Pius XII, Letter to Semaines Sociales, 18 July 1947, ibid.
Pius XII, Address to the International Union of Family Organisations, 20 September 1949, ibid.
Pius XII, Letter to Catholic International Congresses for Social Study and Social Action, 3 June 1950, ibid.
Pius XII, Letter to Austrian Catholics, 14 September 1952, ibid.
Pius XII, Christmas Message 1955, ibid.
Pius XII, Letter to Directors of Chemical Products Organisations, 10 January 1958, ibid.
'Socialisation', 1948, Social Justice Statement of the Australian Catholic Bishops, in *Justice Now! Social Justice Statements of the Australian Catholic Bishops First Series: 1940–1966*.
Statement of the Bishops of Ohio, 20 March 1958, in Cronin, *Social Principles and Economic Life*.
Vatican Council II, Closing Speeches and Messages, 8 December 1965, Human Life International CD Library.

Books and periodicals
Alford, Helen J. and Naughton, Michael J., *Managing as if Faith Matters: Christian Social Principles in Modern Organisation*, University of Notre Dame Press, Notre Dame, Indiana, 2001.
Algisi, Leoni, *John the Twentythird*, The Catholic Book Club, London, 1963.
Anderson-Scott, C. A., *New Testament Ethics: An Introduction*, The Hulsean Lectures 1929, Cambridge University Press, 1948.
Antonides, Harry, *Multinationals and the Peaceable Kingdom*, Clark Irwin & Co. Ltd, Toronto, 1978.
Aquinas, Sister Thomas, GO. (tr.), *St John Chrysostom – Commentary on St John the Apostle and Evangelist,* Homilies 1–47, Fathers of the Church Inc., New York, 1957.
Auden, W. H. (ed.), *G. K. Chesterton. A Selection from his Non-fictional Prose*, Faber & Faber, London, 1970.
Australian Government Parliament Reports, Hansard 1, 15 March 2005.

Avila, Charles, *Ownership: Early Christian Teaching*, Sheed & Ward, London, 1984.

Babcock, William S. (ed.), *The Ethics of St. Augustine*, Scholars Press, Atlanta, 1991.

Bartchy, S. Scott, *First Century of Slavery & The Interpretation of 1 Corinthians 7:21*, Society of Biblical Literature, Visitation Series 11, 1973.

Baum, Gregory, *Essays in Critical Theology*, Sheed & Ward, Kansas City, 1994.

BBC Horizon, written and produced by Dominic Flessati, BBC, 1980.

Belloc, Hilaire, *The Crisis of Our Civilisation*, Fordham University Press, New York, 1937.

Belloc, Hilaire, *The Servile State*, Constable & Company Ltd, London, 1948.

Bettenson, Henry (tr.), *Augustine,* Penguin Books, England, 1984.

Birrell, Bob, Virginia Rapson and Clare Hourigan, *Men and Women Apart: Partnering in Australia*, Centre for Population and Urban Research & Australian Family Association, 2004.

Black, Antony, *Guilds & Civil Society in European Political Thought from the 12th century to the present*, Methuen & Company Ltd, New York, 1984.

Blanpain, Roger (ed.), *Bulletin of Labour Relations No.45 – 2002*, Klewuer Law International, The Hague, 2002.

Bloch, Marc, *Slavery & Serfdom in the Middle Ages*, Selected Essays, University of California Press, 1975.

Bonnassie, Pierre, *From Slavery to Feudalism in South-Western Europe,* tr. Jean Birrell, Cambridge University Press, Cambridge, 1991.

Boswell, J. S., McHugh, F. P. and Verstraeten, J. (eds), *Catholic Social Thought, Twilight or Renaissance?* Leuven University Press, 2000.

Borne, Etienne and Francois Henry, *A Philosophy of Work*, Sheed & Ward, London.

Brentano, Lujo, *On the History and Development of Guilds and the Origin of Trade Unions*, Birt Franklin Publishers, New York, 1969.

Brown, Raymond E., Fitzmyer, Joseph A. and Murphy, Roland E. (eds), *The New Jerome Biblical Commentary*, Geoffrey Chapman Publishers, London, 1990.

Byers, David M. (ed.), 'Present Crisis', Pastoral Letter of the American Hierarchy, 25 April 1933, in *Justice in the Marketplace: Collected Statements of the Vatican and the United States Catholic Bishops on Economic Policy,*

1891–1984, United States Catholic Conference Inc., Washington DC, 1985.

Byron, John, *Slavery Metaphors in Early Judaism and Pauline Christianity: A Traditio-Historical and Exegetical Examination*, Mohr Siebeck, Tübingen, 2003.

Cahill, Thomas, *How the Irish Saved Civilisation, The Untold Story of Ireland's Heroic Role from the Fall of Rome to the Rise of Medieval Europe*, Doubleday Press, New York, 1995.

Cahill, Reverend E., *The Framework of a Christian State*, Roman Catholic Books, Fort Collins, Colorado, 1932.

Calvez, Jean-Yves, *The Social Thought of John XXIII, Mater et Magistra*, Burns & Oates, London, 1964.

Canovan, Margaret, *G. K. Chesterton, Radical Populist*, Harcourt Brace Jovanovich, New York & London, 1977.

Carpenter, The Very Rev. S. C., Anglican Dean of Exeter, *The Bible View of Life*, Ayr & Spottiswood, London, 1937.

Charles, Rodger, *An Introduction to Catholic Social Teaching*, Family Publications, Oxford, 1999.

Chesterton, G. K., *A Miscellany of Men*, Methuen & Co. Ltd, London, 1920.

Chesterton, G. K., *The Well and the Shallows*, Sheed & Ward, London, 1935.

Chesterton, G. K., *As I was Saying*: A Book of Essays, Methuen & Co. Ltd, London, 1936.

Chesterton, G. K., *The Father Brown Stories*, Cassell, London, 1960.

Chesterton, G. K., *Stories, Essays & Poems*, Everyman's Library, London, 1965.

Chesterton, G. K., *The Outline of Sanity*, Methuen & Co. Ltd, London, 1926.

Christo, Gus George (tr.), *St John Chrysostom – On Repentance and Alms Giving*, The Catholic University of America Press, Washington DC, 1998.

Cobbett, William, *A History of the Protestant Reformation in England and Ireland*, James Duffy Publishers, Dublin and London, 1878.

Cole, G. D. H., *Guild Socialism Restated*, Leonard Parsons Publisher, London, 1920.

Compendium of the Social Doctrine of the Church, Pontifical Council for Justice and Peace, Libreria Editrice Vaticana, 2004.

Conlon, D. J. (ed.), *G.K. Chesterton, A Half Century of His Views*, Oxford University Press, Oxford & New York, 1987.

Cronin, John F., *Christianity and Social Progress: A*

Commentary on Mater et Magistra, Helicon, Baltimore and Dublin, 1965.

Cronin, John F. and Harry W. Flannery, *Labour and The Church*, Burns & Oates, London, 1965.

Curran, Charles E., *Catholic Social Teaching 1891–present: A Historical, Theological and Ethical Analysis*, Georgetown University Press, Washington DC, 2002.

Danielou, Jean, *Prayer as a Political Problem*, ed. J. Kirwan, Sheed & Ward, New York, 1965.

Davies, Leryldo W., *Prophecy and Ethics: Isaiah and the Ethical Traditions of Israel,* Jsot Press, University of Sheffield, 1981.

Deberri, Edward P. and Hug, James H., *Catholic Social Teaching: Our Best Kept Secret*, Orbis Books, New York, 2003.

d'Entreves, Alexander Passerin, *The Medieval Contribution to Political Thought,* The Humanities Press, New York, 1959.

de Selincourt, Aubrey (tr.), *Herodotus, The Histories*, Penguin Books, Harmondsworth, 1978.

Dockès, Pierre, *Medieval Slavery & Liberation*, University of Chicago Press, 1982.

Dowd, John F., *The Bible, The Church and Social Justice*, Liguori Publications, USA, 1983.

Do We Agree? A Debate between G. K. Chesterton and Bernard Shaw with Hilaire Belloc in the Chair, Cecil Palmer, London, 1928.

Dwyer, Judith A. (ed.), *The New Dictionary of Catholic Social Thought*, The Liturgical Press, Collegeville, Minnesota, 1994.

Dwyer, Judith A. (ed.), *Questions of Special Urgency: The Church in the Modern World Two Decades after Vatican II,* Georgetown University Press, Washington DC, 1986.

'Encounter', ABC, transcript, 27 July 2003.

Engerman, Stanley, Drescher, Seymour and Paquette, Robert (eds), *Slavery*, Oxford University Press, Oxford, 2001.

Evans, Joseph W. and Ward, Leo R., *The Social and Political Philosophy of Jacques Maritain*, University of Notre Dame Press, Notre Dame, Indiana, 1976.

Fathers of the English Dominican Province (trs), *The Summa Theologica of St Thomas Aquinas*, Vol. II, William Benton Publisher, 1952.

Finnis, John, *Aquinas, Moral, Political and Legal Theory*, Oxford University Press, 1998.

Flannery, Austin (ed.), *Vatican Council II, The Conciliar and Post-Conciliar Documents*, Dominican Publications, Dublin, 1992.

Gauthier, Paul, *Christ, The Church and The Poor,* Geoffrey Chapman, London, 1964.

Gide, Charles and Rist, Charles, *A History of Economic Doctrines,* George G. Harrup & Company Ltd, London, 1948.

Gollan, Paul, ed., *Globalisation and Its Impact on the World of Work.* Papers presented at a meeting of the Australian Participants in the Asia-Pacific Network of National Institutes for Labour Studies, held at the University of Sydney, August 1995, ISBN 0-86758-899-3.

Gonzalez, Justo L., *Faith and Wealth: A History of Early Christian Ideas on the Origin, Significance and use of Money,* Harper & Rowe Publishers, San Francisco, 1990.

Goosen, Gideon, *The Theology of Work*, Clergy Book Service, Wisconsin, 1974.

Graef, Hilda C. (tr.), *St Gregory of Nyssa, The Lord's Prayer and the Beatitudes,* The Newman Press, Longmans Green & Co., London, 1954.

Gregg, Samuel, *Challenging the Modern World: Karol Wojtyla/John Paul II and the Development of Catholic Social Teaching*, Lexington Books, Lanham, 2002.

Guido, Gonella, *A World to Reconstruct: Pius XII on Peace and Reconstruction*, The Bruce Publishing Company, Milwaukee, 1944.

Harries, Richard, *Is There a Gospel for the Rich? The Christian in a Capitalist World*, Mowbray, London, 1992.

Harrill, J. Albert, *The Manumission of Slaves in Early Christianity*, J. C. B. Mohr Publishers, Tübingen, 1995.

Haughey, John C. (ed.), *The Faith That Does Justice: Examining the Christian Sources for Social Change*, Paulist Press, New York, 1977.

Hertz, Moreena, *The Silent Takeover: Global Capitalism and The Death of Democracy,* William Heinemann, London, 2001.

Hessel, Dieter T. (ed.), *The Church's Public Role: Retrospective and Prospect*, William B. Eardmans Publishing Company, Grand Rapids, 1993.

Hines, Kenneth R., *Responses to 101 Questions on Catholic Social Teaching*, Paulist Press, New York, 2001.

Hogan, Michael (ed.), 'Peace in Industry', 1947, Social Justice statement of the Australian Catholic Bishops, in *Justice Now! Social Justice Statements of the Australian Catholic Bishops First Series: 1940-1966*, Department of Government & Public Administration, University of Sydney, 1990.

Holland, Joe, *Modern Catholic Social Teaching: The Popes Confront the Industrial Age 1740-1958*, Paulist Press, New York, 2003.

Houck, John W. and Williams, Oliver F. (eds), *Catholic Social*

Teaching in the United States Economy: Working Papers for a Bishops' Pastoral, University Press of America, Washington DC, 1984.

Houlden, J. L., *Ethics & The New Testament*, Penguin Books, Middlesex, 1973.

Howell, Clifford, *The Work of Our Redemption*, The Catholic Social Guild, Oxford, 1961.

Hutton, Will, *The World We're In*, Abacus, London, 2003.

Jowett, Benjamin (tr.), *The Essential Plato*, South Pack Preview, 1999.

Keyes, Clinton W. (tr.), *Cicero, De Republica & De Legibus*, William Heinemann Ltd., London, 1948.

Klipper, Lawrence J., *G. K. Chesterton*, Twayne Publishers Incorporated, New York, 1974.

Krier Mich, Marvin L., *Catholic Social Teaching & Movements*, John XXIII Publications, Mystic, 1998.

Cortright, S. A. (ed.), *Labour, Solidarity and the Common Good: Essays on the Ethical Foundations of Management*, Carolina Academic Press, Durham, 2001.

Lecky, William Edward Hartspole, *History of European Morals, from Augustus to Charlemagne, Vol. II*, D. Appleton & Co., New York, 1913.

Lecky, W. E. H., *History of European Morals – From Augustus to Charlemagne, Vol. II*, George Brazizzer Publishers, New York, 1955.

Lee, R. W., *The Institutes of Justinian*, Street and Maxwell, London, 1946.

Leeson, R. A., *Travelling Brothers: The Six Centuries Road from Craft Fellowship to Trade Unions*, George Allen & Unwin Ltd, London, 1979.

Leisink, Peter (ed.), *Globalisation and Labour Relations*, Edward Elgar, Cheltenham, 1999.

Livingstone, Tess, *George Pell*, Duffy & Snellgrove, Sydney, 2002.

Lombardi, Riccardo, *Church and Kingdom of God*, tr. Kathleen England, East Asian Pastoral Institute, Manila, 1977.

Lutz, Charles P. (ed.), *God Goods and the Common Good: 11 Perspectives on Economic Justice in Dialogue with the Roman Catholic Bishops Pastoral Letter*, Augsburg Publishing House, Minneapolis, 1987.

McCarthy, George E. and Royal W. Rhodes, *Eclipse of Justice: Ethics, Economics and the Lost Traditions of American Catholicism*, Orbis Books, New York, 1992.

McDonald, Sister Mary Frances, OP (tr.), *Lactantius, The Divine*

Institutes, The Catholic University of America Press, Washington DC, 1964.

McDowall, Reverend Patrick, *The Church and Economics: An Essay on the Development of Catholic Economic Teaching*, Sheed & Ward, London, 1928.

McMurtry, John, *Value Wars: The Global Market versus the Life Economy*, Pluto Press, London, 2002.

Maritain, Jacques, *True Humanism*, Geoffrey Bles, London, 1954.

Martin, Dale B., *Slavery as Salvation: The Metaphore of Slavery in Pauline Christianity*, Yale University Press, New Haven, 1990.

Mayor, Stephen, *The Churches and the Labour Movement*, Independent Press Ltd., London, 1967.

Mechmann, Edward T., *God, Society and the Human Person: The Basics of Catholic Social Teaching*, Alba House, New York, 2000.

Mishra, Ramesh, *Globalisation and the Welfare State*, Edward Elgar, Cheltenham, 1999.

Metlake, George, *Ketteler's Social Reform,* The Dolphin Press, Philadelphia, 1912.

Neal, Marie Augusta, *The Just Demands of the Poor: Essays in Socio-Theology*, Paulist Press, New York, 1987.

Neuhaus, Richard John, *Doing Well and Doing Good: The Challenge to the Christian Capitalist*, Doubleday, New York, 1992.

New York Times, 28 November 1993.

New York Times, 5 September 1999.

News Weekly, 31 July 1999.

News Weekly, 15 July 2000.

Novak, Michael, *The Spirit of Democratic Capitalism*, An American Enterprise/Simon & Schuster Publication, New York, 1982.

Novak, Michael, *The Catholic Ethic and the Spirit of Capitalism*, The Free Press, New York, 1993.

O'Brien, George, *An Essay on the Economic Effects of the Reformation*, IHS Press, Norfolk, 2003.

O'Donovan, Oliver, *The Desire of the Nations, Rediscovering the Roots of Political Theology,* Cambridge University Press, 1996.

O'Grady, John, *The Catholic Church and the Destitute,* Burns Oates & Washbourne Ltd., Publishers to the Holy See, London, 1929.

Parker, John Henry, *St John Chrysostom – On the Gospel of*

Matthew, Prest, Oxford Press, MDCCLXLIV, J. G. F. & J. Rivington, 1843–1851. 1.
On the Duties of the Clergy, Book 1, Chapter 2 in *Early Church Fathers and Other Works,* W. M. B. Eerdmans Publishing Co., Edinburgh, 1867.
People and Places, January 2000.
Pesch, Heinrich, *Ethics and the National Economy*, IHS Press, Norfolk, Virginia, 2004.
Petrie, John (tr.), *The Worker-Priests: A Collective Documentation* Routledge & Kegan Paul, London, 1956.
Phan, Peter C. *Message of the Fathers of the Church*, Michael Glazier Inc., Wilmington, Delaware, 1984.
Pohlsander, Hans A., *The Emperor Constantine*, Routledge Publishers, London, 1996.
Pollock, Robert C. (ed.), *The Mind of Pius XII*, The Fireside Press, London, 1955.
Ragner, Sister M. Monica, CSC (tr.), *St Basil Ascetical Works*, The Catholic University of America Press, Washington DC, 1962.
Rankin, Charles (ed.), *The Pope Speaks*, Faber & Faber Ltd, London, 1940.
Richardson, Cyril C. (ed., tr.,) *Early Christian Fathers*, Collier Books, New York, 1970.
Richardson, Cyril C. (tr.) *Early Christian Fathers, Vol. I*, SCM Press Ltd, London, 1953.
Roberts, Rev. Alexander, DD and Donaldson, James, LLD (eds), *Translations of the Writings of the Fathers*, Vol. 23, T & T Clark, Edinburgh, 1872.
Roberts, Rev. Alexander, DD and Robertson, James, LLD (eds), *The Ante-Nicene Fathers,* W. M. B. Eerdmans Publishing Company, Grand Rapids, Michigan, 1981.
Rodrik, Danni, *Has Globalisation Gone Too Far?* Institute for International Economics, Washington DC, 1997.
Rogerson, John W., Davies, Margaret and Carroll, M. Daniel (eds), *The Bible in Ethics: The Second Sheffield Colloquium*, Sheffield Academic Press, 1995.
Rosner, Brian S., *Paul, Scripture & Ethics: A Study of 1 Corinthians 5–7*, U. J. Brill, Leiden, 1994.
Roth, Catherine P. (tr.), *St John Chrysostom – On Wealth & Poverty*, St Vladimir's Seminary Press, New York, 1984.
Savage, John C., *St Ambrose, Hexameron, Paradise and Cain and Able,* Fathers of the Church Inc., New York, 1961.
Schuck, Michael J., *That They Be One: The Social Teaching of the Papal Encyclicals 1740–1989,* Georgetown University Press, Washington DC.

Sennett, Richard, *The Corrosion of Character: The Personal Consequences of Work in the New Capitalism,* W. W. Norton & Company, New York, 1998.
Sheridan, E. F (ed.), *Love Kindness! The Social Teaching of the Canadian Catholic Bishops 1958–1989,* Editiones Paulines, Toronto, 1991.
Simons, Robert, G., *Competing Gospels: Public Theology and Economic Theory,* E. J. Dwyer, Alexandria, 1995.
Soros, George, *The Crisis of Global Capitalism: Open Society Endangered,* Public Affairs, New York, 1998.
Soros, George, *George Soros on Globalisation,* Public Affairs, New York, 1998.
Standing, Guy, *Global Labour Flexibility: Seeking Distributive Justice,* Macmillan Press, London, 1999.
Szulc, Tad., *John Paul II, The Biography,* Scribner Publishers, New York, 1995.
Tabb, William K., *Unequal Partners: A Primer on Globalisation,* The New York Press, New York, 2002.
The Age, 19 November 2000.
The Catholic Leader, Brisbane, 12 March 2006.
Townsend, Henry, *Society and the Gospel,* The Mercier Press, Dublin & Cork, 1976.
Troeltsch, Ernst, *The Social Teaching of the Christian Churches,* translated by Olive Wyon, Westminster, John Knox Press, Louisville, 1992.
Tropman, John E., *The Catholic Ethic in American Society: An Exploration of Values,* Jossey-Bass Publishers, San Francisco, 1995.
Turley, David, *Slavery,* Blackwell Publishers, Oxford, 2000.
Vermes, Geza, *The Complete Dead Sea Scrolls in English,* Penguin Books, London, 1998.
Vigongiari, Dino (ed.), *The Political Ideas of St Thomas Aquinas,* Harper Press, New York, 1973.
Vischer, Lukas, *The Work of Human Beings as Creatures of God,* a lecture sponsored by the Ecumenical Leadership Foundation, The Second Visser T'Hooft Memorial Consultation, June 1955.
von Nell-Breuning, Oswald, *Re-organisation of the Social Economy: The Social Encyclical Developed and Explained,* The Bruce Publishing Company, New York, 1939.
Wall St Journal, 1 October 1999.
Walsh, Michael, *John Paul II, A Biography,* HarperCollins Publishers, London, 1995.
Weigel, George and Royal, Robert (eds), *A Century of Catholic*

Social Thought: Essays on Rerum Novarum and Nine other Key Documents, Ethics & Public Policy Centre, Washington DC, 1991.

Whyte, William Foote and Whyte, Kathleen King, *Making Mondragon: The Growth and Dynamics of the Worker Co-operative Complex,* ILR Press, New York 1991.

Wiedemann, Thomas, *Greek & Roman Slavery*, Croom Helm Ltd, Kent, 1981.

Wojtyla, Karol, *The Acting Person*, tr. Andrzej Potocki, D. Reidel Publishing Co., Dordrecht, 1979.

INDEX

Affre, Denis-Auguste, Bishop of Paris 89–90
agriculture 12, 23, 47, 60
Alalakh Tablets 23
Albertus Magnus 78
Alford, Helen and Naughton, Michael 249
alienation, in *Centesimus Annus* 211–12, 214
Ambrose of Milan, and common good 51–2, 259
anawim (the poor), in Old Testament 9, 15
Anderson-Scott, C. A. 30–1
Antonides, Harry 250
apprentices, in guild system 70, 73–4
Aquinas, Thomas 68–9, 84
  and distributive justice 109
  and just law 105
  and just price 76
  and just wage 78
  and means of production 203
  and private property 108
aristocracy, and social Catholicism 92, 94
Aristotle 18–19, 49, 68
Ashford, Robert 249
association, right of *see* trade unions
associations, workers' 136–7
Augros, Fr Louis 128
Augustine of Hippo, and justice 42, 43
Australia
  bishops' conferences 158–63, 224–7
  and casualization of employment 240–1
  and income inequality 239–40
  and trade unions 218
avarice, condemnation 100

Bagshawe, Edward Gilpin, Bishop of Nottingham 95
Basil the Great 46, 259

Baum, Gregory 175, 204, 205–6, 217
Belloc, Hilaire
  and capitalism 81–2, 84, 119, 127
  and distributism 116, 122, 123–6
  and guild system 64, 66, 69–70, 71, 72–3
  and industrialization 85–8
  and proletariat 121
  and property 121
  and Protestantism 81–2, 84
  and servile state 122–3, 254
  and social order 116–17
  and socialism 122, 127
Benedict XVI, Pope 195
  Deus Caritas Est 229
Bethune-Baker, J. F. 31
Birrell, Bob, Rapson, Virginia and Hourigan, Clare 118, 130 n.7, 240
Black, Antony 71, 72
Bloch, Marc 61, 62–3
Boland, Vivienne 166
Bonald, Louis de, Cardinal Archbishop of Lyons 92
Bonald, Louis Gabriel Ambroise, Viscount de 92
Bonnassie, Pierre 63–4
Borne, Etienne and Henry, François 19–20, 67–9
Bovone, Alberto 221
Brentano, Lujo 71
Buchez, Philippe 89, 92
Burke, Edmund 119
Byron, John 20

Cahill, E. 64–7, 74, 78
Calvez, Jean-Yves 171
Calvinism
  and capitalism 83–4
  and wealth 84–5
Campbell, Duncan 242
Canada, bishops' statements 163, 222–4, 227

Canovan, Margaret 126
capitalism
  and Belloc 119, 122–3, 127
  and Calvinism 83–4
  in *Centesimus Annus* 213–14
  and Chesterton 117–20, 127
  and contract with worker 81–2, 106–7, 233
  and the family 118–19, 241
  globalization 136, 205–6, 232–3, 234, 235–7
  and guild system 71, 118
  and individualism 121, 204, 225
  and industrialization 85–7
  and just price 76–7
  and Pius XII 151, 155
  and profit sharing 92, 138, 157–8, 168, 218, 248–9
  and rise of proletariat 84–8, 112
  and servile state 120–3
  and social dimension of work 25
  and unemployment 117, 119, 123, 132, 155, 217, 222
  and wages 106
  see also labour and capital; laissez-faire; neoliberalism
Carolingian period, and slavery 63
Carpenter, S. C. 16–17
Catechism of the Catholic Church 140, 260
Catholic Action 128, 130
Catholic social movement
  in England 95–6
  in France 89–90, 92–4
  and Fribourg Union 94–5
  in Germany 89, 90–1
  and proletariat 89–98
Catholic Social Studies Movement 160
Centesimus Annus 114, 185, 211–14, 227
  and alienation 211–12, 214
  and capitalism 213–14
  and role of the state 211, 213, 228
  and worker participation 213
charity, and justice 140
Charles, Rodger 88, 203–4, 212
chasès 63

Chateaubriand, François-René de 92
Chesterbelloc era 116–30
Chesterton, Cecil 123
Chesterton, Gilbert Keith 116–17
  and capitalism 117–20, 121, 127
  and communism 120, 122, 127
  and distributism 116, 122, 123–6
  and proletariat and the servile state 120–3
child labour 91, 108
Christian Democratic movements 132
Christian Labour Catechism 91
Christian socialism 89
Chrysostom, St John
  and equality before God 48
  and trades and crafts 47
  and wealth and poverty 47–8, 258
  and work and toil 48
Church Fathers
  and justice 50
  and slavery 42, 43, 46, 50, 53–6
  and solidarity 46, 47–8
  and stewardship of property 42, 44–9, 258–9
Cicero, Marcus Tullius, and justice 42, 43
civil society 112, 145
Clancy, Cardinal Edward Bede 225
class, social
  in Church Fathers 45, 49
  in Greek thought 7–8, 42–3
  hollowing out of middle class 3, 119, 123, 240
  in medieval thought 68–9
  in New Testament 26, 31–2, 35
  and vocational groups 144–6
  see also proletariat; working class
class war 2, 98, 102, 125, 134, 154–5, 161–2, 194, 198–9, 210
Clement of Rome 45–6
Clement XIV, Pope, *Cum Summi* 100
Clines, David J. A. 22–3

Index

Cobbett, William 85, 119, 121
Code Social (1927) 133
Code of Social Principles 133
codetermination *see* worker participation
Cole, G. D. H. 70
Coleman, John A. 170-1
Columbanus, St 59-60
common good
　in Aquinas 76
　in Church Fathers 43, 45-6, 51-2, 259
　episcopal statements 220, 228-9
　in *Gaudium et Spes* 182, 183, 185
　and guild system 76, 78
　in *Laborem Exercens* 145-6, 202, 210
　in *Mater et Magistra* 168, 169, 172, 175
　and neoliberalism 254
　in *Quadragesimo Anno* 140, 142-4, 145
　in *Rerum Norarum* 104, 110, 112
　and state intervention 175-6, 235
Communion of Saints 83
communism
　and Chesterton 120
　and class struggle 154-5, 161
　collapse 113, 214
　see also socialism
Communist Manifesto (Marx and Engels) 90, 97
community, and stock ownership 249
community of work
　and John Paul II 204
　and John XXIII 172-3, 182
　and Paul VI 189, 191
　and Pius XII 153, 172
competition
　and capitalism 87, 225, 234
　and guild system 71, 78, 81-2
　and wage levels 158, 238
conciliation, workplace 226-7
conditions of work 107-8, 183-4, 209, 218, 220, 228
conferences, national episcopal 157-64, 217-24

Constantine the Great 54
consumerism 211
contemplation, and work 68-9
contract
　of partnership 138-9
　and status 81-2
　and wage 106-7, 138-9, 157-8, 233
cooperation
　in Church Fathers 46
　in guild system 70, 71, 81
　in medieval monasticism 62
cooperatives 92, 173-4, 226
　in *Mater et Magistra* 173-5
　Mondragon 174-5, 226, 252-3
copani (medieval cooperative) 67
corporations
　and globalism 232-3, 234-5, 237
　and guild system 68-9
　and the media 253
　reform 250-1
　and subsidiarity principle 157
corporativism *see* solidarism
Coux, Charles de 93
Cronin, John 168, 169, 173
Cunningham, Dr 83
Curran, Charles E. 167
Cuthbert, Fr 100

Damascus Document (Dead Sea Scrolls) 17-18
Daniel, Abbé Yvan 127-8
Davidson, Kenneth 244
Dead Sea Scrolls, Damascus Document 17-18
Deberri, Edward P. and Hug, James H. 176
Decurtins, Gaspard 90, 94
democracy
　and fatherhood of God 126
　and guild system 72, 81
　and neoliberal capitalism 235-6
　and participation 190, 249
Destro, Robert A. 206
Deus Caritas Est (Benedict XVI) 229
Deuteronomy, and social justice 10, 17-18
Didache 44
dignity, human 1, 3-4, 38-9,

218, 222, 227-8, 260
  and Catholic social movement
    91
  in Church Fathers 46-7, 48-9,
    55
  in *Gaudium et Spes* 179, 180,
    181, 182
  and guild system 69
  in *Laborem Exercens* 196
  in *Pacem in Terris* 170
  in *Rerum Novarum* 103, 110,
    111
dignity of work
  and Canadian bishops'
    statements 222-3
  in Chesterbelloc period 120-1,
    124
  and Church Fathers 42
  in *Gaudium et Spes* 180-1,
    186
  in medieval monasteries 62
  and neoliberalism 237
  in New Testament 34
  in Old Testament 8, 11, 20
  and Pius XII 152-3
  and US bishops' statement
    1919 132-3
distributism 108, 116, 122, 23-7
Distributive League 123-4
division of labour 68, 117
dock strike (London) 95-6, 99
Dockès, Pierre 61
doctrine, and economic teaching
  27-8
Dowd, John F. 29, 35
Duhig, James, Archbishop of
  Brisbane 160

Ecclesiasticus, and social justice
  11-12, 258
economics
  and doctrinal teaching 27-8,
    228
  economic rationalism 168-9,
    219, 225-7, 228
  and ethics 50
  and free market 154, 214,
    220, 225, 227, 228-9
  and *Gaudium et Spes* 178-9,
    181, 183-4
  laissez-faire 93, 97, 111, 232,
    233-6, 254

see also neoliberalism
economism, materialistic 204-6,
  214
Ederer, Rupert 204
education of workers 171-2,
  210, 219
Edward I, King of England 66
employer, indirect 206-7, 223-4,
  227, 233, 243-4
employment
  casualization 240-1
  insecurity 217, 237-8, 241,
    244, 246
  part-time 237, 239-40,
    246-7
Engels, Friedrich 88, 90
Engerman, Stanley, Drescher,
  Seymour and Paquette,
  Robert 24
England and Wales, bishops'
  conference (1996) 228-9
Enlightenment, and laissez-faire
  economics 88
Epistles, and work 31-4
equality
  in Chesterbelloc period 126
  in Church Fathers 42, 46-7,
    48-9, 54-5
  in Middle Ages 61
  in New Testament 32, 36,
    38-9, 258
  in Old Testament 24
  in *Rerum Novarum* 103
  and Second Vatican Council 179
Eshnunna, law code 23
ethics, and economics 50
Exodus event, and Israelite
  attitudes to slavery 20-1, 24
exploitation 8, 86, 111, 182, 183,
  194, 212, 214, 219, 227

factory system *see*
  industrialization
family
  and capitalism 118-19, 241
  family wage 95, 140-2, 150-1,
    155, 158, 160, 169, 208,
    222
  in *Laborem Exercens* 208-9
  and property ownership 163
  in *Quadragesimo Anno* 140,
    155

Index

in *Rerum Novarum* 102, 208
family allowances 141, 156, 208
fascism 132, 134
fatherhood of God 28, 38–9, 258
Feltin, Cardinal Maurice 129
Finn, Daniel 182
Flynn, John J. 250
France
   and Catholic social movement 89–90, 92–4
   and worker priest movement 127–30, 193
Fribourg Union 94–5, 99, 101, 133

gainsharing 248–9
Garriguet, 27–8
Gates, Jeff 249
Gaudium et Spes 178–86, 188, 196
   and economic structures 180
   and labour and capital 181, 184–5
   and *Rerum Novarum* 182
   and role of women 209
   and trade unions 183, 184–5, 210
   and wages 182–3, 190
   and worker participation 183, 184–6
Gauthier, Paul 6–7, 8
Genesis, and role of work 5–6, 8, 12, 195–6, 205
George, Henry, *Progress and Poverty* 99
Gerlier, Pierre-Marie 129
Germany
   and Catholic social movement 89, 90–1
   and worker participation 139, 170–1, 226
Gibbons, Cardinal James 81, 97, 99
gleaning 17, 18
Glendon, Mary Ann 147–8
globalism 170, 232–3
globalization of capitalism 136, 205–6, 232–3, 234, 235–7
Godin, Abbé Henri 127–8
golden rule 28, 49–50, 257
Goosen, Gideon 5–6, 7, 14, 18, 32–3, 37

Gospels, and work 24–31
Great Depression 251
   and *Quadragesimo Anno* 132, 134, 143
Greece
   attitudes to work 7–8, 19–20
   and slavery 18–19
Gregg, Samuel 200, 204, 210, 212
Gregory XVI, Pope, *Mirari Vos* 93
Gregory, R. G. 239–40
Gregory of Nazianzus, and property ownership 48, 258–9
Gregory of Nyssa, and slavery 50, 54
guild system 69–75, 250
   classes 70, 73–4
   craft guilds 70
   decline 81
   everyday practice 71–5
   and just price 70, 75–7, 82
   and just wage 77–8
   merchant guilds 70
   and Reformation 85
   and religion 74–5
   revival 92
Gundlach, Gustav 134, 167

Hammurabi, law code 21–2, 23
Harding, Anne 240
Haughey, John C. 112
Head, Simon 238–9
Healy, Ernest 239
Hehir, J. Bryan 185–6
Herodotus, and role of labour 7–8
Hertz, Moreena 234–5
Hillenbrand, Reymold 147
Hines, Kenneth R. 196, 220
Holland, Joe 92, 96–7, 112, 147
Hollenbach, David 111
home ownership 125–6
Houlden, J. L. 36–7
Howell, Clifford 84
Huet, Francis 89
Human Rights Watch 245
Husslein, Joseph 107
Hutton, Will 247

idleness
   in Church Fathers 44

in the Gospels 24, 25
in Old Testament 18
Ignatius of Antioch 46
image of God 8, 49, 50, 152, 195–6
income inequality 170, 225–6, 236–40, 249; see also just wage; wages
individualism
  and capitalism 121, 204, 225
  and Reformation 83–4
industrial relations 226–7; see also strikes; trade unions
industrialization
  and capitalism 85–7
  and child labour 91, 108
  and worker participation 138–40
industry
  industrial councils 159–60
  and nationalization 162–3
inspectors, factory 91
The Instruction on Christian Freedom and Liberation 221–2
International Labour Organization 173, 206, 242
International Monetary Fund 232–3, 237
International Union of Family Organizations 156
International Union for Social Studies 133
Ireland, John, Archbishop of St Paul 97
Irenaeus of Lyons 44–5

Jacobini, Cardinal Luigi 101
Janssen, Johann 74
Jesus Christ
  and slavery 34–5
  and work 26–31, 103, 180, 257
  as worker 6, 26, 103, 178, 181, 186, 258
job creation 222
John Paul II, Pope 193–215
  Centesimus Annus 114, 185, 211–14, 227, 228
  Laborem Exercens 6, 145–6, 185, 194–210, 219
  and labour and capital 254
  and Paul VI 193
  and personalism 202, 214–15, 222
  and Second Vatican Council 193
  Solicitudo Rei Socialis 104, 115 n.21
  and solidarity 104
  as Worker Pope 193
  and worker priest movement 193–4
John XXIII, Pope
  Mater et Magistra 139–40, 166–70, 184
  Pacem in Terris 170, 176
  and Second Vatican Council 178
  and worker priest movement 166, 193
journeymen, in guild system 70, 73–4
just price 75–7, 82
just wage 77–8, 82, 95, 150–1
  in *Gaudium et Spes* 182–3, 190
  and guild system 77–8
  in *Laborem Exercens* 207–9
  in *Mater et Magistra* 78, 167–70
  and neoliberalism 237
  and *Octogesima Adveniens* 190
  and Old Testament 12
  in *Pacem in Terris* 176
  and Pius XII 150–1, 155–6
  in *Quadragesimo Anno* 140–3, 157–8
  in *Rerum Novarum* 78, 102, 106–7, 141, 148
  and the state 95, 102, 106, 110
  and US bishops' statements 220, 228
justice
  in Church Fathers 42, 50, 51–2
  commutative 140, 141
  distributive 109, 146
  in New Testament 38, 257
  in Old Testament 9–10, 14–17, 257
  in Palto 42–3
  and wealth 47
Justinian, Emperor 55

Index

Katholikentag 170
Ketteler, Wilhelm Emmanuel von, bishop of Mainz 90–1, 99
kingdom of God 26, 28, 30, 178
Knights of Labour (US) 97, 99
koinonia, and private property 52
Krier Mich, Marvin L. 94, 134, 147, 167
Krugman, Paul 239
Kuefstein, Count Franz von 94
Kurland, Norman 249

La Tour Du Pin, René de 93–4
Laborem Exercens 6, 145–6, 185, 194–210, 214
  and indirect employer 206–7, 223–4, 233, 243
  and just wage 207–9
  and labour and capital 198–200
  and materialistic economism 204–6, 214
  and personalism 202, 214–15, 222
  and trade unions 209–10, 219–20
  and worker participation 200–4
  and the Worker Question 197–8
labour
  and contemplation 68–9
  eschatological value 27
  individual and social character 138–40
  in *Populorum Progressio* 188–9
  redemptive role 6–7, 67–8, 181, 186, 197
  and Reformation 82–4
  and service 25, 26, 29, 37, 257–8
  and society 138–40, 152–3
  substitutability 242–3
  theology of 195–7, 237
  and toil 48, 102, 107, 197
  as willed by God 6–7
  see also dignity of work
labour and capital
  and Canadian bishops 223
  in *Deus Caritas Est* 229
  in *Gaudium et Spes* 181, 184–5
  in *Laborem Exercens* 198–200, 202
  in *Mater et Magistra* 167–8, 170–3
  in *Quadragesimo Anno* 45, 135–6, 138–9, 140, 148, 172
  in *Rerum Novarum* 45, 102–3, 112, 135, 138, 172
  and US bishops 132
  and vocational groups 144–6
labour law 143–4
labour market, flexibility 117, 119, 221, 223, 238, 246
labour movement 91
  England 95–7
  United States 97
  see also trade unions
Lacordaire, Jean Baptiste Henri Dominique 92–3
Lactantius
  and human dignity 46–7, 48–9
  and stewardship 259
laissez-faire 93, 97
  and Enlightenment 88
  and neoliberalism 232, 233–6, 254
  and Puritanism 83–4
  and *Rerum Novarum* 111
Lamennais, Abbé Félicité Robert de 89, 93
landownership
  concentration 86
  and contract system 81–2
  and monasteries 85–6
  in Old Testament 14, 16
law
  labour 143–4
  Roman 82
Lecky, W. E. H. 55, 59
Ledochowski, Fr Wlodimir 134
Leeson, R. A. 72
Lehmkuhl, August 95
Leisibnk, Peter 242
Leo XIII, Pope
  and Catholic social movement 99–100, 101
  and Fribourg Union 95, 99
  and Workers' Pope 2, 101, 193
  see also Rerum Novarum
Leviticus, and love of neighbour 10
liberalism
  and social Catholicism 92–3

and social contract theories 100
Liberatore, Matteo 101
Lienart, Cardinal Achille 129
Lombardi, Riccardo 178
Louis Philippe of France 93
Louis the Pious, Holy Roman Emperor and King of the Franks 61
love of neighbour
 in New Testament 32
 in Old Testament 10
Lowenstein, Prince Karl von 94

McCarthy, George E. and Rhodes, Royal W. 88, 113
McDowall, Patrick 28, 38, 50
McMurtry, John 253
magisterium, and social teaching 201, 208, 209–10, 230, 232, 260
Malines Union 133–4
management, and worker participation 138–9, 146–8, 150, 153, 158, 171, 184, 190, 201
Manchester School of economics 135
Mann, Thomas 96
Manning, Cardinal Henry Edward 95–6, 97, 99, 112–13
manumission of slaves 20, 54–6, 63
Marget, Abbé Henri 93
Maritain, Jacques 172–3, 249–50
market fundamentalism 233–4
marriage, and capitalism 118–19
Martin, Dale 20
Marx, Karl 88, 90, 97–8
Marxism
 and alienation 211–12
 and labour 7, 90, 113, 135–6
 and private ownership 111
masters, in guild system 70, 73
Mater et Magistra 166–76, 182
 and education of workers 171–2, 210
 and International Labour Organization 173
 and just wage 78, 167–70
 and *Rerum Novarum* 166
 and role of the laity 176

 and state intervention 175–6
 and trade unions 173
 and worker cooperatives 173–5
 and worker participation 139–40, 170–3, 176, 184, 190, 191, 202
materialism
 economic 88, 204–6, 214
 and John Paul II 194, 204–6, 214
Mazzella, Cardinal Camillo 101
means of production, ownership
 in Australian bishops' statements 158–9, 161
 in Belloc 87, 122
 in Chesterton 119, 124–5
 in *Laborem Exercens* 200–4, 210
 in *Mater et Magistra* 173
 in *Quadragesimo Anno* 127
 in *Rerum Novarum* 111
Mechmann, Edward 195
Melun, Armand de 92
Mercier, Cardinal Desiré Joseph 133
mercy, in Church Fathers 49, 51
Mermillod, Cardinal Gaspar 94, 95, 99, 101
Mickwitz, Gunnar 71
middle class, hollowing out 3, 119, 123, 240
Millicent, Louis 94
Mishra, Ramesh 235–6, 237–8
Mission to Paris 128
missionaries, medieval 59–60
monasteries
 dissolution 85–8
 and landownership 85–6
 and manual labour 62
 and medieval slavery 59–62
Mondragon (Spain), worker cooperatives 174–5, 226, 252–3
monetarism 205, 217
morality, social 14–15, 16–17
mothers, role 208–9
Mun, Albert de 93–4
Murphy, James 247–8
Murphy, William 89, 90–1, 99

Nader, Ralph 250

Index

nationalization, of industry 162–3
natural law 18, 51, 61, 68–9, 116
  and community 151–2
  and just price 75
  and *Mater et Magistra* 167
Nell-Breuning, Fr Oswald von 134, 137–8, 139, 141, 144, 145, 167
neoliberalism
  and Catholic social teaching 232–55
  and collapse of communism 214
  and dignity of work 237
  and episcopal statements 217, 219, 221–2, 223–4, 225
  and family wage 158
  and laissez-faire 232, 233–6, 254
  and social security 238
  and trade unions 242–7
  and worker participation 247–50
Neuhaus, Richard John 112
New Testament
  Epistles 31–4
  Gospels 24–31
  and slavery 34–7
  and work 24–7
Nisbet, Robert 119
Novak, Michael 147, 235

O'Brien, George 83
Octogesima Adveniens
  and just wage 190
  and trade unions 190
  and urban proletariat 189–90
  and worker participation 190, 191
O'Donovan, Oliver 14, 53, 54
OECD, and trade unions 242
Old Testament
  and agriculture 12
  labour and justice in 9–18, 257
  and slavery 18–24
  and trades and crafts 11, 12–14
  and Yahweh as worker 5–6, 13
oligopolies 234, 235
Organization for Economic Cooperation and Development *see* OECD
Origen, and trades and crafts 44
original sin, and work as punishment 6–7, 67–8, 152
Oswald, Rudi 217–18
Owen, Robert 252
Ozanam, Frederick 92–3

partnership, labour and capital 138–9, 148
Paul, St
  and dignity of the person 260
  and slavery 36–7
  and slavery to the gospel 20, 35, 37
  and work 31–4, 136, 258
Paul VI, Pope 188–91
  and John Paul II 193
  Octogesima Adveniens 189–90
  Populorum Progressio 188–9
  and Synod of Bishops 191
Pavan, Pietro 166
peasantry
  and contract system 82
  and guild system 81
  and industrial capitalism 118
  and proletariat 86
  and serfdom 64
  and wage labour 82
Pell, George, Cardinal Archbishop of Sydney 113
personalism, and John Paul II 202, 214–15, 222, 237
Pesch, Heinrich 134, 167, 204
Pius IX, Pope
  Nostis et Nobiscum 100
  Quanta Cura 100
  Quanto Conficiamur Moerore 100
  Qui Pluribus 100
  Quod Apostolici Muneris 100, 101
Pius XI, Pope 133–4
  Caritate Christi Compulsi 146
  Casti Conubii 140
  Nova Impendet 134
  Quadragesimo Anno 42, 45, 78, 127, 132–48
  Ubi Arcano dei Consilio 134
Pius XII, Pope 150–7
  and capitalism 151, 155
  and class struggle 154–5

and community and natural law
  151–2
and community of work 153,
  172
and dignity of work 152–3
Optatissima Pax 155
Sertum Laetitiae 150
and wages 150–1, 155–6
and worker participation 153–4
and worker priest movement
  129
Plato, and justice 42–3
politics
  and the common good 112,
    210
  and industrial capitalism 119
  and labour 243
  political strikes 190, 191
  and social contract theories
    100
Populorum Progressio 188–9
  and trade unions 189
  and work 188–9
  and worker participation 189,
    190, 191
post-industrialism 220
poverty
  in Chesterbelloc period 116
  and Church Fathers 47–8, 51
  and neoliberalism 236–7
  in New Testament 103
  in Old Testament 9, 15, 17
price, just 70, 75–7, 82
privatization 225, 233
production *see* means of
  production
productivity, and wages 170,
  176, 244, 248
productivity wage index 170,
  176, 248
profit sharing 92, 138, 157–8,
  168, 170–1, 218, 248–9
progress, social and economic
  169
proletariat
  and Catholic social movement
    89–98
  and *Octogesima Adveniens*
    189–90
  and property ownership 123–5
  rise 84–8
  and servile state 120–3
  urban 189–90, 191
  and worker-priest movement
    127–30
property
  in bishops' statements 159,
    163
  in Chesterbelloc period 121,
    123–5
  in Church Fathers 42, 44,
    48–52
  and *koinonia* 52
  in *Laborem Exercens* 200
  in *Mater et Magistra* 170
  in New Testament 31
  in Old Testament 14
  in papal encyclicals 100
  and Pius XII 151, 156, 157
  in *Quadragesimo Anno* 136,
    142–3, 144, 146
  in *Rerum Novarum* 108–14
  see also means of production
prophets, and social morality
  14–17
Protestantism, and work ethic
  82–4
Psalms, and justice 9–10, 257
Puritanism, and individualism
  83–4

Quadragesimo Anno 42, 114,
  132–48
  and Belloc and Chesterton 127
  drafts 134
  and fascism 134
  influences on 133
  and just wage 78, 140–3, 148,
    157
  and labour and capital 45,
    135–6, 138–9
  and labour law 143–4
  and property 136, 142–3, 144
  and *Rerum Novarum* 134, 135,
    147–8
  and socialism 135
  and trade unions 104, 136–8
  and vocational groups 144–6,
    160, 202
  and worker participation
    138–40, 146–7, 170, 172,
    191
Quebec, bishops' statement 163

rationalism, economic 168-9, 219, 225-7
Ratzinger, Cardinal Joseph 221; see also Benedict XVI, Pope
Reagan, Ronald 234
redemption
  and individualism 84
  role of labour 6-7, 67-8, 181, 186, 197
  see also salvation
Reformation
  and decline of the guild system 81-2
  and dissolution of the monasteries 85-8
  and individualism 83-4
  and rise of the proletariat 85-8
  and wealth 84-5
Rerum Novarum 42, 101-8, 132, 255
  and biblical references 110
  events leading to 95, 99-101
  on the family 102, 208
  and just wage 78, 102, 106-7, 141
  and labour and capital 45, 102-3, 138, 172
  and Marxism 98
  and *Octogesima Adveniens* 189
  and private property 108-14
  and *Quadragesimo Anno* 134, 135, 147-8
  and solidarity 104
  and state intervention 102, 104-5, 106, 109-10, 112
  and trade unions 104-5, 113, 136-7, 246
  and working conditions 107-8
responsibility, corporate 250
riches see wealth
Riffel, Kaspar 89
right to work 164, 186, 222, 223, 243
righteousness, in Old Testament 15-16
Rodrik, Danni 237, 242-3
Roman Committee of Social Studies 101
Roman Empire
  and craft colleges 71
  and role of work 7
  and slavery 53-6

Roosevelt, Franklin D. 147
Rotondi, Fr 129
Rudd, Kevin 218
runaway shops 246
Ruskin, John 117

Sacred Congregation for the Doctrine of the Faith 221-2
salvation
  and private judgement 83, 84
  and social issues 112
  see also redemption
Santamaria, B. A. 160, 161, 206
Saunders, Bishop Christopher 241
Schuck, Michael 100
Second Vatican Council
  and John Paul II 193, 196
  see also *Gaudium et Spes*
Semaines Sociales 152-3, 167
Sennett, Richard 238-9
serfdom 62, 64-7
Sermon on the Mount 28
service
  and guild system 70
  and work 25, 26, 29, 37, 257-8
servus casatus 63
shareholding, worker 124, 168, 176, 201, 218-19, 220, 248
Shepherd of Hermas 45
Simons, Robert 234
slavery
  to Christ 20
  and Church Fathers 42, 43, 46, 50, 53-6
  medieval 59-64
  in New Testament 34-7, 38-9
  in Old Testament 18-24
  pagan attitudes to 18-19
  in Roman Empire 53-4
  runaway slaves 22-3
  and serfdom 62, 64-7
Smith, Adam 229, 251
sociability, in Church Fathers 49-50
social security
  in *Mater et Magistra* 170
  and neoliberalism 237-8
  in Old Testament 17-18
socialism
  and Bolshevik revolution 132

and Chesterbelloc period 122, 124, 127
and *Rerum Novarum* 112-13
and solidarity 100
see also communism
socialization 154, 161-2, 200-3
society
and the Church 151-2
in Church Fathers 46
and labour 138-40, 152-3
and servile state 123
and social structures 180
transformation 91
Sodano, Cardinal Angelo 227
solidarism 145-6, 147, 159, 202
solidarity
and Catholicism 83, 247
in Church Fathers 46, 47-8
in *Laborem Exercens* 197-8, 210
and Pius XII 151
in *Rerum Novarum* 104
and socialism 100
Solidarity trade union 195, 209
Solzhenitsyn, Alexander 254
Soros, George 233-4
sovereignty, popular 116
Sparta, and role of labour 8
specialism, in Chesterton 117
Standing, Guy 241, 244, 246, 249
state
in *Centesimus Annus* 228
collective 122, 125, 202, 211
distributive 124
and distributive justice 109-10, 112, 157
and free market 154, 214, 220, 225, 227, 228
and full employment 221, 223
as indirect employer 233, 243-4
and just wage 95, 102, 106, 110
and justice 42-3
and labour law 143-4
and multinational corporations 235
and nationalization of industries 162-3
neoliberal 238
servile 120-3, 254
and trade unions 104-5
and unemployment 175, 221, 226-7
status
and contract 81-2
in Middle Ages 72-3
stewardship
in Chesterbelloc period 116
in early Church 14, 42, 44-9, 103, 258-9
in New Testament 25
in Old Testament 14
and Pius XII 157
Stilwell, Frank 225
stoicism
and slavery 54
and the state 42
strikes
just 160-1, 183, 210
political 190, 191
and role of the state 110
subsidiarity
and Australian bishops 163
in *Quadragesimo Anno* 147
and US bishops 157
Suhard, Cardinal Emmanuel Célestin, Archbishop of Paris 127-8
Switzerland, and Catholic social movement 94
Synod of Bishops (1971) 191
Szulc, Tad 193

Tabb, William 243, 245-6
Tacitus, Publius Cornelius 62-3
talents, parable of 25
tariff reduction, effects 227, 233
Thatcher, Margaret 234
Theodosius I, Emperor 54
theology of work 195-7
Tillett, Ben 112-13
Townsend, Henry 15-16, 30, 34, 111, 179
Townsend, Robert 250-1
trade
fair 243
free 205, 223-4, 243
trade unions
and Australian bishops 160-1, 225-6
and Canadian bishops 163
and Catholic social movements 9, 96-7

in *Centesimus Annus* 213
compulsory unionism 164
declining membership 242, 244
in *Gaudium et Spes* 183, 184–5, 210
and indirect employers 207
in *Laborem Exercens* 209–10, 219–20
in *Mater et Magistra* 173
and neoliberalism 238, 242–7
in *Octogesima Adveniens* 190
in *Populorum Progressio* 189
in *Quadragesimo Anno* 104, 136–8
in *Rerum Novarum* 104–5, 113, 136, 246
restrictions on 123
and US bishops 157, 164, 217–18, 219–20, 228
and worker-priests 128, 129
trades and crafts
  in ancient Greece 19
  in Church Fathers 42, 44, 47
  and cooperatives 174
  medieval 65
  in New Testament 26
  in Old Testament 11, 12–14
  see also guild system
training, vocational 171
tribunals, industrial 110, 133, 184
Trithemius, Johannes 76–7
Troeltsch, Ernst 64, 68, 75
Tropman, John 82–3

ultramontanism 95–7
unemployment
  and capitalism 117, 119, 123, 132, 143, 155, 217, 222
  insurance 223
  in *Laborem Exercens* 207
  and state intervention 175, 221
  structural 198, 217, 221, 223, 226–7
United Nations
  Declaration of Human Rights 147
  as indirect employer 206
United States
  bishops of Ohio 164
  and Catholic social movement 97, 99

episcopal conferences and statements 157–8, 217–21, 227–8
and *Gaudium et Spes* 179
and income inequality 237–9
and International Labour Organization 173
and labour and capital 132–3, 150, 244–6
and *Quadragesimo Anno* 147
and trade unions 157, 164, 217–18, 219–20, 244–7
urbanization, and proletariat 189–90, 191
usefulness, and wealth 45, 52

van Roy, Cardinal Josef Ernest 133
Velasquez, Manuel 185
Veuillot, Louis 92
Ville-Neuve-Burgement, Viscomte 92
Vischer, Lukas 185, 214
vocational groups, and *Quadragesimo Anno* 144–6, 160, 202

wages
  entry-level 241
  family wage 95, 140–2, 150–1, 155, 158, 160, 169, 208
  and New Testament 28, 32
  and poverty 236–7
  and productivity 170, 176, 244, 248
  and unemployment 143
  withholding 32
  see also just wage
wealth
  and Calvinism 84–5
  in Church Fathers 44, 45, 46–7
  concentration 86–7, 117, 122–3, 146–7, 214
  distribution 123, 144, 146, 251
  in encyclicals 100
  and justice 47
  in New Testament 24–5, 29
  in Old Testament 24
  and sufficiency 45
  and workers 10, 108
wisdom literature, and changing attitudes to work 18

Wojtila, Karol, *The Acting Person* 194, 211–12; *see also* John Paul II, Pope
women
　and the family 208–9
　in workforce 227
Wood, H. G. 83–4
work *see* dignity of work; labour
work, right to 164, 186, 222, 223, 243
worker participation 247–50
　in Australian bishops' statements 226
　in *Centesimus Annus* 213
　in *Gaudium et Spes* 183, 184–6
　in *Laborem Exercens* 200–4
　in *Mater et Magistra* 170–3, 176, 184, 190, 191, 202
　in *Octogesima Adveniens* 190, 191
　and Pius XII 153–4, 170–1
　in *Populorum Progressio* 189, 191
　in *Quadragesimo Anno* 138–40, 146–8, 170, 172, 191
　in US bishops' statements 218–19
worker-priest movement 127–30, 166, 193–4

working class
　and Catholic social movement 81, 91–3, 95–7
　and the Church 127–30
　and *Deus Caritas Est* 229
　Irish 96–7
　and Marxism 132
　and property 108–14, 123–7, 136, 142–3, 144, 146, 157, 170
　and *Rerum Novarum* 101–8, 112–14
　and working conditions 107–8, 183–4, 218, 220, 228
　see also proletariat
working hours
　increased 237, 239, 247
　limitation 91, 107–8
World Bank 237
World Summit on Social Development (Copenhagen 1995) 227
World Trade Organization 232–3, 253

Xenophon, and role of labour 7

Yahweh, as worker 5–6, 13

Zigliara, Cardinal Tommaso 101

INDEX OF BIBLICAL CITATIONS

Genesis
  1:28 6, 29, 195, 215 n.10
  2:2 107, 115 n.31
  2:7 5
  3:17 6, 102
  3:19 5, 28
  4:22 13

Exodus
  20:8 107, 115 n.30
  21:1-11 21
  21:1-7 39 n.24
  21:2 20
  21:5-11 22
  21:26-7 40 n.34
  22:1-4 39 n.25
  35:30-5 13, 39 n.8

Leviticus
  19:13 32
  19:18 10
  25:3-6 12
  25:23 14
  25:44-6 21

Deuteronomy
  4:7 13
  15:12-15 21, 22
  15:16-17 22
  23:15-16 22
  23:25-6 17, 18
  24:14-15 10
  24:14 32
  24:17 17
  24:19 17
  24:20 17
  24:21 17

Joshua
  24:13 14

Judges
  6:11 12

Ruth
  2:4 23

1 Kings
  6:13

1 Chronicles
  22:1-8 13

Nehemiah
  5:1-5 39 n.26

Job
  1:21 51

Psalms
  15 9
  15:5 10
  37:21 10
  37:29 14
  41 9
  41:1-2 10
  58 10
  72 9
  72:1-2 9
  72:4 9
  72:12-14 9
  82 9, 10
  94 9, 10
  99:4 9
  106:2 10
  112:5 10

Proverbs
  10:4 18
  13:4 18
  16:26 18
  18:19 104
  19:1 18
  21:25 18
  22:29 18
  24:30 18

Ecclesiastes
  5:9-10 104, 115 n.19
  7:15-16 18
  9:16 18
  22:2 18
  33:31-3 23
  34:22 32
  40:18 18

Ecclesiasticus
  4:1 47, 258
  34:21-2 12

38:24–39 11, 44
38:39 40 n.55

Ezekiel
  47:13 16
  47:21–2 16
  48:1–7 16
  48:23–9 16

Amos
  1:1 12

New Testament

Matthew
  4:45 48
  5:3 15, 103, 115 n.15
  5:6 257
  5:14–30 40 n.48
  5:42 30–1
  6:2 254, 266 n.56
  6:24 24, 25, 28, 40 n.45
  6:33–4 28
  7:9 40 n.52
  7:12 28, 257
  10:17–27 41 n.82
  11:28 103, 115 n.16
  13:55–6 26, 40 n.54
  14:16 31
  16:24–5 25, 40 n.47
  20:3 40 n.42
  20:28 26
  21:33–43 34
  22:1–14 34
  25:31–6 40 n.49

Mark
  6:3 103, 115 n.14
  6:37 31
  10:23 40 n.44
  10:43–5 29, 257

Luke
  9:13 31
  11:5 40 n.53
  12:16–21 24
  13:20–1 26
  14:33 25, 40 n.46
  16 40 n.43
  19:11–26 40 n.48
  22:25–7 29, 257

John
  1:26 50
  13:2–17 35
  13:13–15 29, 257
  15:1–5 45
  15:15 35

Romans
  8:29 103

1 Corinthians
  7:21–4 35
  9:16–19 40 n.29
  12:21 46
  12:22 46
  15:23 46

Galatians
  3:26–9 36, 258

Ephesians
  4:1–6 32, 258, 260

Philippians
  2:3–4 28, 32
  2:6–8 32, 258

Colossians
  3:22–5 36
  4:1 36

2 Thessalonians
  3:7–9 32, 40 n.66
  3:10 33, 136, 148 n.9
  3:12 32
  3:14–15 33

1 Timothy
  6:2 46

Philemon
  16 37

James
  1:22 25, 40 n.50
  2:1 31
  2:8 32
  2:17 25, 40 n.51
  5:4 32

1 Peter
  2:18–20 37

2 Peter
  3:13 215 n.17

1 John
  4:20–1 32

Revelation
  21:1 215 n.17

www.ingramcontent.com/pod-product-compliance
Lightning Source LLC
Chambersburg PA
CBHW070937230426
43666CB00011B/2470